2015 上半年
First Half of 2015

中国国际收支报告
China's Balance of Payments Report

国家外汇管理局国际收支分析小组
BOP Analysis Group
State Administration of Foreign Exchange

中国金融出版社
China Financial Publishing House

责任编辑：张翠华
责任校对：孙　蕊
责任印制：程　颖

图书在版编目（CIP）数据

2015 上半年中国国际收支报告／国家外汇管理局国际收支分析小组．—北京：中国金融
出版社，2016.1
　ISBN 978-7-5049-8342-8

　Ⅰ．① 2… 　Ⅱ．①国… 　Ⅲ．①国际收支—研究报告—中国—2015
Ⅳ．① F812.4

　中国版本图书馆 CIP 数据核字（2015）第 320671 号

出版
发行　中国金融出版社

社址　北京市丰台区益泽路 2 号
市场开发部　（010）63266347，63805472，63439533（传真）
网上书店　http://www.chinafph.com　（010）63286832，63365686（传真）
读者服务部　（010）66070833，62568380
邮编　100071
经销　新华书店
印刷　天津银博印刷有限公司
尺寸　210 毫米 ×285 毫米
印张　12.25
字数　190 千
版次　2016 年 1 月第 1 版
印次　2016 年 1 月第 1 次印刷
印数　1—2000
定价　80.00 元
ISBN 978-7-5049-8342-8/F.7902
如出现印装错误本社负责调换　联系电话：（010）63263947

国家外汇管理局
国际收支分析小组人员名单

组　　长：易　纲

副 组 长：邓先宏　方上浦　王小奕　杨国中　韩红梅

审　　稿：王允贵　杜　鹏　郭　松　张生会　崔汉忠

统　　稿：王春英　方　文　温建东　周　济　赵玉超

执　　笔：

第一部分：刘　畅　高　铮　赵玉超

第二部分：余　猛　李玲青　胡　红　张青青　马玉娟

第三部分：常国栋　张青青

第四部分：贾　宁　梁　艳

第五部分：管恩杰

专　　栏：杨　灿　周　济　赵玉超　邵国安　王　凯
　　　　　梁　艳　高　铮

附录整理：覃砾颉

英文翻译：周海文　王　亮　胡　红

英文审校：Nancy Hearst（美国哈佛大学费正清东亚研究中心）

Contributors to This Report

Head
Yi Gang

Deputy Head
Deng Xianhong   Fang Shangpu   Wang Xiaoyi   Yang Guozhong   Han Hongmei

Readers
Wang Yungui   Du Peng   Guo Song   Zhang Shenghui   Cui Hanzhong

Editors
Wang Chunying   Fang Wen   Wen Jiandong   Zhou Ji   Zhao Yuchao

Authors
Part One: Liu Chang Gao Zheng   Zhao Yuchao
Part Two: Yu Meng   Li Lingqing   Hu Hong   Zhang Qingqing   Ma Yujuan
Part Three: Chang Guodong   Zhang Qingqing
Part Four: Jia Ning   Liang Yan
Part Five: Guan Enjie
Boxes: Yang Can   Zhou Ji   Zhao Yuchao   Shao Guoan   Wang Kai
        Liang Yan   Gao Zheng
Appendix: Qin Lijie

Translators: Zhou Haiwen   Wang Liang   Hu Hong

Proofreader: Nancy Hearst (Fairbank Center for East Asian Research,
                Harvard University)

内容摘要

2015 年上半年，国内外经济金融环境依然复杂，主要经济体经济运行存在差异，货币政策继续分化，国际资本流动的波动性加大。国内经济运行缓中趋稳，总体处于合理区间，人民币汇率保持基本稳定。

我国经常账户持续较大顺差，但仍处于国际公认的合理水平之内。2015 年上半年顺差 1 486 亿美元，较 2014 年同期增长 85%，与 GDP 之比为 3.1%，同比上升 1.3 个百分点。主要是由于货物贸易顺差 2 566 亿美元，较上年同期大幅增长 73%。此外，服务贸易逆差 945 亿美元，较上年同期进一步扩大 53%。跨境资本延续净流出态势，但第二季度趋向基本平衡。上半年，资本和金融账户（不含储备资产，下同）逆差 1 256 亿美元，其中，第一和第二季度逆差分别为 981 亿和 275 亿美元。上半年的资本和金融账户逆差主要反映了境内主体本外币资产负债结构的优化调整。一方面，境内机构和个人的境外资产有所增多，体现了"藏汇于民"的积极效果；另一方面，境内主体进一步减少境外负债，逐步降低高杠杆经营等风险。2015 年上半年，我国外汇储备资产减少 666 亿美元，其中，第一季度下降 795 亿美元，第二季度增加 130 亿美元。

2015 年下半年，预计我国国际收支将延续"经常账户顺差、资本和金融账户逆差"的格局，国际收支自主平衡能力进一步提高。外汇管理部门将坚持统筹兼顾、改革创新，继续大力简政放权，深化外汇管理重点领域改革；完善跨境资金流动监测分析预警，严厉打击外汇领域违法违规行为，强化风险防范。

Abstract

During the first half of 2015, both the domestic and the international economic and financial situations remained complicated, with different economic circumstances and diversified monetary policies in the major economies and increased fluctuations of international capital flows. The Chinese national economy was stabilized at an overall reasonably low range and the RMB exchange rate remained stable.

China's current account continued to record a substantial surplus, which was still recognized internationally as a reasonable level. During the first half of the year, the surplus totaled USD 148.6 billion, increasing by 85 percent year on year. The ratio to GDP was 3.1 percent, 1.3 percentage points higher year on year. The increase in the surplus was derived from the surplus in trade in goods, which amounted to USD 256.6 billion, 73 percent higher year on year. In the meantime, the deficit in trade in services totaled USD 94.5 billion, increasing by 53 percent year on year. Cross-border capital continued to record a net outflow, although in the second quarter capital flows tended to be more balanced. In the first half of the year, the capital and financial account (excluding reserve assets) recorded a deficit of USD 125.6 billion. In particular, the first quarter and the second quarter recorded a deficit of USD 98.1 billion and USD 27.5 billion respectively. The deficit reflected domestic adjustments of the assets and liabilities in both the domestic and foreign currencies. Domestic institutions and individuals increased their holdings of foreign assets, which indicated a positive effect of the strategy to encourage residents to hold external assets. In addition, domestic entities deleveraged by further reducing their external liabilities. In the first half of the year, China's foreign-reserve assets decreased by USD 66.6 billion, with the first quarter and second quarters seeing a decrease of USD 79.5 billion and an increase of USD 13 billion respectively.

In the second half of the year, China's balance of payments was projected to record a surplus in the current account and a deficit in the capital and financial account. China will see improved self-adjustments with respect to the balance of payments. The SAFE will further streamline its administrative processes and continue its reforms in important areas. Moreover, it will improve risk prevention by enhancing its monitoring of cross-border capital movements and fighting against illegal operations in the foreign-exchange market.

目 录

一、国际收支概况

（一）国际收支运行环境 ……………………………………… 2

（二）国际收支主要状况 ……………………………………… 4

（三）国际收支运行评价 ……………………………………… 13

二、国际收支主要项目分析

（一）货物贸易 ………………………………………………… 20

（二）服务贸易 ………………………………………………… 22

（三）直接投资 ………………………………………………… 26

（四）证券投资 ………………………………………………… 32

（五）其他投资 ………………………………………………… 33

三、国际投资头寸状况

四、外汇市场运行与人民币汇率

（一）人民币汇率走势 ………………………………………… 44

（二）外汇市场交易 …………………………………………… 49

五、国际收支形势展望

附 录 统计资料

一、国际收支 ………………………………………………… 134

二、对外贸易 ………………………………………………… 154

三、外汇市场和人民币汇率 ………………………………… 167

四、利用外资 ………………………………………………… 173

五、外债 ……………………………………………………… 175

六、国际旅游 ………………………………………………… 177

七、世界经济增长状况 ……………………………………… 178

八、国际金融市场状况 ……………………………………… 180

专栏

专栏 1《国际收支手册》(第六版)标准下的国际收支统计变化 … 8

专栏 2 如何看待近期我国黄金储备变动 ………………… 12

专栏 3 外汇储备余额下降的主要影响因素 ……………… 16

专栏 4 我国企业"走出去"具有顺周期性 ……………… 30

专栏 5 我国按照 SDDS 要求公布全口径外债数据 ……… 34

专栏 6 汇改十年的外汇市场发展及面临的挑战 ………… 53

专栏 7 美联储加息周期对新兴经济体跨境资本流动的差异化影响 … 59

图

图 1-1 2007-2015 年上半年主要经济体经济增长率 ……… 2

图 1-2 2007 年以来国际金融市场利率和货币波动率水平 … 3

图 1-3 2012 年以来全球股票、债券和商品市场价格 …… 3

图 1-4 2008-2015 年上半年我国季度 GDP 和月度 CPI 增长率 … 4

图 1-5 2001-2015 年上半年经常账户主要子项目的收支状况 …… 5

图 1-6 2001-2015 年上半年资本和金融账户主要子项目的收支
状况 ………………………………………………… 6

图 1-7 2001-2015 年上半年外汇储备资产变动额 ……… 7

图 1-8 1990-2015 年上半年经常账户差额与 GDP 之比及其结构 … 14

图 1-9 2005-2015 年第二季度国际收支差额与外汇储备资产变动 14

图 1-10 2005-2015 年第二季度证券投资和其他投资项下资本
流动情况 ………………………………………… 15

图 C3-1 外汇储备余额变动的主要影响因素 ……………… 17

图 2-1 2001-2015 年上半年我国进出口差额与外贸依存度 …… 20

图 2-2 2000-2015 年上半年我国按贸易方式货物贸易差额构成 21

图 2–3 2000–2015 年上半年我国按贸易主体货物贸易差额构成 …… 21

图 2–4 2002–2015 年上半年我国出口商品在发达经济体的市场
份额变动 ……………………………………………… 22

图 2–5 进出口差额同比变动中的数量与价格因素 …………… 23

图 2–6 2004–2015 年上半年货物贸易和服务贸易收支总额比较… 23

图 2–7 2004–2015 年上半年服务贸易收支情况………………… 24

图 2–8 2009–2015 年上半年旅行逆差对服务贸易逆差贡献度…… 25

图 2–9 2015 年上半年我国对主要贸易伙伴服务贸易收支情况 … 25

图 2–10 2000–2015 年上半年直接投资差额 ………………… 26

图 2–11 2000–2015 年上半年对外直接投资状况 ……………… 27

图 2–12 2015 年上半年我国非金融部门对外直接投资流出分布
（按国内行业、投资目的国划分）…………………… 28

图 2–13 2000–2015 年上半年来华直接投资状况 ……………… 29

图 C4–1 2005–2015 年 6 月大宗商品价格与海外并购交易量
趋势 …………………………………………………… 30

图 2–14 2001–2015 年上半年跨境证券投资净额 ……………… 32

图 2–15 2000–2015 年上半年其他投资净额 …………………… 34

图 3–1 2004–2015 年 6 月末我国对外资产结构变化…………… 38

图 3–2 2004–2015 年 6 月末我国对外负债结构变化…………… 39

图 3–3 2004–2015 年 6 月末我国对外资产、负债及净资产状况… 40

图 3–4 2005–2015 年 6 月我国对外资产负债收益率…………… 41

图 4–1 2015 年上半年境内外人民币对美元即期汇率走势 ……… 44

图 4–2 2015 年上半年全球主要发达和新兴市场货币对美元双边
汇率变动 ……………………………………………… 45

图 4–3 1994 年 1 月 –2015 年 6 月人民币有效汇率走势 ………… 45

图 4–4 2015 年上半年全球主要发达和新兴市场货币有效汇率变动 … 46

图 4–5 境内外人民币对美元即期汇率价差 …………………… 46

图 4–6 2013 年以来境内外人民币对美元远期市场 1 年期美元升
贴水点数 ……………………………………………… 47

图 4–7 2013 年以来境内人民币与美元利差（6 个月期限）……… 48

图 4–8 2015 年上半年银行间外汇市场人民币对美元即期交易价
波动情况 ……………………………………………… 48

图 4–9 2012 年以来人民币对美元汇率 6 个月隐含波动率 …… 49

图 4-10 中国与全球外汇市场的交易产品构成比较 ……………… 50

图 4-11 2012-2015 年上半年银行对客户远期结售汇交易量 …… 51

图 4-12 2015 年上半年银行对客户远期结售汇的交易期限结构 … 51

图 4-13 中国外汇市场的参与者结构 ……………………………… 53

图 C6-1 中国外汇市场交易量概况 …………………………………… 54

图 C7-1 1990 年以来美国联邦基金利率与美元指数走势………… 59

表

表 1-1 2010-2015 年上半年中国国际收支顺差结构 ……………… 5

表 1-2 2015 年上半年中国国际收支平衡表 ……………………… 10

表 3-1 2015 年 6 月末中国国际投资头寸表 ……………………… 41

表 4-1 2015 年上半年人民币外汇市场交易概况 ………………… 52

Content

I. Overview of the Balance of Payments

(I) The Balance-of-Payments Environment ·········· 64

(II) The Main Characteristics of the Balance of Payments ·········· 67

(III) Evaluation of the Balance of Payments ·········· 78

II. Analysis of the Major Items in the Balance of Payments

(I) Trade in Goods ·········· 84

(II) Trade in Services ·········· 87

(III) Direct Investments ·········· 91

(IV) Portfolio Investments ·········· 98

(V) Other Investments ·········· 100

III. International Investment Position

IV. Operation of the Foreign-exchange Market and the RMB Exchange Rate

(I) Trends in the RMB Exchange Rate ·········· 112

(II) Transactions in the Foreign-Exchange Market ·········· 117

V. Outlook for the Balance of Payments

Appendix Statistics

I. Balance of Payments ·········· 134

II. Foreign Trade ·········· 154

Ⅲ. Foreign Exchange Market and Exchange Rate of Renminbi ················ 167

Ⅳ. Foreign Investment Utilization ································· 173

Ⅴ. External Debt ··· 175

Ⅵ. International Tourism ··· 177

VII. Growth of World Economics ·· 178

VIII. International Financial Market·· 180

Boxes

Box 1   Statistical changes under the framework of the *Balance of Payments and*

International Investment Position Manual (Sixth Edition) ···················· 71

Box 2   A perspective on recent changes in China's gold reserves ················ 76

Box 3   The main factors contributing to the decrease in foreign-exchange

reserve assets ·· 80

Box 4   Procyclicality of ODI investments ································ 95

Box 5   China dissemination of its external debt data according to the SDDS ··· 101

Box 6   The ten-year development of foreign-exchange markets since the regime

reform and Future Challenges ································· 123

Box 7   The differentiated impact of the rising cycle in interest rates by the FED

on cross-border capital flows of the emerging economies ·············· 129

Charts

Chart 1-1   Growth rates of the major economies since 2007 ···················· 64

Chart 1-2   Fluctuations in interest rates and exchange rates in international

financial markets since 2007 ································· 65

Chart 1-3   Indices of stocks, bonds, and goods since 2012 ···················· 65

Chart 1-4   Growth rate of the quarterly GDP and the monthly CPI since 2008 ··· 66

Chart 1-5   Major items under the current account since 2001 ·················· 68

Chart 1-6   Major items under the capital and financial account since 2001 ······ 69

Chart 1-7 Foreign reserve position and growth since 2001 ······················ 70

Chart 1-8 The ratio of the current account balance to GDP and its composition

since 1990 ··· 78

Chart 1-9 The BOP balance and foreign-reserve assets since 2005 ·············· 79

Chart 1-10 Portfolio investments and other investments since 2005 ·············· 80

Chart C3-1 The main factors contributing to changes in China's foreign-

exchange reserves ·· 82

Chart 2-1 Foreign trade balance and dependence since 2001 ···················· 84

Chart 2-2 Composition of trade in terms of trade patterns since 2000 ·········· 85

Chart 2-3 Composition of trade in goods in terms of trade participants since 2000··· 85

Chart 2-4 Market shares in the advanced economies since 2002 ················ 86

Chart 2-5 The influence of volume and price on the trade balance ·············· 87

Chart 2-6 Trade in goods and trade in services since 2004 ······················ 88

Chart 2-7 Trade in services since 2004 ··· 89

Chart 2-8 Contribution of travel to the deficit of trade in services since 2009 ··· 90

Chart 2-9 Trade in services in terms of trading partners during the first half of 2015 ··· 90

Chart 2-10 The balance of direct investments since 2000·························· 92

Chart 2-11 Outward direct investments since 2000 ································ 92

Chart 2-12 The distribution of outward direct investments by the non-financial

sector in the first half of 2015(in terms of industries and destinations) ···93

Chart 2-13 FDI since 2000 ··· 95

Chart C4-1 Prices of staple goods and overseas M&As since 2005 ·············· 96

Chart 2-14 Net portfolio investments since 2001 ·································· 98

Chart 2-15 Net other investments from 2000 to 2015 ···························· 100

Chart 3-1 The structure of external assets structure since 2004 ·············· 106

Chart 3-2 The structure of external liabilities from 2004 to 2015 ·············· 107

Chart 3-3 External assets, liabilities, and net assets since 2004 ·············· 108

Chart 3-4 The yields of external assets and liabilities since 2005·············· 109

Chart 4-1 Trends in the spot RMB exchange rate against the USD in the domestic

and offshore markets, first half of 2015 ·································· 112

Chart 4-2 Changes in the exchange rates of the major developed economies

		and the emerging markets against the USD, first half of 2015 ⋯⋯	113
Chart 4–3	Trends in the RMB effective exchange rate, January 1994 to June 2015	⋯ 113
Chart 4–4	Changes in the effective exchange rates of the major developed economies and the emerging markets, first half of 2015 ⋯⋯⋯⋯	114
Chart 4–5	Spread of the spot RMB exchange rates against the USD in the domestic and offshore markets, first half of 2015 ⋯⋯⋯⋯⋯⋯	114
Chart 4–6	The premium and discount of the 1–year RMB forward rate against the USD in the domestic and offshore markets since 2013 ⋯⋯⋯	116
Chart 4–7	The 6–month interest–rate spread of the domestic RMB and the USD since 2013 ⋯⋯⋯⋯⋯⋯⋯⋯⋯⋯⋯⋯⋯⋯	116
Chart 4–8	The volatility of the spot RMB exchange rate against the USD in the inter–bank foreign–exchange market, first half of 2015 ⋯⋯⋯	117
Chart 4–9	The 6–month implied volatility of the RMB exchange rate against the USD since 2012 ⋯⋯⋯⋯⋯⋯⋯⋯⋯⋯⋯⋯⋯	118
Chart 4–10	A comparison of the structure of products in the domestic and global foreign–exchange markets ⋯⋯⋯⋯⋯⋯⋯⋯⋯⋯	118
Chart 4–11	The trading volume of forward foreign–exchange transactions in the client market, 2012 to the first half of 2015 ⋯⋯⋯⋯⋯	120
Chart 4–12	The term structure of forward transactions of foreign–exchange purchases and sales in the client market, first half of 2015 ⋯⋯⋯	121
Chart 4–13	The structure of participants in China's foreign–exchange markets ⋯⋯	123
Chart C6–1	An overview of the trading volume of China's foreign–exchange market ⋯⋯⋯⋯⋯⋯⋯⋯⋯⋯⋯⋯⋯⋯⋯⋯⋯	125
Chart C7–1	Trends in the federal funds rate and the USD index, from 1990 ⋯	132

Tables

Table 1–1	The structure of the BOP surplus since 2010 ⋯⋯⋯⋯⋯⋯⋯⋯	67
Table 1–2	Balance of payments in the first half of 2015 ⋯⋯⋯⋯⋯⋯⋯	73
Table 3–1	The IIP at the end of June 2015 ⋯⋯⋯⋯⋯⋯⋯⋯⋯⋯⋯	110
Table 4–1	Transactions in the RMB/foreign–exchange market, first half of 2015⋯⋯	121

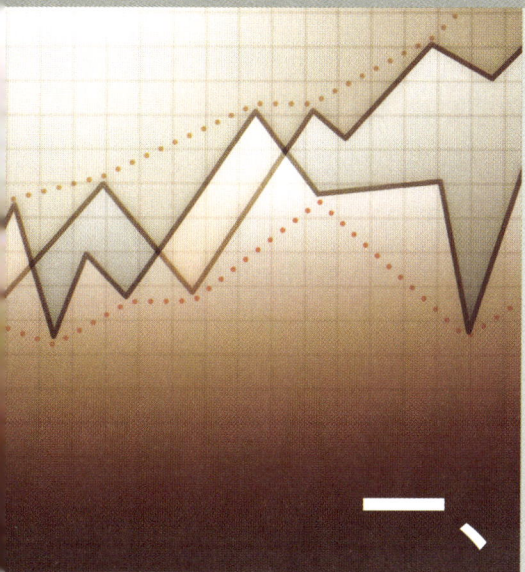

一、国际收支概况

（一）国际收支运行环境

2015 年上半年，我国面临的国际国内经济金融环境复杂，国际资本流动波动加大，国内经济保持在合理区间运行，国际收支在振荡中保持基本平衡。

从国际看，上半年世界经济延续不平衡的缓慢复苏，各经济体经济运行存在差异和分化（见图 1-1）。美国经济先抑后扬，第二季度经济复苏势头进一步巩固，市场普遍预期美联储加息；欧元区经济出现部分复苏迹象，欧央行宽松货币政策令经济下行风险有所缓解，市场信心总体提升；日本经济重回正增长，日本央行量化和质化宽松货币政策刺激日元贬值，推动对外贸易有所好转；新兴经济体增长动能总体减弱，部分经济体金融市场波动加剧，更多经济体开始放松货币政策，但同时又面临资本外流的担忧。错综复杂的全球经济和货币政策交织，加大了国际金融市场波动。上半年，美元震荡走强，多数发达和新兴经济体货币走弱，大宗商品价格普遍下挫，发达经济体股票、债券市场表现总体好于新兴经济体（见图 1-2、图 1-3）。

从国内看，我国经济增长与预期目标相符，主要经济指标环比有所回升（见图 1-4）。上半年，就业形势基本稳定，城乡居民收入和消费平稳增长，社会融资成本下行，但工业生产增速回落，外需疲弱导致出口增速放缓，依靠政府投资推动的经

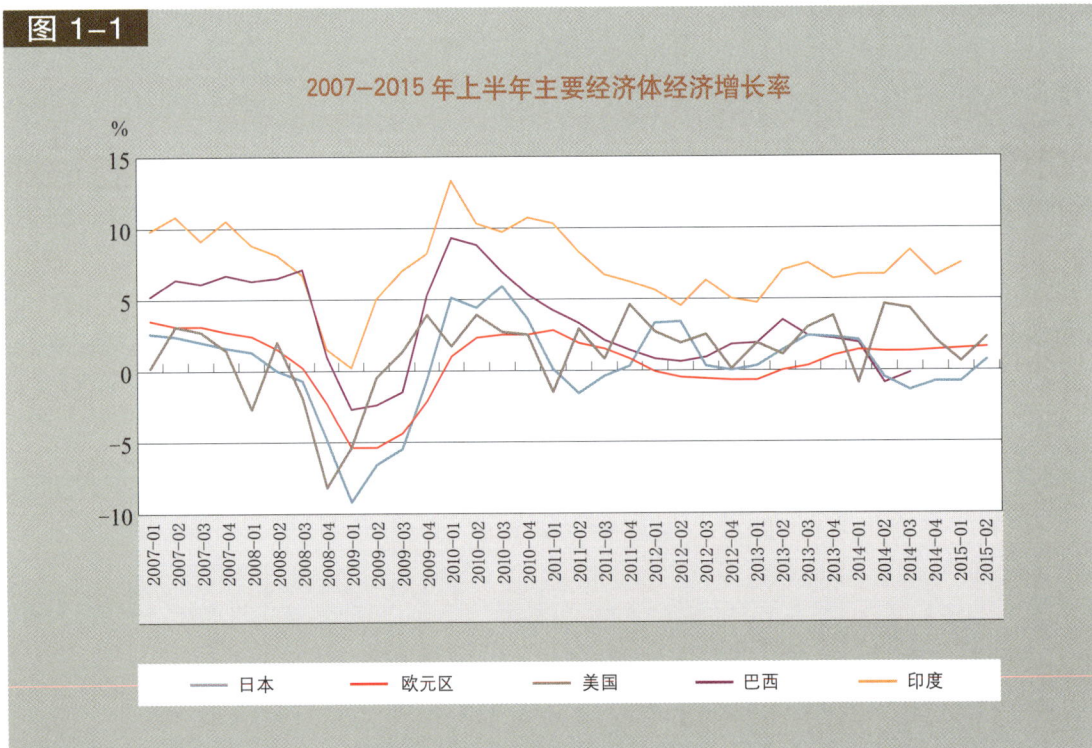

图 1-1

2007—2015 年上半年主要经济体经济增长率

图例：日本　欧元区　美国　巴西　印度

注：美国数据为季度环比折年率，其他经济体数据为季度同比。

数据来源：环亚经济数据库。

图 1-2

2007 年以来国际金融市场利率和货币波动率水平

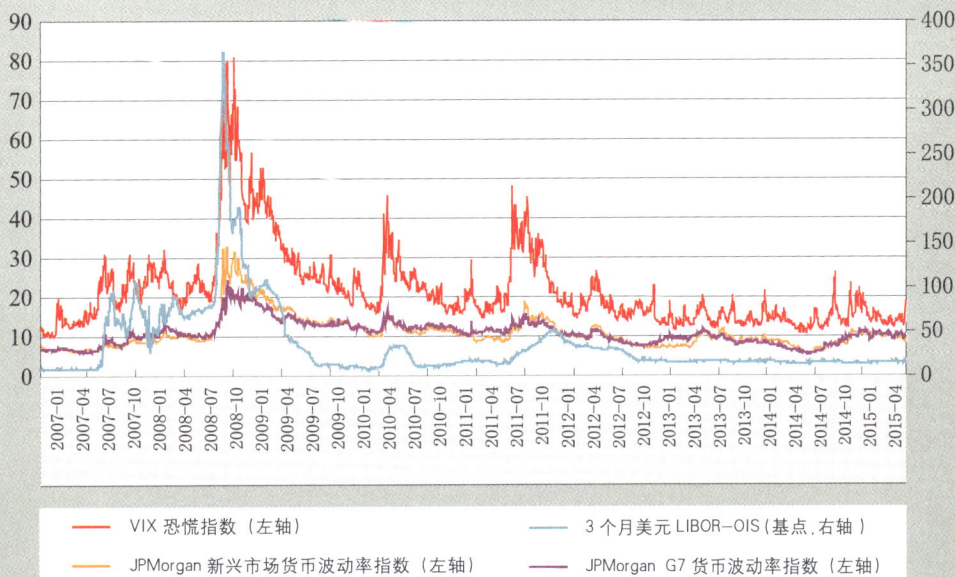

VIX 恐慌指数（左轴）　　　　　3 个月美元 LIBOR-OIS（基点，右轴）
JPMorgan 新兴市场货币波动率指数（左轴）　　JPMorgan G7 货币波动率指数（左轴）

数据来源：彭博资讯。

图 1-3

2012 年以来全球股票、债券和商品市场价格

SX5E　　　　BGSV　　　　MXEF
SPX　　　　SPGSCI　　　　BEMS

注：BEMS 和 BGSV 分别为彭博新兴市场和发达国家主权债券指数，MXEF 为 MSCI 新兴市场股指，SPX 为美国标准普尔 500 股指，SX5E 为欧元区斯托克 50 股指，SPGSCI 为标准普尔 GSCI 商品价格指数，均以 2012 年初值为 100。
数据来源：彭博资讯。

图 1-4

2008—2015 年上半年我国季度 GDP 和月度 CPI 增长率

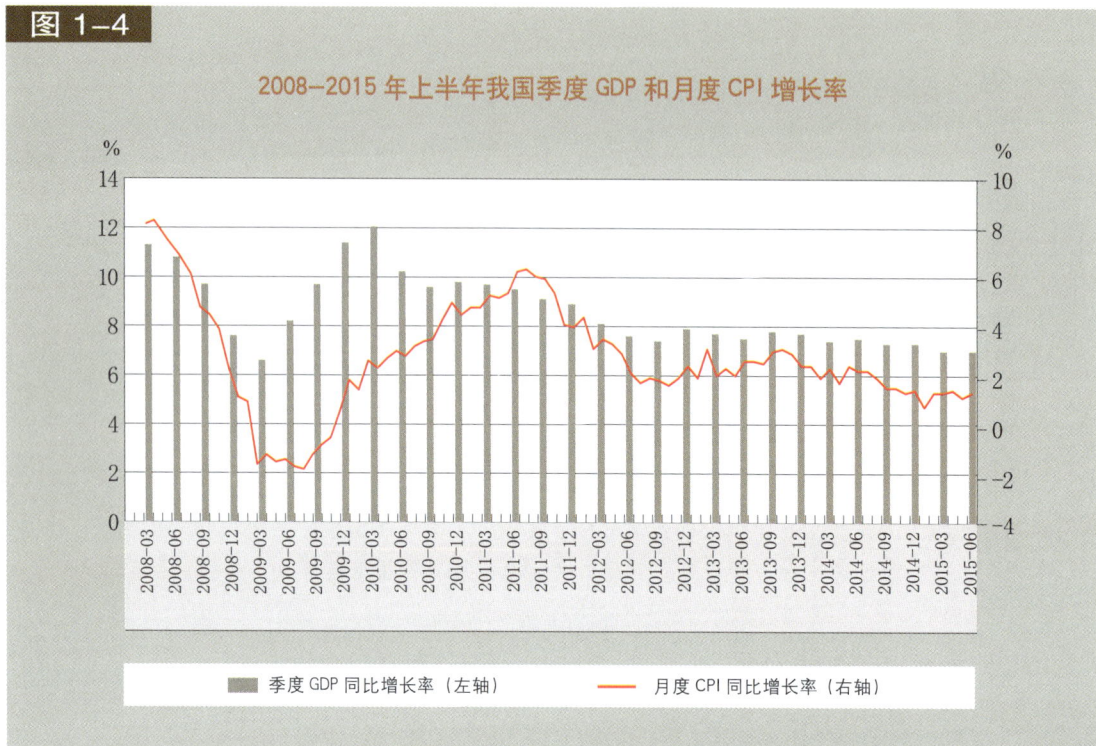

季度 GDP 同比增长率（左轴）　　月度 CPI 同比增长率（右轴）

数据来源：国家统计局。

济增长扩张空间有限。在增速换挡、结构调整和前期政策消化三期叠加阶段，结构调整为中长期的经济增长注入动力，但短期看仍面临下行调整压力。

（二）国际收支主要状况

2015 年上半年，我国国际收支总差额[①]230 亿美元，同比下降 85%（见表1-1）。其中，经常账户顺差 1 486 亿美元，增长 85%；资本和金融账户（不含储备资产，下同）逆差 1 256 亿美元，2014 年同期为顺差 778 亿美元。

货物贸易顺差增长较快。按国际收支统计口径[②]，2015 年上半年，我国货物贸易出口 10 112 亿美元，进口 7 546 亿美元，同比分别下降 2% 和 15%；顺差 2 566 亿美元，增长 73%（见图 1-5）。

---

① 国际收支总差额 = 经常账户差额 + 资本和金融账户差额（不含储备资产）。

② 本口径与海关口径的主要差异在于：一是国际收支中的货物只记录所有权发生了转移的货物（如一般贸易、进料加工贸易等贸易方式的货物），所有权未发生转移的货物（如来料加工或出料加工贸易）不纳入货物统计，而纳入服务贸易统计；二是计价方面，国际收支统计要求进出口货值均按离岸价格记录，海关出口货值为离岸价格，但进口货值为到岸价格，因此国际收支统计从海关进口货值中调出国际运保费支出，并纳入服务贸易统计；三是补充部分进出口退运等数据；四是补充了海关未统计的转手买卖下的货物净出口数据。

表 1-1 2010-2015 年上半年中国国际收支顺差结构　　　　　　　　　　单位：亿美元，%

项 目	2010 年	2011 年	2012 年	2013 年	2014 年	2015 年上半年
国际收支总差额	5 247	4 016	1 836	4 943	2 579	230
经常账户差额	2 378	1 361	2 154	1 482	2 197	1 486
占国际收支总差额比重	45	34	117	30	85	646
与 GDP 之比	4.0	1.9	2.6	1.6	2.1	3.1
资本和金融账户差额	2 869	2 655	−318	3 461	382	−1 256
占国际收支总差额比重	55	66	−17	70	15	−546
与 GDP 之比	4.8	3.6	−0.4	3.6	0.4	−2.6

数据来源：国家外汇管理局，国家统计局。

服务贸易逆差继续扩大。2015 年上半年，服务贸易收入 1 122 亿美元，同比增长 1%；支出 2 067 亿美元，增长 20%；逆差 945 亿美元，扩大 53%，其中运输项目逆差收窄 24%，旅行项目逆差延续扩大态势，增长 103%（见图 1-5）。

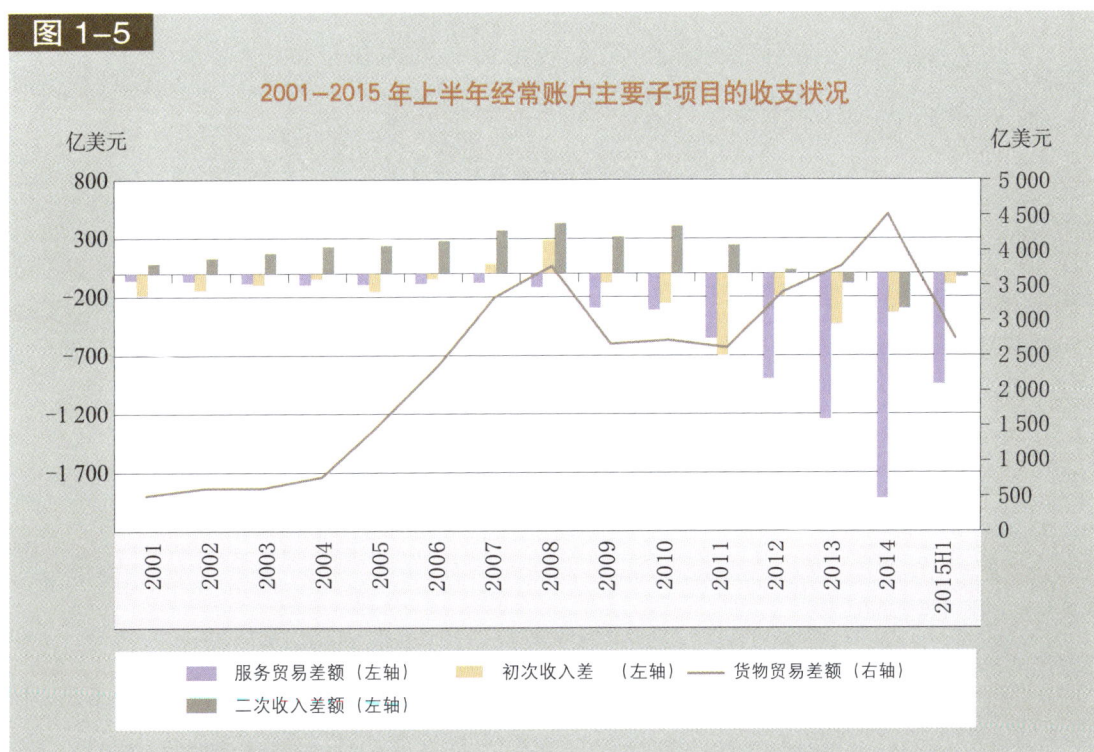

图 1-5 2001-2015 年上半年经常账户主要子项目的收支状况

数据来源：国家外汇管理局。

　　初次收入① **项目转为逆差。** 2015年上半年，初次收入项下收入1 310亿美元，同比增长20%；支出1 414亿美元，增长36%；逆差104亿美元，上年同期为顺差55亿美元。其中，雇员报酬顺差151亿美元，增长47%；投资收益逆差258亿美元，扩大4.5倍（见图1-5）。投资收益为负不代表我国对外投资损失，实际上，上半年我国对外投资的收益为1 127亿美元，同比增长15%；外国来华投资利润利息、股息红利等支出1 385亿美元，扩大35%。

　　二次收入项目逆差大幅收窄。 2015年上半年，二次收入项下收入184亿美元，同比下降22%；支出215亿美元，下降39%；逆差32亿美元，同比收窄73%（见图1-5）。二次收入主要包括捐赠、赔偿、社会保障、税收、罚款以及博彩等。自2013年起，二次收入由顺差转为逆差，主要反映了随着居民收入的提高，境内企业和个人对境外的捐赠有所增多。

　　直接投资顺差小幅下降。 按国际收支统计口径，2015年上半年，直接投资② 顺差920亿美元，同比下降1%（见图1-6）。其中，对外直接投资净流出即直接投资资产净增加529亿美元，增长70%；外国来华直接投资净流入即直接投资负债净增

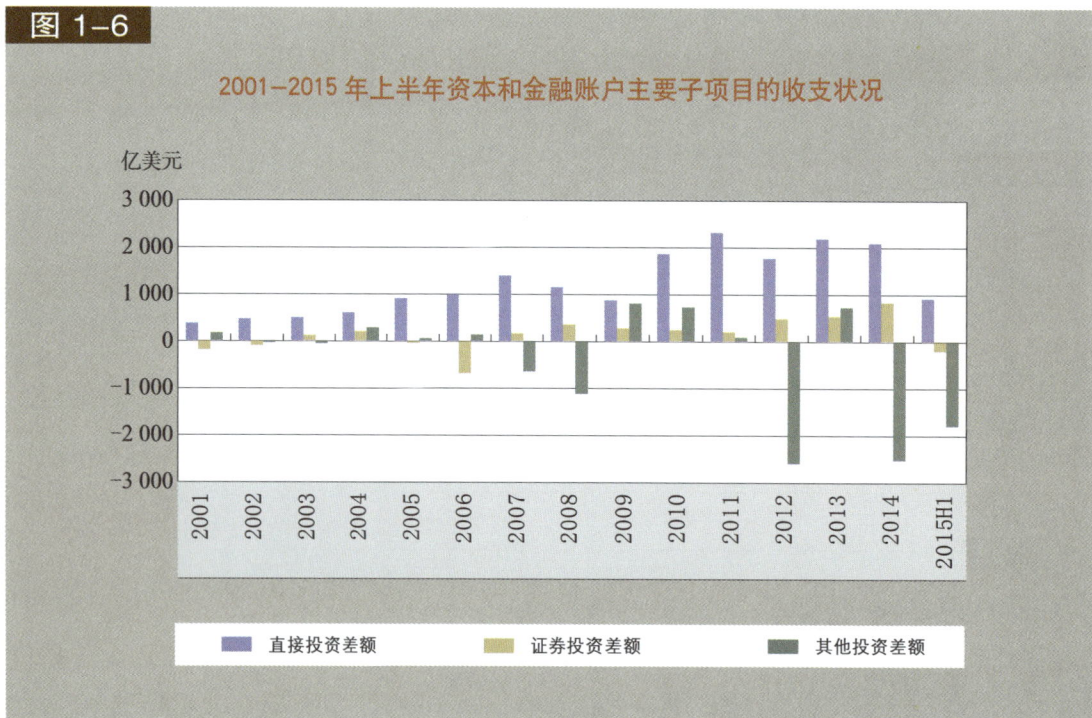

图 1-6

2001-2015年上半年资本和金融账户主要子项目的收支状况

数据来源：国家外汇管理局。

---

　　① 国际货币基金组织《国际收支和国际投资头寸手册》（第六版）将经常项下的"收益"名称改为"初次收入"，将"经常转移"名称改为"二次收入"。

　　② 本口径与商务部公布的数据主要差异在于，国际收支统计中还包括了外商投资企业的未分配利润、已分配未汇出利润、盈余公积、股东贷款、金融机构吸收外资、非居民购买不动产等内容。

图 1-7

2001-2015 年上半年外汇储备资产变动额

亿美元

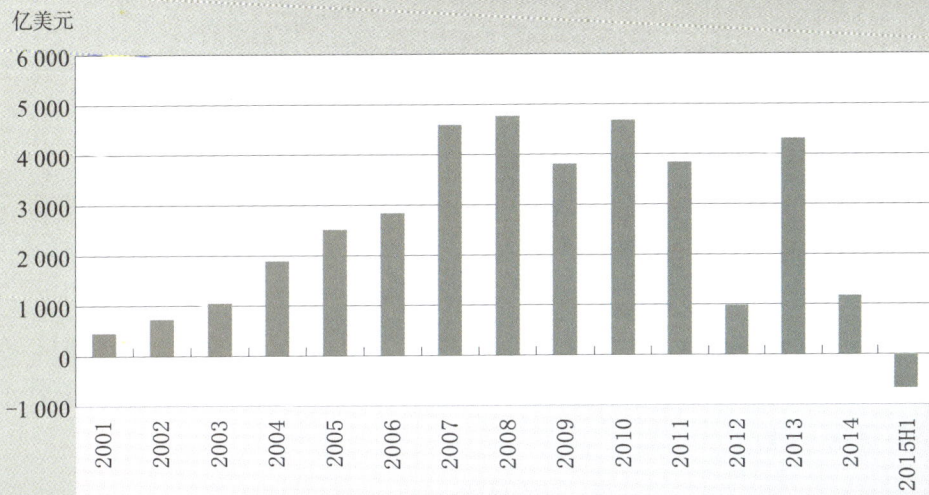

数据来源：国家外汇管理局。

加 1 449 亿美元，增长 17%。

证券投资转为逆差。2015 年上半年，证券投资为逆差 241 亿美元，上年同期为顺差 369 亿美元（见图 1-6）。其中，我国对外证券投资净流出 572 亿美元，上年同期为净流入 25 亿美元；境外对我国证券投资净流入 331 亿美元，同比下降 4%。

其他投资逆差大幅扩大。2015 年上半年，其他投资为逆差 1 931 亿美元，同比扩大 2.7 倍（见图 1-6）。其中，我国对外的贷款、贸易信贷和资金存放等资产净增加 632 亿美元，同比下降 61%；境外对我国的贷款、贸易信贷和资金存放等负债净减少 1 299 亿美元，上年同期为净增加 1 124 亿美元。

储备资产有所下降。2015 年上半年，我国储备资产（剔除汇率、价格等非交易价值变动影响，下同）减少 671 亿美元，上年同期为增加 1 479 亿美元，其中，外汇储备资产减少 666 亿美元（见图 1-7），上年同期为增加 1 486 亿美元。

专栏 1

《国际收支手册》(第六版)标准下的国际收支统计变化

我国从 2015 年开始按照《国际收支和国际投资头寸手册》(第六版)的标准编制和公布国际收支平衡表和国际投资头寸表。与第五版相比,第六版加强了对经济体脆弱性和可持续性的分析和监测,更加关注国际投资头寸和资产负债表情况。主要变化有:

一、主要项目名称有所调整

一类调整是项目的中文翻译改变,如"经常项目"改为"经常账户","资本和金融项目"改为"资本和金融账户"。另一类调整是项目的英文名称改变,为与国民账户体系等其他国际统计标准的相关概念相协调。如经常账户下的"收益"改为"初次收入"、"经常转移"改为"二次收入"等。

二、项目归属及分类变化

一是"来料加工"在第五版下按照进口和出口分别记录在货物贸易贷方和借方,而第六版是按照"工缴费"净额记录在服务贸易贷方;"转手买卖"由服务贸易调整至货物贸易下,按净额记录在贷方。以 2013 年国际收支平衡表为例,"来料加工"出口 925 亿美元、进口 828 亿美元,根据第五版分别记录在货物贸易贷方和借方下;而根据第六版,应按净额即 97 亿美元记录在服务贸易的贷方,在货物贸易中不再出现。2013 年"转手买卖"净收入 686 亿美元,根据第五版记录在服务贸易贷方项下;而根据第六版,应记录在货物贸易的贷方,在服务贸易中不再出现。二是将"金融衍生工具"从证券投资中单列出来,成为与证券投资并列的分类。三是将储备资产列于金融账户下。为兼顾公众的使用习惯,我国在金融账户下设"非储备性质的金融账户"和"储备资产"两个大项,前者口径与以往公布表式的金融账户相同。2015 年上半年资本和金融账户逆差 583 亿美元,其中"非储备性质的金融账户"逆差 1 259 亿美元。

三、列示方法变化

一是使用一列方式列示数据。以往我们在公布国际收支平衡表时按贷方、借方、差额三列列示数据,2015 年起按照一列列示数据。这种列示方法有助于进行时间序列分析。二是金融账户按差额列示而不再列示借贷方。主要是因为金融交易往往非常频繁,规模非常大,分析资产和负债的净变化比总流量更有意义。并且，总流量通常很难统计，很多时候需根据存量变化推算流量。另外，第六版给出了金融账户新的记录方法，可将资产和负债的增加均记录为正值，减少均记录为负值。考虑公众的使用习惯，我国仍采用以往的记录方法，即将金融账户资产净增加记借方（以负值表示），负债净增加记贷方（以正值表示），例如2014年储备资产增加记为 −1 178亿美元。

四、直接投资的统计方法发生变化

新版直接投资统计的变化主要体现在对直接投资企业对境外母公司投资（逆向投资）的处理方法上。第五版中，根据投资方向，直接投资被划分为"我国对外直接投资"（ODI）和"外国来华直接投资"（FDI），其中ODI下既包括我国对外直接投资的资产，也包括我国对外直接投资的负债（逆向投资），并按照资产减负债的轧差方式记录对外直接投资净资产；同样，FDI项下则采用外国来华直接投资负债减去外国来华直接投资资产（逆向投资）的统计原则。根据该原则，如当年境内直接投资者对境外子公司股权和债权投资100亿美元，接受境外子公司贷款或股权投资（逆向投资）30亿美元，则这30亿美元负债将作为ODI资产的扣减项处理，最终当年ODI净增加70亿美元。FDI项下按同样原则处理。第六版中，直接投资不再对逆向投资进行轧差处理，而是根据该投资是形成资产还是产生负债分别加以记录。如境外子公司对境内股东的股权和债务投资，记录在"负债"项下；外商投资企业对外国股东的股权和债务投资，记录在"资产"项下。还是上例，第六版中境内直接投资者对境外子公司的100亿美元投资将纳入我国对外直接投资统计，30亿美元的逆向投资将纳入外国来华直接投资统计。

五、改进了部分存量数据统计方法

根据手册的最新标准，我们全面采用市值法统计和编制我国国际投资头寸表中的各项数据，替代以往个别项目历史流量累计的方法。但是，由于部分重要数据的统计制度都是在近期开始实施，历史数据无法获得，因此，往期数据未能进行追溯调整，这样2014年前后的IIP数据存在不可比的情况。例如，2014年及以前的证券投资股权负债数据采用历史成本法，对于上市企业在境外发行的股票按发行价格记录存量。2015年起我们采用了市场价值法，即按期末的股票市场价格进行记录。由于估值方法改变，造成2014年前后的该部分数据不可比。

表 1-2 2015 年上半年中国国际收支平衡表　　　　　　　　　　单位：亿美元

项　目	行次	2015 年上半年
1. 经常账户	**1**	**1 486**
贷方	2	12 728
借方	3	−11 242
1.A 货物和服务	4	1 621
贷方	5	11 234
借方	6	−9 613
1.A.a 货物	7	2 566
贷方	8	10 112
借方	9	−7 546
1.A.b 服务	10	−945
贷方	11	1 122
借方	12	−2 067
1.A.b.1 加工服务	13	97
贷方	14	98
借方	15	−1
1.A.b.2 维护和维修服务	16	11
贷方	17	17
借方	18	−6
1.A.b.3 运输	19	−220
贷方	20	198
借方	21	−418
1.A.b.4 旅行	22	−892
贷方	23	277
借方	24	−1 169
1.A.b.5 建设	25	31
贷方	26	82
借方	27	−51
1.A.b.6 保险和养老金服务	28	−14
贷方	29	20
借方	30	−34
1.A.b.7 金融服务	31	−4
贷方	32	11
借方	33	−15
1.A.b.8 知识产权使用费	34	−99
贷方	35	6
借方	36	−105
1.A.b.9 电信、计算机和信息服务	37	59
贷方	38	114
借方	39	−55
1.A.b.10 其他商业服务	40	100
贷方	41	290
借方	42	−190
1.A.b.11 个人、文化和娱乐服务	43	−4
贷方	44	4
借方	45	−8
1.A.b.12 别处未提及的政府服务	46	−9
贷方	47	5
借方	48	−14
1.B 初次收入	49	−104
贷方	50	1 310
借方	51	−1 414
1.B.1 雇员报酬	52	151
贷方	53	179
借方	54	−28
1.B.2 投资收益	55	−258
贷方	56	1 127
借方	57	−1 385
1.B.3 其他初次收入	58	4
贷方	59	4

续表

项 目	行次	2015 年上半年
借方	60	−1
1 C 二次收入	61	−32
贷方	62	184
借方	63	−215
2. 资本和金融账户	**64**	**−585**
2.1 资本账户	65	3
贷方	66	4
借方	67	−1
2.2 金融账户	68	−587
资产	69	−1 084
负债	70	497
2.2.1 非储备性质的金融账户	71	−1 259
资产	72	−1 756
负债	73	497
2.2.1.1 直接投资	74	920
2.2.1.1.1 直接投资资产	75	−529
2.2.1.1.1.1 股权	76	−495
2.2.1.1.1.2 关联企业债务	77	−34
2.2.1.1.2 直接投资负债	78	1 449
2.2.1.1.2.1 股权	79	1 233
2.2.1.1.2.2 关联企业债务	80	215
2.2.1.2 证券投资	81	−241
2.2.1.2.1 资产	82	−572
2.2.1.2.1.1 股权	83	−326
2.2.1.2.1.2 债券	84	−247
2.2.1.2.2 负债	85	331
2.2.1.2.2.1 股权	86	212
2.2.1.2.2.2 债券	87	120
2.2.1.3 金融衍生工具	88	−7
2.2.1.3.1 资产	89	−23
2.2.1.3.2 负债	90	16
2.2.1.4 其他投资	91	−1 931
2.2.1.4.1 资产	92	−632
2.2.1.4.1.1 其他股权	93	0
2.2.1.4.1.2 货币和存款	94	−152
2.2.1.4.1.3 贷款	95	−541
2.2.1.4.1.4 保险和养老金	96	−56
2.2.1.4.1.5 贸易信贷	97	130
2.2.1.4.1.6 其他应收款	98	−13
2.2.1.4.2 负债	99	−1 299
2.2.1.4.2.1 其他股权	100	0
2.2.1.4.2.2 货币和存款	101	−175
2.2.1.4.2.3 贷款	102	−759
2.2.1.4.2.4 保险和养老金	103	14
2.2.1.4.2.5 贸易信贷	104	−357
2.2.1.4.2.6 其他应付款	105	−23
2.2.1.4.2.7 特别提款权	106	0
2.2.2 储备资产	107	671
2.2.2.1 货币黄金	108	0
2.2.2.2 特别提款权	109	−4
2.2.2.3 在国际货币基金组织的储备头寸	110	10
2.2.2.4 外汇储备	111	666
2.2.2.5 其他储备资产	112	0
3. 净误差与遗漏	**113**	**−901**

注：1. 本表根据《国际收支和国际投资头寸手册》(第六版)编制。
　　2. "贷方"按正值列示，"借方"按负值列示，差额等于"贷方"加上"借方"。本表除标注"贷方"和"借方"的
　　　 项目外，其他项目均指差额。
　　3. 本表计数采用四舍五入原则。
数据来源：国家外汇管理局。

专栏 2

如何看待近期我国黄金储备变动

近期，人民银行按照国际货币基金组织数据公布特殊标准（SDDS）公布了黄金储备数据。截至 2015 年 6 月末，我国黄金储备规模为 1 658 吨，较上次（2009 年 4 月）公布规模增加了 604 吨。

根据国际收支统计原则，黄金分为货币黄金与非货币黄金，前者由央行持有，是一种金融资产，在金融账户的储备资产项下记录；后者由其他部门持有，是一种实物资产，在经常账户下的货物进出口中记录。央行增持黄金储备，根据交易对手可分为国内交易和国外交易。国内交易不需要在国际收支平衡表中进行记录。国外交易需区分交易对手进行记录，只有与国外央行或国际组织的交易才记录货币黄金，从其他商业机构购买属于非货币黄金进口，记录在货物项下，这些非货币黄金通过黄金货币化（非交易变动）最后形成央行的货币黄金储备。

我国本次增持黄金的渠道主要包括国内杂金提纯、生产收贮、国内外市场交易等方式。其中，国内杂金提纯、生产收贮以及国内市场购买都属于国内交易，不需要在国际收支平衡表中进行记录。国外市场购买黄金的交易对手均是国外商业机构，而非央行或国际组织，因此不应记录为货币黄金增加，而应记录为货物进口。考虑到本次增持黄金是多年来逐步累积的，进行追溯调整较为困难，因此国际收支平衡表中不再对这些交易进行记录和调整，未来发生交易时根据实际情况进行记录。存量方面，央行的黄金储备余额记录在国际投资头寸表的储备资产项下，2015 年第二季度货币黄金余额变化与流量之间的差异形成约 220 亿美元的非交易变动，其中包括黄金货币化以及往期存量黄金的价格变化等。2015 年 6 月末，我国黄金储备余额 624 亿美元，与外汇储备之比为 1.7%。

虽然与 3 万多亿美元的外汇储备相比，我国黄金储备的规模不大，与外汇储备之比不足 2%。但是，从绝对量来看，我国的规模并不低。根据世界黄金协会（WCG）7 月公布的数据，中国已超越俄罗斯成为全球第五大黄金储备国。排在前四位的美国、德国、意大利以及法国由于其本币均是可自由兑换货币，同时外汇储备规模较低，因此黄金储备与外汇储备之比较高。而我国作为尚未实现完全可兑换的发展中国家，外汇储备规模较大，黄金储备比例自然较低，因此不能仅以这一比例高低来衡量黄金储备规模是否合适。作为外汇储备全球第二大国的日本，其黄金储备的占比也只有2%。

黄金作为一种特殊的资产，具有金融和商品的多重属性，与其他资产一起配置，有助于调节和优化国际储备组合的整体风险收益特性。但是，相对于其他外汇资产，黄金储备也有着一定的局限性。比如，黄金的价格波动较大，市场容量小，持有成本高，流动性欠缺等。从价格方面来看，国际金价波动较大。2009年初以来，黄金由每盎司800美元左右逐步上升到2011年中的高点接近1 900美元，之后不到两年又回落到1 200美元左右。价格的大幅波动不利于储备资产保持安全性。从市场容量和流动性看，国际外汇市场的日成交量在5万亿美元以上，债券市场仅美国余额就有约50万亿美元，而国际黄金市场日成交量仅有约0.3万亿美元。因此大规模持有黄金作为储备资产难以满足随时变现的需要。从资产的保值增值性来看，持有黄金储备不仅不能生息，还要支付托管费用以及存储费用等成本。

此外，中国已成为世界第一大黄金生产国，也是黄金消费大国。2015年上半年，我国累计生产黄金229吨，消费黄金561吨，其中，首饰制造用金412吨，金条及金币用金102吨，工业及其他用金47吨。可见，"藏金于民"成效显著，而从国家储备角度来讲，也没有必要和老百姓"争"金。

（三）国际收支运行评价

经常账户顺差增加但仍处于国际公认的合理水平之内。2015年上半年，我国经常账户顺差与GDP之比为3.1%，同比上升1.3个百分点。主要是由于货物贸易顺差增长较快，与GDP之比为5.3%，同比上升2.0个百分点；服务贸易和投资收益逆差与GDP之比分别为2.0%和0.5%，同比扩大0.6个和0.4个百分点（见图1-8）。此外，上半年经常账户和直接投资顺差合计2 406亿美元，较上年同期增长39%，说明我国抵御跨境资本流动冲击的基础依然较强。

跨境资本延续流出势头但第二季度大幅缓解并趋向基本平衡。2015年第一季度，资本和金融账户逆差981亿美元，较2014年第四季度扩大677亿美元；外汇储

图 1-8

1990—2015 年上半年经常账户差额与 GDP 之比及其结构

数据来源：国家外汇管理局、国家统计局。

图 1-9

2005—2015 年第二季度国际收支差额与外汇储备资产变动

数据来源：国家外汇管理局。

図 1-10

2005-2015 年第二季度证券投资和其他投资项下资本流动情况

亿美元

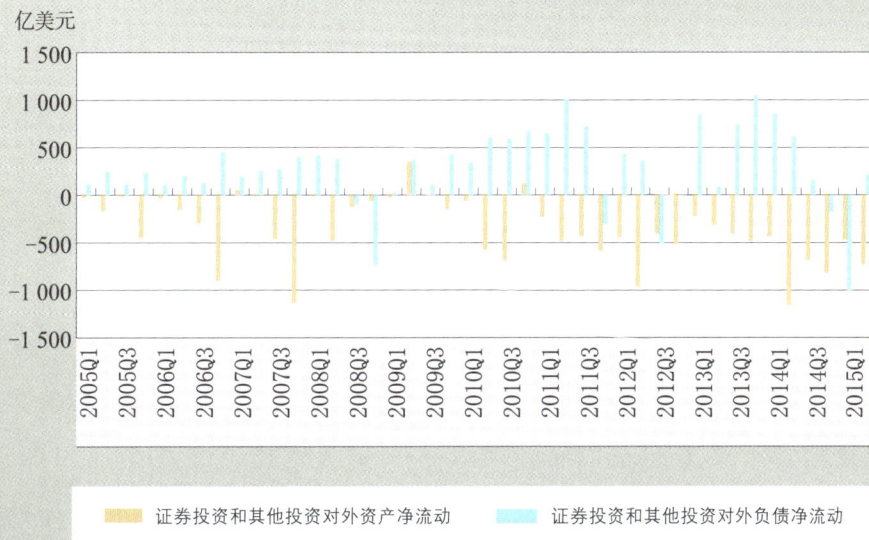

数据来源：国家外汇管理局。

备资产减少 795 亿美元，环比多降了 502 亿美元。第二季度跨境资本流出明显放缓，资本和金融账户逆差 275 亿美元，较第一季度收窄 707 亿美元；外汇储备资产由第一季度的下降转为增加 130 亿美元（见图 1-9）。

境内主体本外币资产负债结构优化调整是跨境资本流动变化的主导因素。一方面，"藏汇于民"效果明显，境内机构和个人的对外资产有所增多。2015 年上半年，我国企业对外直接投资项下净流出即对外资产净增加 529 亿美元，同比增长 70%；对外证券投资项下净流出即对外资产净增加 572 亿美元，2014 年同期为净回流 25 亿美元（见图 1-10）。另一方面，境内主体进一步减少对外负债，逐步降低高杠杆经营等风险。上半年，境外贷款净流出 759 亿美元，2014 年同期为净流入 769 亿美元；贸易信贷项下净流出即对外负债净减少 357 亿美元，同比增长 3.3 倍。此外，境内主体对外债务去杠杆化进程也根据市场情况有所调整，随着人民币汇率走势及预期逐步企稳，第二季度境外贷款和贸易信贷净流出即对外负债净下降 179 亿和 136 亿美元，分别较第一季度净流出规模下降 69% 和 39%。

专栏 3

外汇储备余额下降的主要影响因素

2015 年 6 月末，我国外汇储备余额为 36 938 亿美元，而 2014 年 6 月末为历史最高的 39 932 亿美元。在此一年间，外汇储备余额累计下降了 2 994 亿美元，主要影响因素如下（见图 C3-1）：

一是汇率、价格等非交易价值变动影响使外汇储备账面价值减少 2 000 多亿美元，这些并不是实际的外汇从储备流出。国际收支平衡表显示，2014 年下半年至 2015 年上半年，我国外汇储备资产累计下降 963 亿美元，这都是国际收支实际交易所致（含储备经营收益），其余 2 031 亿美元的外汇储备余额变化均与汇率、价格等估值因素有关。例如，美元指数在此期间上涨 20%，导致外汇储备中的欧元等非美元资产折算成美元时，就会出现美元计价规模下降。

二是我国企业、银行等调整境内本外币资产负债结构，增持外汇资产，减少外汇负债。2014 年下半年至 2015 年上半年，我国企业、个人持汇意愿逐步增强，在境内银行的外汇存款余额先降后升，累计增加了 236 亿美元；同时，企业购汇偿还境内外汇贷款增多，在此一年内的银行境内外汇贷款余额累计下降 328 亿美元，其中，2014 年下半年降幅较大，2015 年上半年有所企稳；此外，由于客户与银行签订的远期售汇合同金额明显大于远期结汇，银行未来需要向客户净卖出外汇，为规避汇率波动风险，银行相应增持了 666 亿美元的外汇头寸。上述调整最终都使我国银行的自身外汇头寸、客户外汇存款等境内外汇资金来源增多，而境内外汇贷款发放等资金运用减少，更多外汇资金被银行运用到境外，在国际收支统计中表现为银行部门增持境外资产或偿还境外负债，均导致资本和金融账户逆差扩大。

三是企业等各类市场主体跨境外汇净支付。2014 年下半年至 2015 年上半年，境内企业、个人等非银行部门跨境外汇净支付 456 亿美元，主要用于境外旅游消费、企业"走出去"投资或偿还境外融资等。但外商直接投资、我国企业境外证券筹资等项下依然是外汇较大净流入，说明真正以长期投资为目的的外汇资金仍在进入我国。同期，银行自身净购汇并对外支付外汇

494亿美元，主要是由于国内客户黄金等贵金属投资和消费需求旺盛，推动了黄金进口以及贵金属投资形成的汇率敞口平盘购汇，体现了"藏金于民"的效果。

此外，外汇储备经营收益等还会增加外汇储备，2014年下半年至2015年上半年，国际收支平衡表中的投资收益项目累计收入（即贷方）1 979亿美元，其中的储备经营收益贡献较大。总的来看，近期我国外汇储备余额下降，汇率、价格等估值因素影响较大，其他主要是由于境内主体本外币资产负债结构的优化调整。

图 C3-1

外汇储备余额变动的主要影响因素

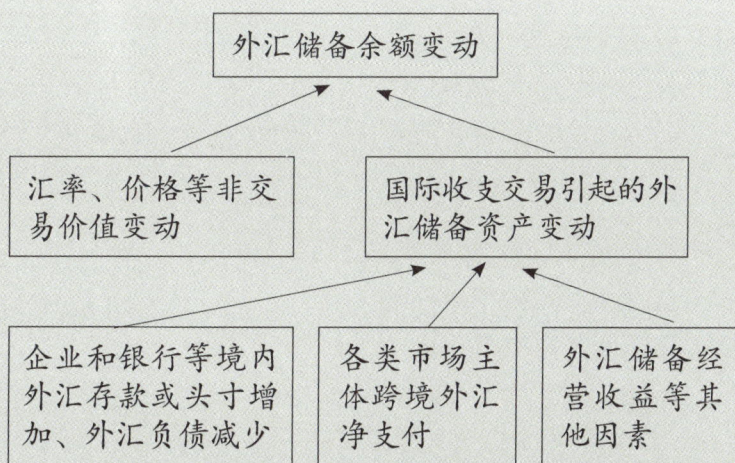

二、国际收支主要
项目分析

（一）货物贸易

货物进出口呈现较大顺差，外贸依存度进一步下降。根据海关统计，2015 年上半年，我国出口同比增长 0.7%，进口同比下降 15.7%，进出口顺差 2 622 亿美元，同比增长 1.5 倍，与同期 GDP 的比为 5.4%，较上年同期提高 3.1 个百分点。上半年，我国外贸依存度（进出口总额 /GDP）为 38.8%，较 2014 年同期下降 5.7 个百分点（见图 2-1）。

一般贸易差额由逆转顺，私营企业进出口顺差增长较快。2015 年上半年，我国一般贸易顺差 1 261 亿美元，2014 年同期为逆差 136 亿美元；加工贸易顺差 1 625 亿美元，同比略降 2.8%（见图 2-2）。私营企业进出口顺差 2 729 亿美元，同比大幅增长 60.8%；外资企业进出口顺差 769 亿美元，增长 19.0%；国有企业进出口逆差 865 亿美元，同比下降 34.2%。近期，货物贸易顺差中加工贸易、外资企业的比重有所下降（见图 2-3），一方面说明我国对外贸易的内生动力逐步增强，另一方面也反映了一般贸易和内资企业进口成本的降低。

我国出口商品在主要发达市场的份额稳中有升，出口市场多元化积极推进。2015 年上半年，我国对美国出口同比增长 9.3%，对日本和欧盟出口同比分别下降 10.6% 和 2.5%。从欧美日进口来源国情况看，上半年美国进口商品中来自中国的比重为 20.4%，

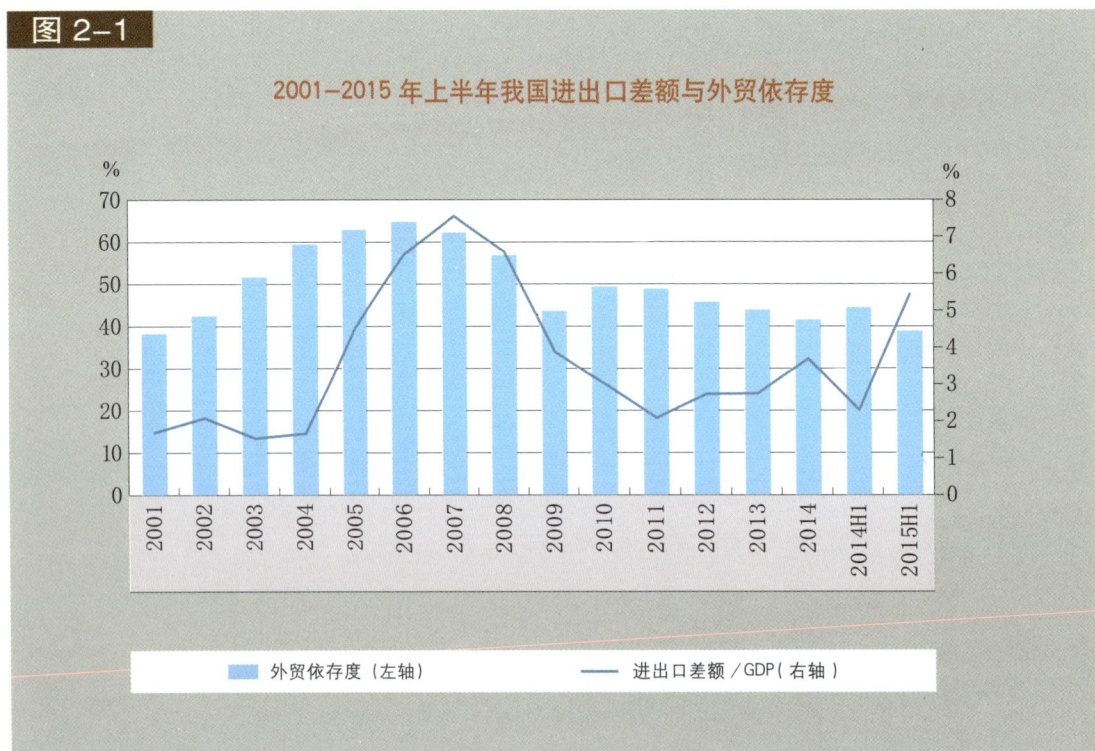

图 2-1

2001-2015 年上半年我国进出口差额与外贸依存度

数据来源：海关总署、国家统计局。

图 2-2

2000—2015 年上半年我国按贸易方式货物贸易差额构成

亿美元

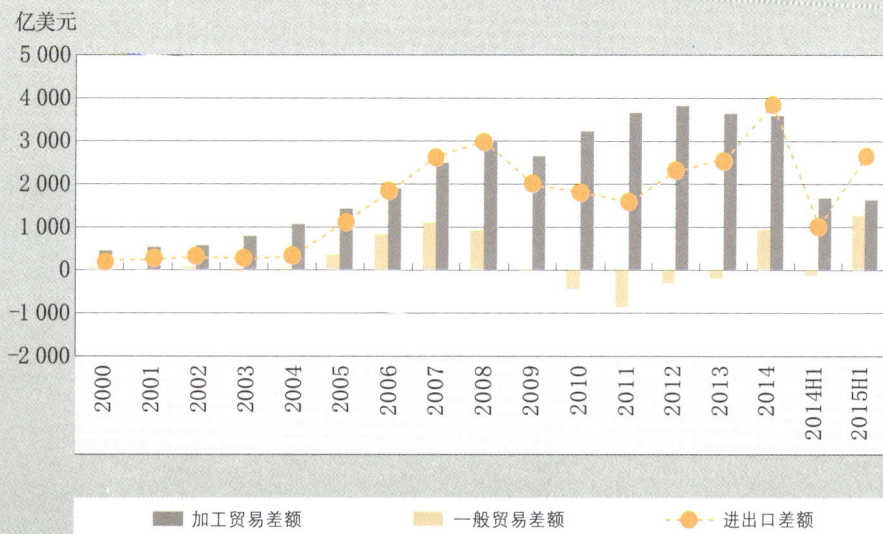

加工贸易差额　　　一般贸易差额　　　·○· 进出口差额

数据来源：海关总署。

图 2-3

2000—2015 年上半年我国按贸易主体货物贸易差额构成

亿美元

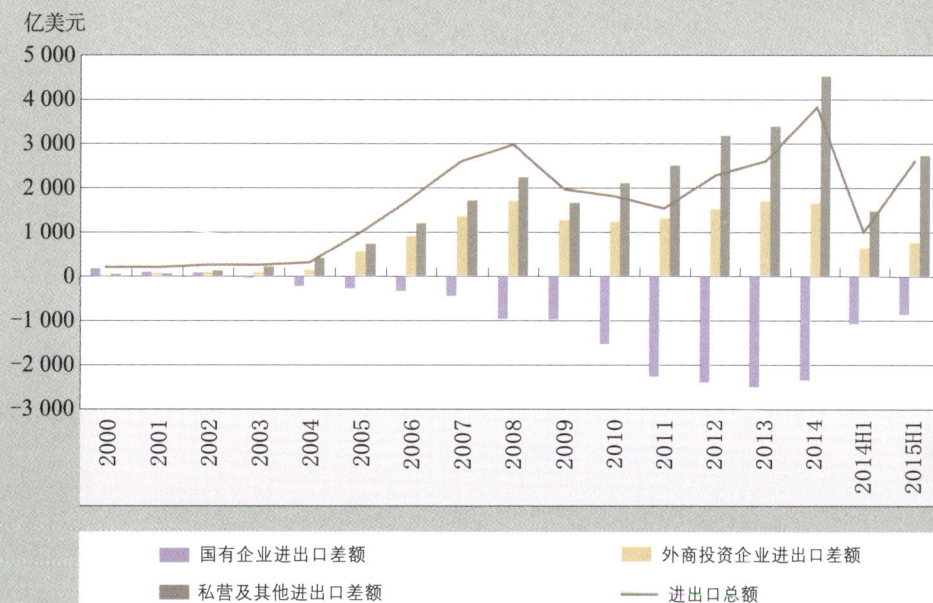

国有企业进出口差额　　　　外商投资企业进出口差额

私营及其他进出口差额　　　—— 进出口总额

数据来源：海关总署。

较 2014 年同期上升 1.8 个百分点；欧盟进口商品中来自中国的比重为 19.3%，同比上升 2.5 个百分点；日本进口商品中来自中国的比重为 23.9%，同比上升 2.2 个百分点。上半年，我国对东盟、印度、拉丁美洲、非洲等新兴市场出口增长较快，增速分别为 9.7%、10.7%、3.7% 和 12.8%，合计占比为 26.1%，同比上升 2.0 个百分点。

进口价格回落对顺差增长贡献较大，贸易条件明显改善。2015 年上半年，进出口顺差同比增加 1 579 亿美元。其中，由于石油、铁矿石等国际大宗商品价格大幅下跌，进口价格指数月均回落 10.7%，对顺差增加的贡献为 64%，即 1 011 亿美元（见图 2-5）。上半年，我国出口价格指数月均下跌 1.1%，贸易条件指数月均为 110.8%，较 2014 年同期明显改善。

（二）服务贸易 [1]

服务贸易规模保持稳定增长趋势，高附加值服务贸易与传统服务贸易齐头并进。在国内经济增速放缓、外贸低迷的背景下，我国服务贸易仍保持较快增长势头。2015 年上半年，服务贸易收支总额达到 3 188 亿美元，同比增长 12%，同期货物贸易总额为下降 8%。服务贸易与货物贸易总额的比例为 18%，较上年同期高 3 个百

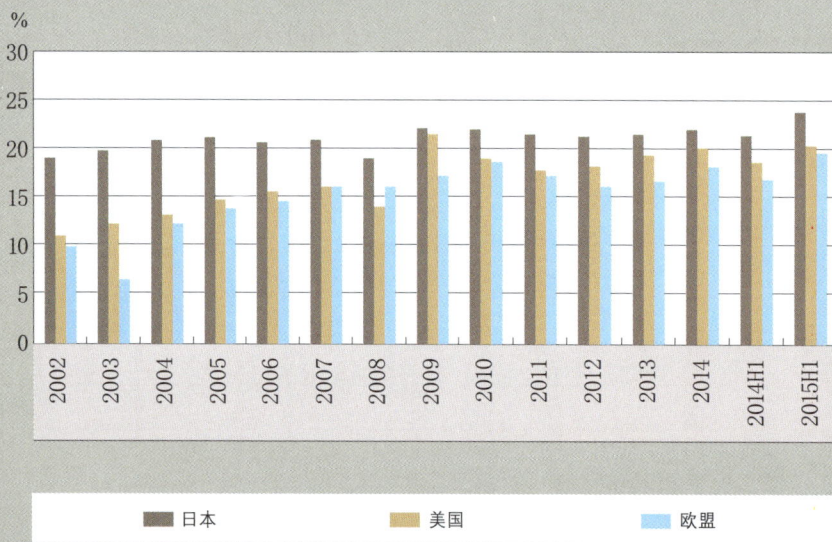

图 2-4

2002–2015 年上半年我国出口商品在发达经济体的市场份额变动

数据来源：海关总署。

---

[1] 按照最新国际标准，国际收支平衡表中服务贸易口径较过去发生变化，加工贸易从货物贸易调整至服务贸易，转手买卖从服务贸易调整至货物贸易。同时，服务贸易分类和细项名称略有调整。

图 2-5

进出口差额同比变动中的数量与价格因素

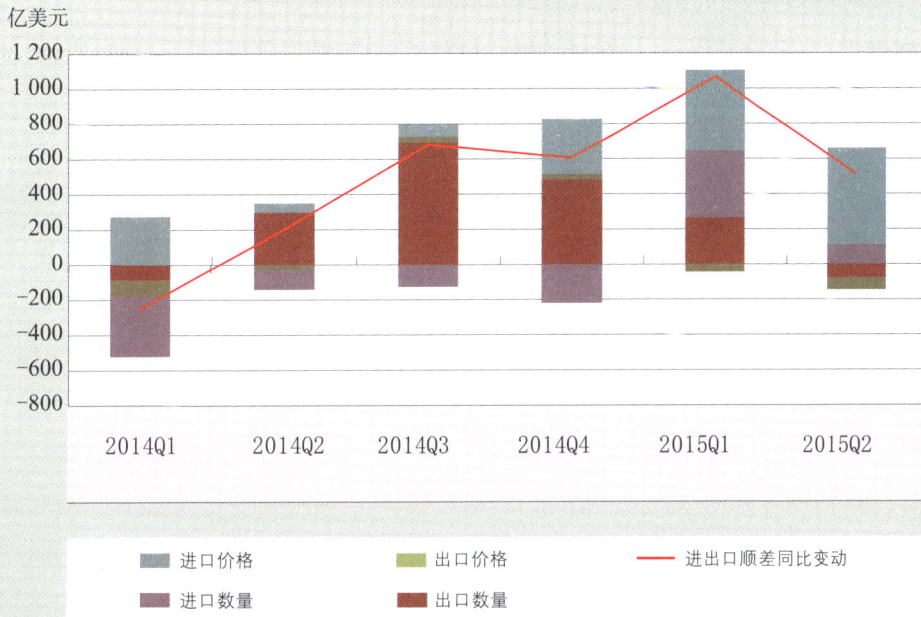

数据来源：环亚经济数据库。

图 2-6

2004-2015 年上半年货物贸易和服务贸易收支总额比较

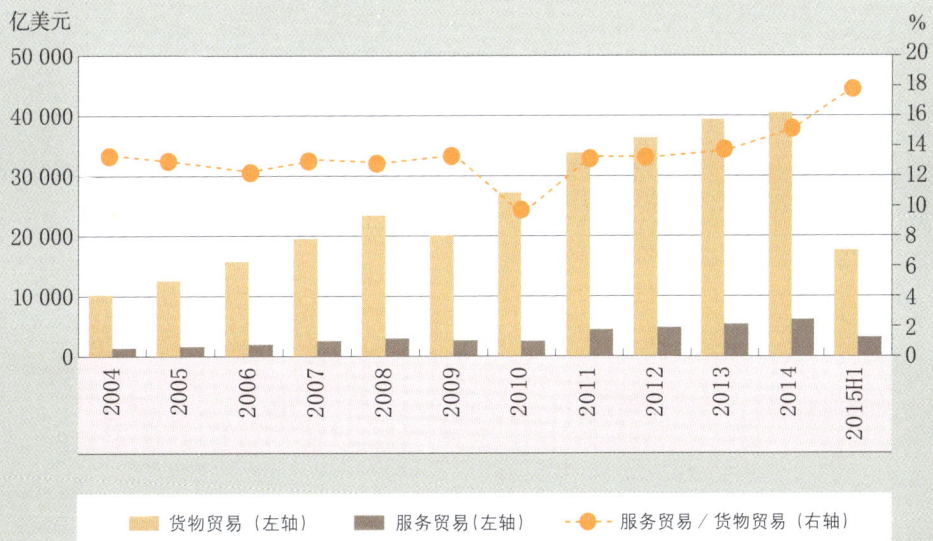

数据来源：国家外汇管理局。

分点（见图 2-6）。在国家优化服务贸易结构，支持高附加值服务发展政策的推动下，我国服务贸易转型升级不断深化。2015 年上半年，电信计算机和信息服务、建设以及文化娱乐等高附加值服务贸易分别增长 19%、79% 和 1.3 倍。

服务贸易收入略有增长，增速有所下滑。2015 年上半年服务贸易收入为 1 122 亿美元，增长 1%（见图 2-7），增速较上年同期下降 13 个百分点。上半年，由于服务贸易的五个主要项目出现分化，使整体服务贸易收入增长大幅放缓。其中，运输、旅行、建设、电信计算机和信息服务收入较上年同期共计增加 97 亿美元，其他商业服务（包括研发服务、专业和管理咨询服务、技术服务、经营性租赁服务等项目）收入较上年同期减少 97 亿美元。

服务贸易支出继续保持较快增长，旅行占比持续上升。2015 年上半年服务贸易支出 2 067 亿美元，增长 20%（见图 2-7）。其中，旅行支出 1 169 亿美元，占服务贸易支出的 57%，是服务贸易支出占比最大项目，且该比例近年还有不断扩大趋势；运输支出和其他商业服务支出分列第二、第三位，分别为 418 亿美元和 190 亿美元。

服务贸易逆差继续扩大，旅行支出快速增长是主因。2015 年上半年服务贸易逆差 945 亿美元，增长 53%，其中在服务贸易总额中占比近半的旅行项目是服务贸易整体逆差扩大的主要来源（见图 2-8）。由于居民可支配收入提高，部分国家签证政策放松，出境留学热潮不减，以及部分国家货币贬值等因素，导致境外购物更具

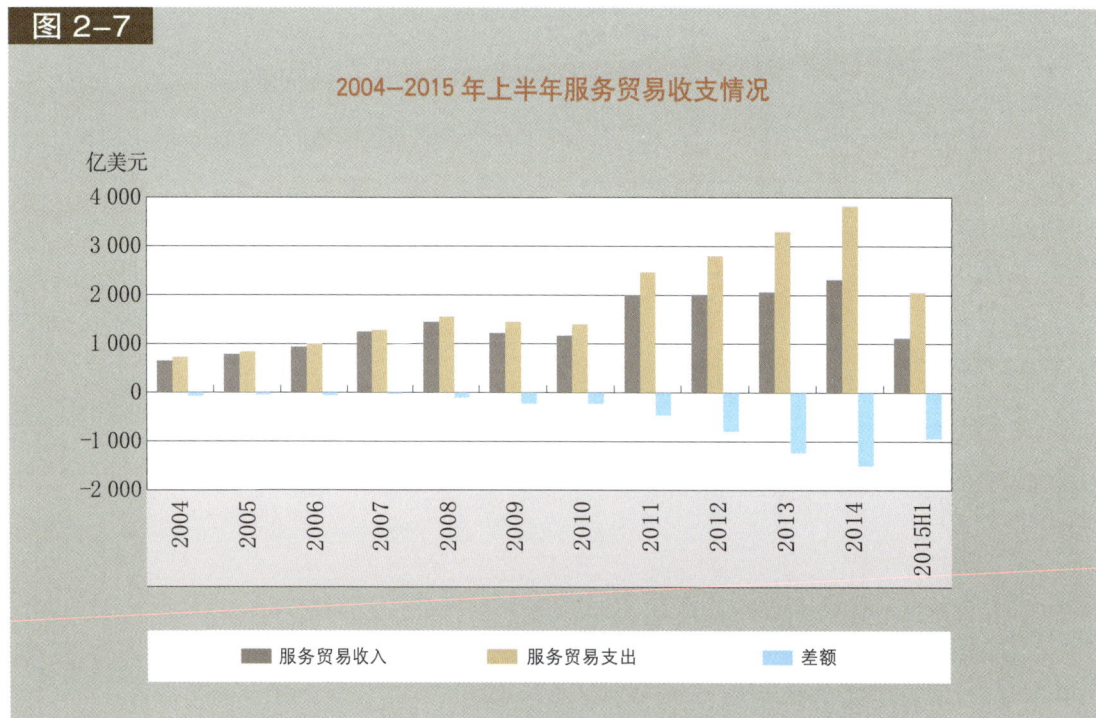

图 2-7

2004—2015 年上半年服务贸易收支情况

数据来源：国家外汇管理局。

图 2-8

2009-2015 年上半年旅行逆差对服务贸易逆差贡献度

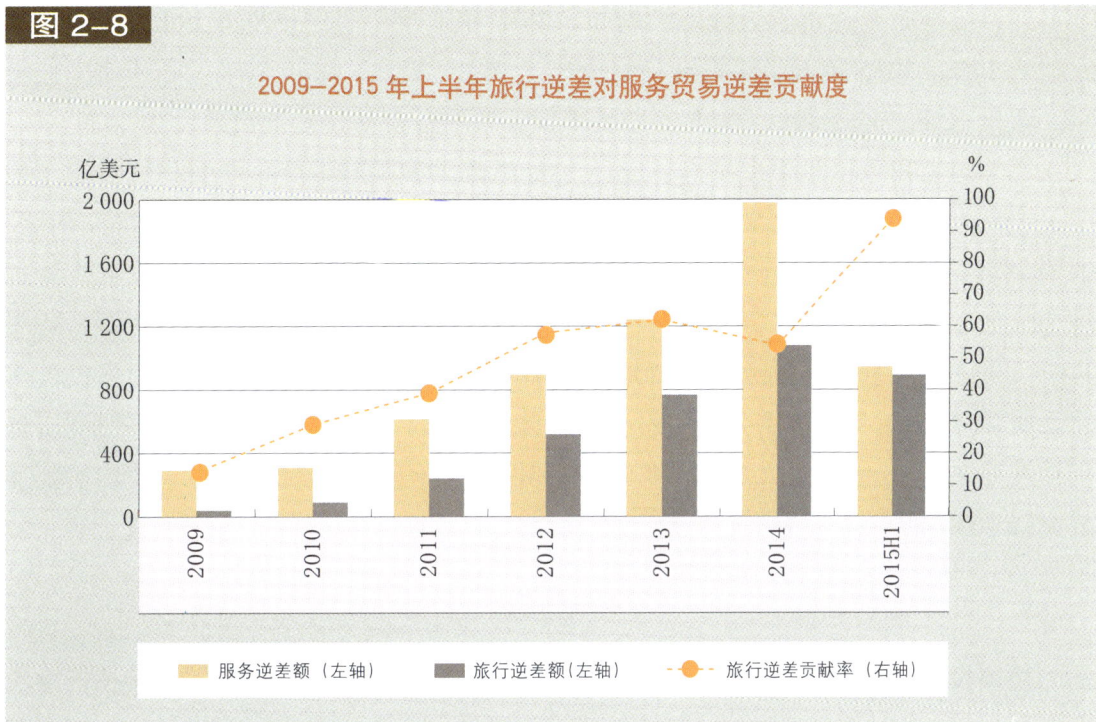

数据来源：国家外汇管理局。

图 2-9

2015 年上半年我国对主要贸易伙伴服务贸易收支情况

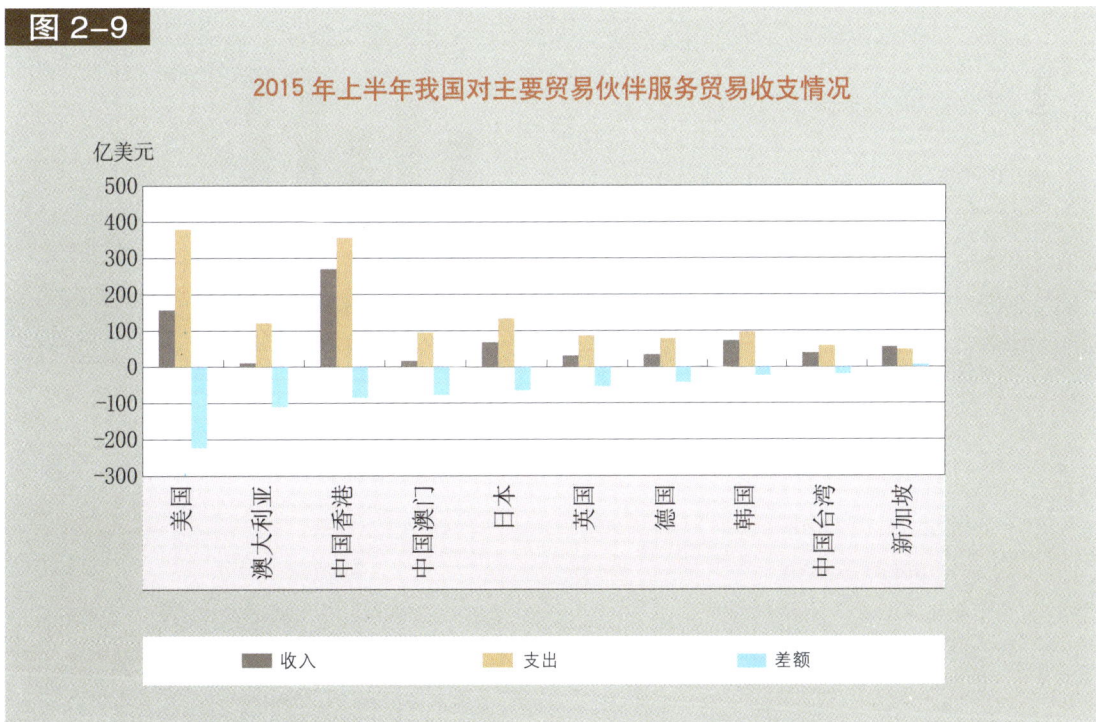

数据来源：国家外汇管理局。

吸引力，出境旅游及留学人数持续增长。2015 年上半年我国出境 6 190 万人次，同比增长 14%。2015 年上半年旅游项目支出 1 169 亿美元，增长 70%；收入 277 亿美元，增长 12%；逆差 892 亿美元，增长 1 倍，对服务贸易逆差的贡献度为 94%。

逆差国家和地区集中度较高。2015 年上半年，我国对十个主要贸易伙伴国（地区）中的九个均呈现逆差，占同期服务贸易逆差 75%。其中，对美国、澳大利亚、中国香港、中国澳门、日本、英国、德国、韩国、中国台湾的服务贸易逆差分别为 223 亿、111 亿、86 亿、78 亿、66 亿、55 亿、44 亿、24 亿和 20 亿美元（见图 2-9）。过去，服务贸易顺差的主要地区是中国香港，由于《国际收支和国际投资头寸手册》（第六版）将转手买卖从服务贸易调至货物贸易，因此上半年我国对港服务贸易转为逆差 86 亿美元，去年同期为顺差 306 亿美元。2015 年上半年，我国对新加坡保持小额顺差，金额为 7 亿美元。

（三）直接投资

直接投资继续呈现净流入 [①]。2015 年上半年，我国国际收支口径的直接投资净流

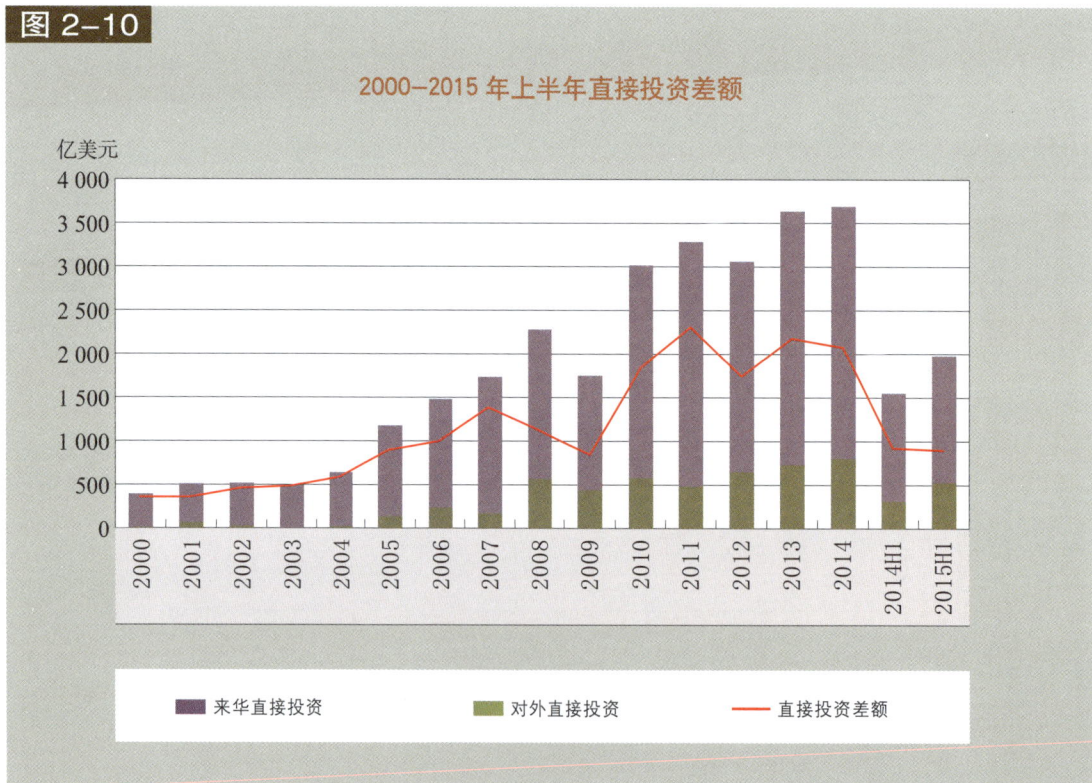

图 2-10

2000-2015 年上半年直接投资差额

亿美元

（图例）■ 来华直接投资　■ 对外直接投资　— 直接投资差额

数据来源：国家外汇管理局。

---

① 直接投资净流动指对外直接投资净增与来华直接投资净增之差。当对外直接投资净增大于来华直接投资净增时，直接投资项目为净流出。当对外直接投资净增小于来华直接投资净增时，直接投资项目为净流入。

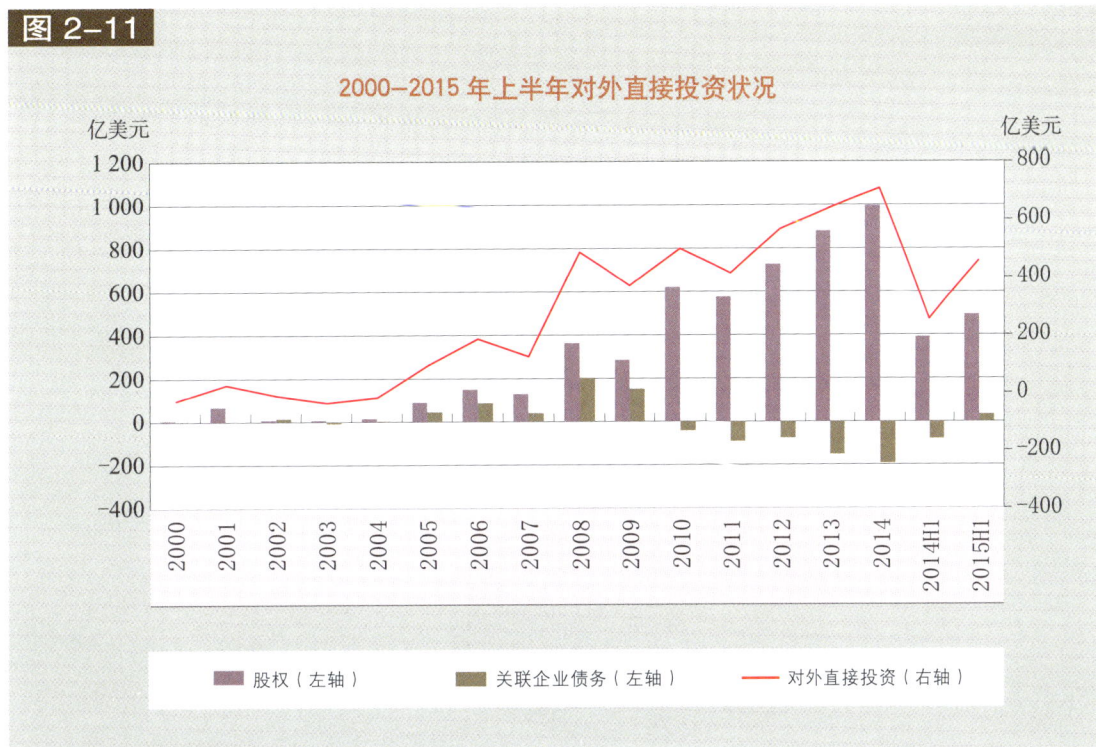

图 2-11

2000—2015 年上半年对外直接投资状况

数据来源：国家外汇管理局。

入 920 亿美元，同比下降 1%。2014 年，全球吸收外来直接投资减少 16%，我国超过美国，成为吸收外来直接投资最多的国家。2015 年以来，直接投资继续较大规模净流入，反映我国在吸引外资流入方面仍具较强竞争力。上半年直接投资净流入同比少增，不在于吸收来华投资下降，而在于我国企业加快"走出去"（见图 2-10）。

对外直接投资大增，显示企业进一步加速海外布局。2015 年上半年，我国对外直接投资净增 529 亿美元，同比增长 70%（见图 2-11），其中，投资新增 774 亿美元，增长 41%，投资回流 245 亿美元，增长 3%。

从投资形式看，逾九成为股权投资净增（495 亿美元），其中新增股权投资和收益再投资均为两位数增长，表明境内企业看好境外投资前景，较好的境外企业盈利状况也推动了对外投资的扩大。对外债权投资净增 34 亿美元，上年同期为净减少 81 亿美元，反映此类投资灵活多变，易受短期市场因素影响。

分部门看，非金融部门对外直接投资净增 399 亿美元，同比增长 57%。上半年，中小规模投资趋于活跃，私营企业对外投资较快增长，"走出去"行业和主要投资目的地相对集中（见图 2-12）。欧美等成熟经济体经济运行出现复苏，对外国投资者吸引力上升。金融部门对外直接投资净增 134 亿美元，增长 1.3 倍，其中七成为银行部门对外投资，其投资资金主要来自收益再投资，主要投资目的地为中国香港，

图 2-12

2015 年上半年我国非金融部门对外直接投资流出分布
（按国内行业、投资目的国划分）

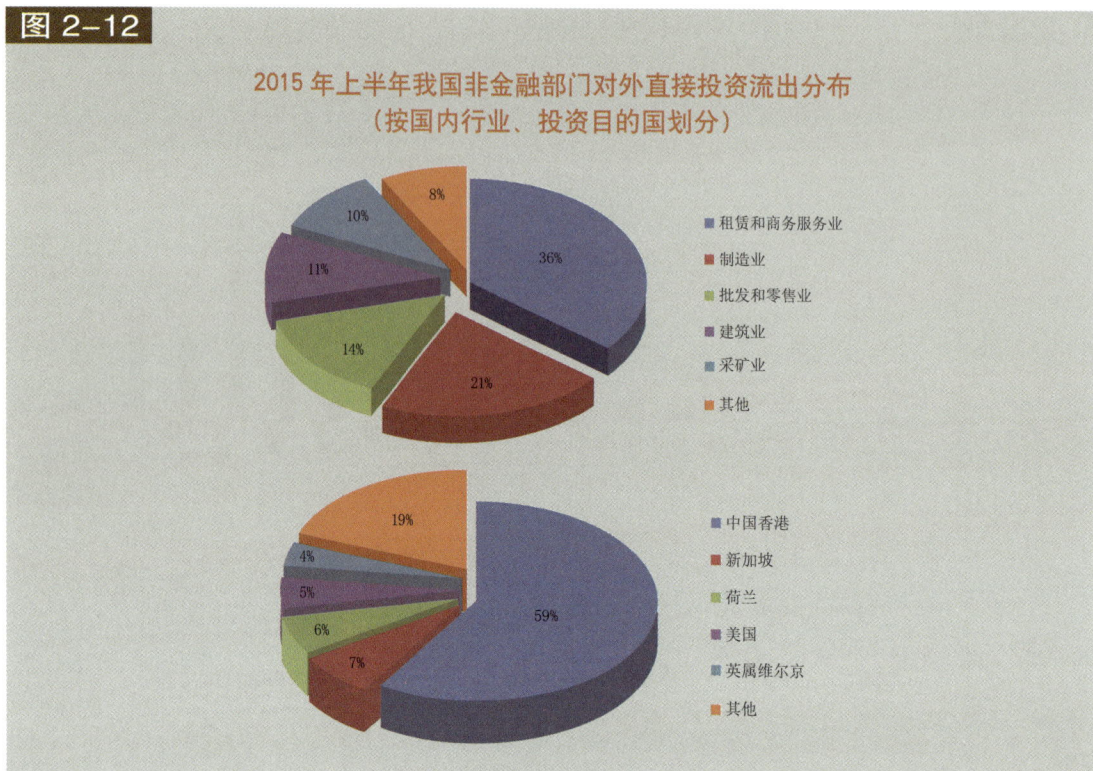

■ 租赁和商务服务业 36%
■ 制造业 21%
■ 批发和零售业 14%
■ 建筑业 11%
■ 采矿业 10%
■ 其他 8%

■ 中国香港 59%
■ 新加坡 7%
■ 荷兰 6%
■ 美国 5%
■ 英属维尔京 4%
■ 其他 19%

数据来源：国家外汇管理局。

表明伴随企业"走出去"不断壮大，金融业持续跟进投资。

从境内外关系[①]看，境内直接投资者对境外被投资企业的投资是我国对外直接投资的主要构成，2015 年上半年净增 492 亿美元，增长 58%，占对外直接投资净增的 93%。此外，外商投资企业对境外直接投资者的投资（逆向投资），以及境内对境外联属机构的投资净增 37 亿美元，虽然仅占对外直接投资净增的 7%，但这类企业在跨国企业集团全球资金汇集中正在逐步形成"资金中心"功能。

来华直接投资稳定增加，反映境外直接投资者继续保持对华投资信心。2015 年上半年，来华直接投资净增 1 449 亿美元，同比增长 17%，其中，投资新增 2 008 亿美元，增长 26%；投资撤回 560 亿美元，增长 56%。继 2014 年超过美国成为全球最大外来直接投资目的地后，我国吸收来华直接投资继续保持增长。

分部门看，上半年非金融部门吸收境外直接投资净增 1 315 亿美元，同比增长 11%，占来华直接投资净增的九成。我国经济结构转型、产能调整、产业升级，促

① 根据《国际收支和国际投资头寸手册》（第六版），直接投资关系分为三类，即直接投资者对直接投资企业的投资、直接投资企业对直接投资者的投资（逆向投资）和联属企业之间的投资。其中，对直接投资资产（对外直接投资）而言，分别为境内直接投资者对境外直接投资企业（ODI 企业）的投资、境内直接投资企业（外商投资企业）对境外直接投资者的投资（逆向投资），以及境内企业对有共同母公司的境外联属企业的投资。

图 2-13

2000~2015 年上半年来华直接投资状况

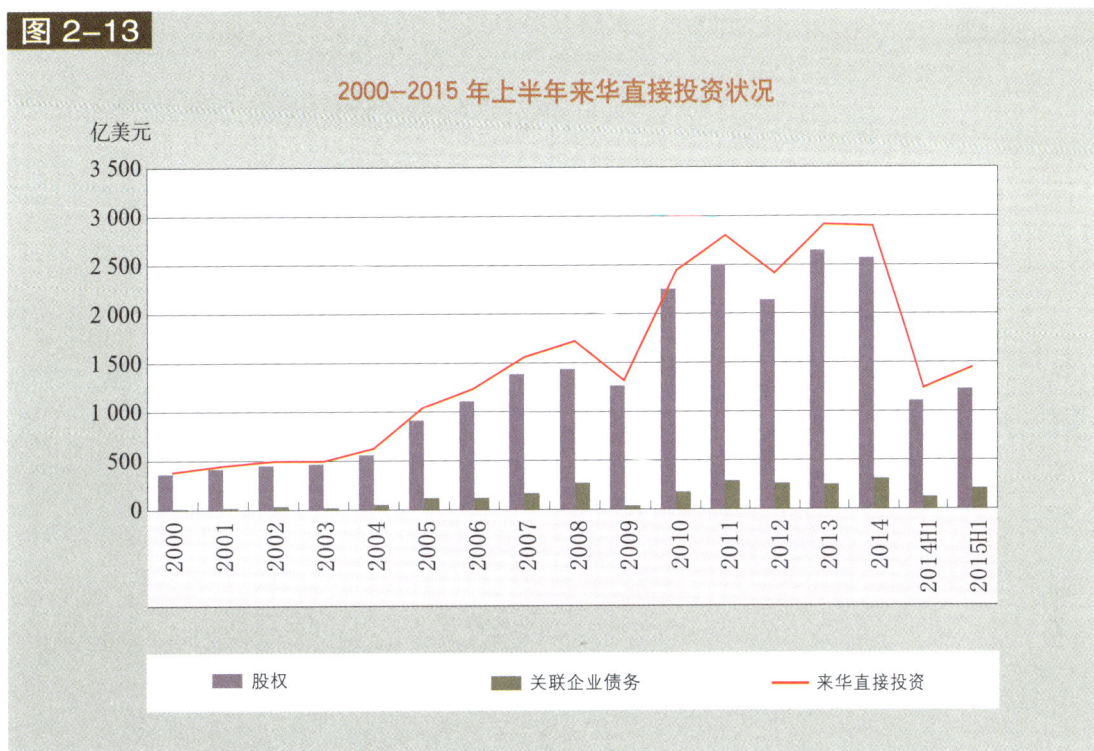

数据来源：国家外汇管理局。

使境外股东不断调整其投向。上半年，制造业吸收来华直接投资占比 29%，同比下降 4 个百分点；商务服务业等第三产业吸收来华直接投资占比上升。金融部门吸收境外投资净增 134 亿美元，增长 1.2 倍，其中过半投向银行业和保险业，且主要为收益再投资，境内机构经营状况较好，境外投资未现大量撤出。

从投资形式看，85% 为股权投资净增（1 233 亿美元），增长 11%（见图 2-13）。在我国经济增速趋缓情况下，来华直接投资中的新增股权投资和收益再投资同比分别增长 8% 和 14%，表明外资继续保持长期投资中国的信心。15% 为债务投资净增（215 亿美元），增长 68%，主要是跨国公司根据境内外市场差异，进行灵活的财务安排。此外，人民币跨境投资不断扩大。52% 的来华直接投资跨境资金净流入为人民币净流入，美元只占 41%。

从境内外关系[1] 看，外商投资企业吸收境外直接投资者的投资是来华直接投资的主要构成，上半年境外投资净增 1 359 亿美元，同比增长 9%，占来华直接投资净增的 94%，表明外资仍保持长期投资中国的信心；境内直接投资者吸收境外被投资企业的投资（逆向投资），以及境内吸收境外联属企业的投资 90 亿美元，占比仅为 6%。

---

[1] 对直接投资负债（来华直接投资）而言，分别为外商投资企业吸收境外直接投资者的投资、境内直接投资者吸收境外直接投资企业（ODI 企业）的投资（逆向投资），以及境内企业吸收境外联属企业的投资。

我国企业"走出去"具有顺周期性

过去十年，随着国家加快实施"走出去"战略，我国企业对外投资步伐提速，大宗商品是主要投资领域之一。自2011年3月，全球大宗商品价格进入下行周期，先前的投资项目受到不同程度影响，我国对外大宗商品投资规模下降，呈现出较强的顺周期性。"走出去"企业在专注项目分析评价的同时，需加强跨周期研判，既做好整体方案设计，又做好不利情形的压力测试，按市场化原则稳健开展对外投资。

大宗商品是我国"走出去"战略的主要领域。过去十年，我国企业"走出去"步伐提速，大宗商品是投资重点之一。据国际数据公司Dealogic统计，2000年至2014年，我国企业海外并购2 130笔，金额合计4 399亿美元，其中大宗商品的并购696笔，占33%；金额合计2 433亿美元，占55%。大宗商品并购集中于能源和矿产，中石油、中石化、中海油并购金额超过1 200亿美元，约占50%。

图 C4-1

2005-2015年6月大宗商品价格与海外并购交易量趋势

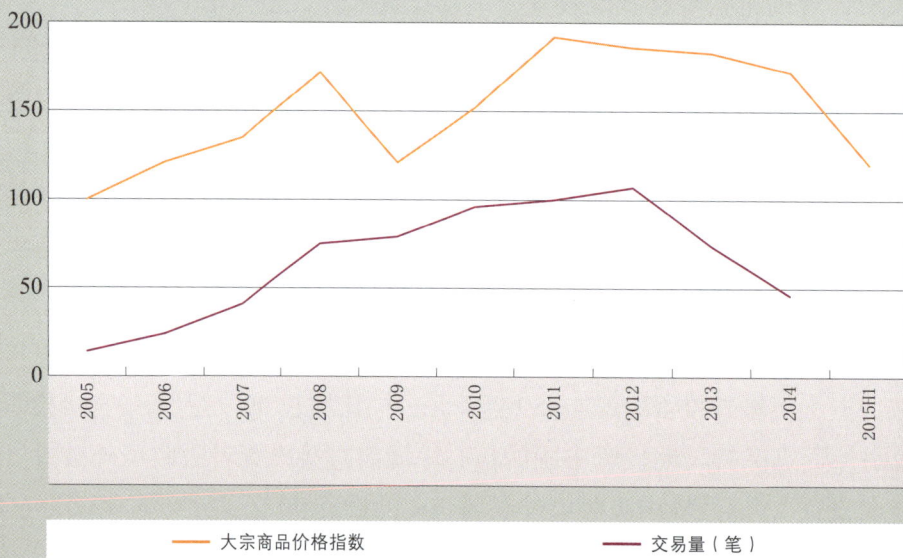

大宗商品价格指数 ——— 交易量（笔）

数据来源：国际货币基金组织、Dealogic公司。

　　我国海外大宗商品投资具有顺周期性。2005—2011 年，随着全球大宗商品价格不断上涨，我国企业海外大宗商品并购笔数显著增长。从 2011 年 3 月开始，全球大宗商品价格进入下行周期，原油、铁矿石、大豆价格均从较高位"腰斩"，我国并购步伐也显著放缓。过去十年我国企业大宗商品并购与同期价格走势呈现明显的正相关性（见图 C4-1）。

　　顺周期性对我国海外投资的负面影响正在显现。价格越涨，我国企业表现出的海外并购欲望越强，一旦价格下跌，不仅导致较大的投资损失，而且还错失在低位进行真正价值投资的宝贵时机。比如，2012 年我国某国有企业出资 12 亿港元，收购加拿大阳光油砂 8% 股权。由于油价下跌，阳光油砂面临经营困境，被迫在价格低位出售部分资产偿还债务。截至 2015 年 6 月底，该笔投资市值缩水超过 80%，浮亏约 10 亿港元。

　　"走出去"要加强对周期性的研判和把握。一是跟踪评估产品供求、国际形势、地缘政治等因素，加强周期研究，增强逆周期的投资能力。二是做好财务测算，保障项目经济可行，保证中长期合理回报。三是把风险和困难估计充分，做好应对预案，采取有效措施应对价格下行风险。

　　"走出去"要继续坚持市场化原则。作为实施主体的企业，需要尊重市场规律，接受市场约束，落实市场主体责任。一是明确项目权责和资金属性，做到产权清晰、责任明确，权责利相一致，谁投资、谁负责，谁承担风险、谁获得收益。二是应受资本金约束，承担合理融资成本，确保现金流覆盖资金成本，落实经济回报，防范投融资风险。三是战略性项目要尽最大限度实行市场化运作，要有正向激励和约束机制，有效防范道德风险，把国家战略利益落到实处。

　　"走出去"要加强多方合作。中国企业海外大宗商品直接投资起步晚，面临投资经验不足、不熟悉当地市场等问题。需要加强多方合作，并采取参股、合营、基金等多种灵活策略开展对外投资。对内需加强统一协调，重视产业链的延伸和衔接。比如一个矿可以多家矿企联合投资，事前协调好国内的配套基建、交通运输等企业。对外需联合国际多边开发机构、国际同业、当地企业，弥补自身短板，发挥各自相对优势。

（四）证券投资

证券投资净资产增加。 2015 年上半年，我国证券投资净资产增加 241 亿美元，上年同期为减少 369 亿美元（见图 2-14）。在我国资本市场对外开放推进以及国际证券市场企稳的影响下，我国对外证券投资和境外对我国证券投资活跃，资金流入流出频率和规模较以往有所加大，尤其是我国对境外证券投资出现较大规模的增加，是我国证券投资净资产增加的主因。

我国对境外证券投资增加较多。 2015 年上半年我国对外证券投资增加 572 亿美元，上年同期为减少 25 亿美元。其中，股本投资和债券投资分别增加 326 亿美元和 247 亿美元。资本市场对外进一步开放以及外部市场条件变化是推动我国对外证券投资大规模增加的主因。一方面，"沪港通"为人民币资本跨境证券投资提供更为便利渠道，2015 年上半年通过"港股通"渠道对外投资增加 107 亿美元，占股本投资增加额的 33%；另一方面，随着美国经济复苏以及国际市场对美国加息预期增强，上半年美国和欧洲主要国家股票和债券市场表现良好，国内主体海外投资热情较高，银行等金融机构自身或通过 QDII 渠道增加对外投资，上半年分别增加 207 亿美元股本投资和 241 亿美元债券投资。

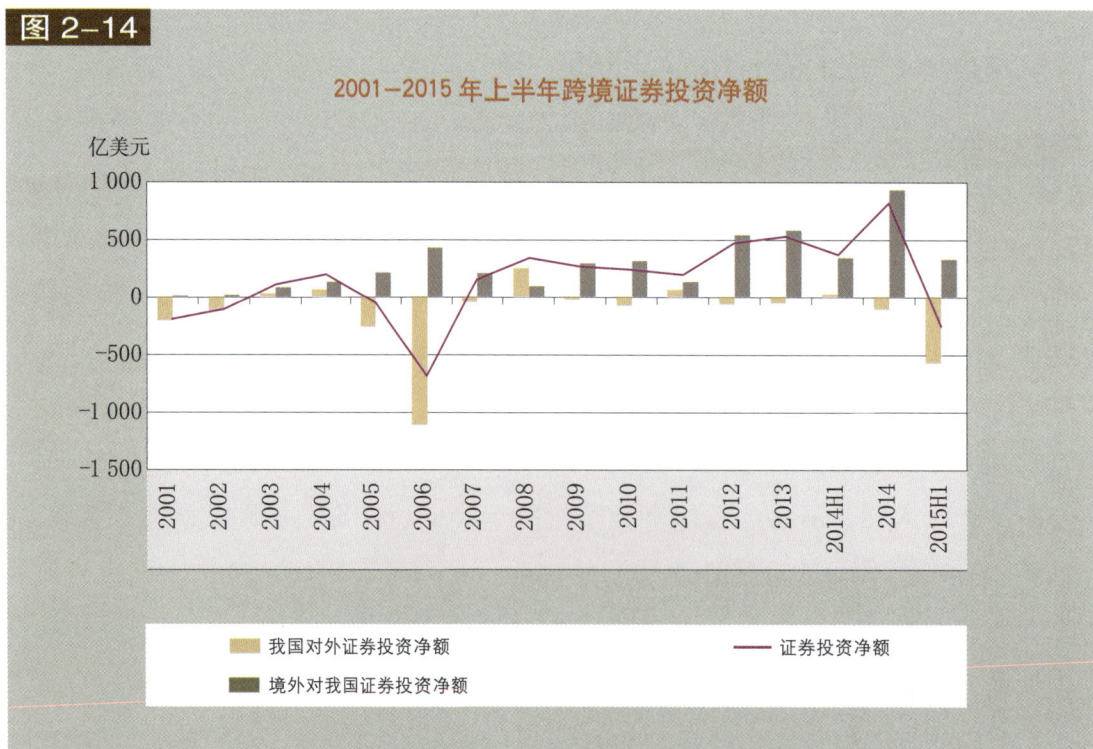

图 2-14

2001－2015 年上半年跨境证券投资净额

亿美元

（图例）
- 我国对外证券投资净额
- 境外对我国证券投资净额
- 证券投资净额

注：我国对外证券投资正值表示减持对外股权或债券，负值表示增持对外股权或债券；境外对我国证券投资正值表示增加对国内股权或债权投资，负值表示减少对国内股权或债券投资。

数据来源：国家外汇管理局。

境外对我国证券投资延续增加。2015 年上半年，境外对我国证券投资增加 331 亿美元，同比减少 4%。其中，境外对我国股本证券投资增加 212 亿美元，债务证券投资增加 120 亿美元。从股本投资来看，一是随着我国企业竞争力提高和境外 IPO 市场稳步繁荣，境内企业境外上市及增发活跃，上半年，境内机构境外筹资 235 亿美元，发行主体主要是广发证券、海通证券等大型金融企业。二是我国对外开放进程加速，通过"沪股通"渠道流入资金规模较大，上半年对我国投资增加 86 亿美元。三是上半年国内股票市场显现"牛市"格局，股指期货指数快速上涨，后期股票市场整体估值推高，部分境外投资者选择获利离场。上半年，合格境外机构投资者（QFII）和人民币合格境外机构投资者（RQFII）股权投资减少 88 亿美元，其中 4 月份减少 47 亿美元，5 月份增加 13 亿美元，6 月份减少 42 亿美元，但 6 月下旬转为增加 11 亿美元。从债券投资来看，银行部门债券投资负债增加，上半年，境外银行、货币当局等投资境内银行部门发行的债券增加 61 亿美元，QFII、RQFII 机构投资境内银行部门发行的债券减少 6 亿美元，境内银行承兑进口相关汇票增加 57 亿美元。

（五）其他投资

其他投资净资产增加。其他投资项下资本流动是影响我国国际收支状况的重要因素。2015 年上半年，我国其他投资项下净资产增加 1 931 亿美元，较上年同期增长 2.7 倍，是资本和金融账户净资产增加规模的 3.3 倍。上半年，其他投资各项均为净资产增加，反映了境内主体对境内外汇率、利率及市场风险等预期的变化。其中，贷款项下由去年同期的净资产减少 203 亿美元转为净资产增加 1 299 亿美元，占其他投资净资产增加总额的 67%；贸易信贷以及货币和存款分别为净资产增加 226 亿美元和 327 亿美元（见图 2–15）。

其他投资项下对外资本输出继续增加。2015 年上半年，我国其他投资项下对外资本输出净增加 632 亿美元，较去年同期少增 61%，反映了银行部门运用于境外的资金虽增长，但增速有所减缓。其中，我国在境外的货币和存款增长 152 亿美元，较上年同期增量下降 87%；对境外贷款增长 541 亿美元，较上年同期增量下降 4%。另外，对外提供的贸易信贷资产减少 130 亿美元（即贸易项下应收和预付下降），较上年同期多减少了 25 亿美元。

其他投资项下对外负债大幅减少。2015 年上半年，境外对我国其他投资项下资本净流出（即我国对外负债净减少）1 299 亿美元，而上年同期为净流入 1 124 亿美元。一是获得境外贷款由上年同期的净增加 769 亿美元转为净减少 759 亿美元，主要是由于去年暴露的信用证风险促使银行加强了对贸易融资业务的风险控制，导

图 2-15

2000-2015 年上半年其他投资净额

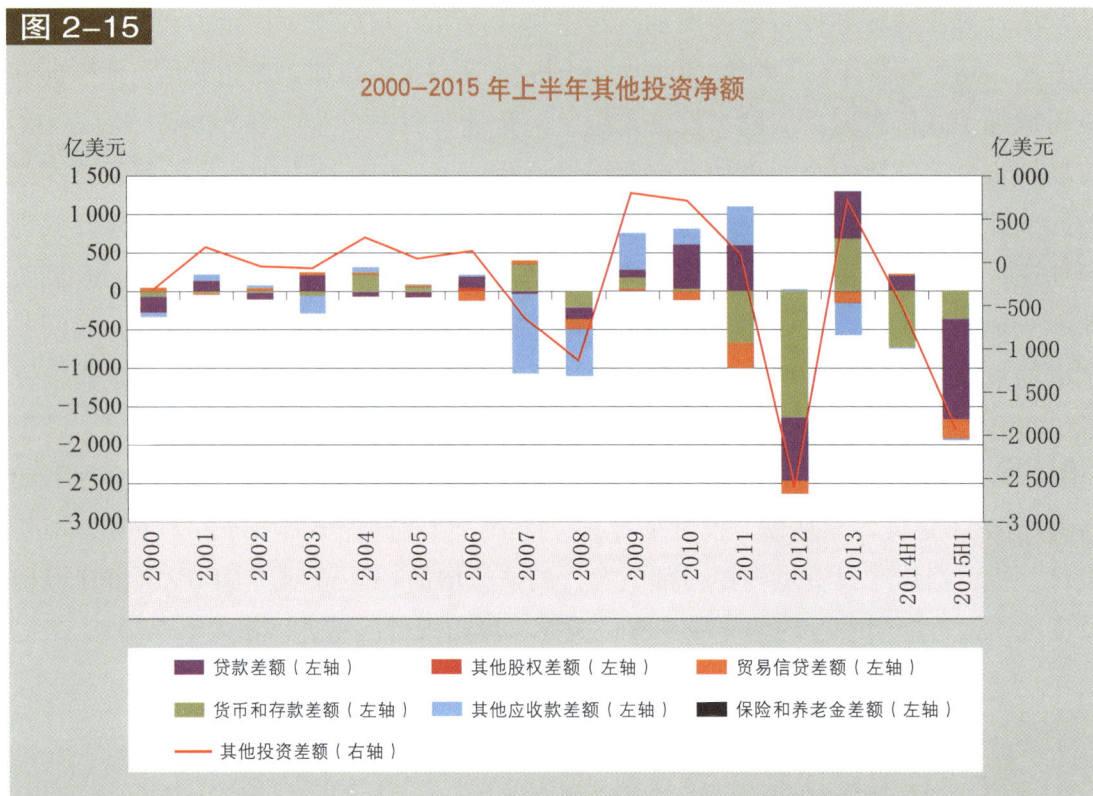

图例：
- 贷款差额（左轴）
- 其他股权差额（左轴）
- 贸易信贷差额（左轴）
- 货币和存款差额（左轴）
- 其他应收款差额（左轴）
- 保险和养老金差额（左轴）
- 其他投资差额（右轴）

数据来源：国家外汇管理局。

致该信用证负债减少 740 亿美元；二是从境外获取的贸易信贷负债减少 357 亿美元（即贸易项下应付和预收下降），较上年同期多减少了 274 亿美元；三是我国吸收的货币和存款类资金减少 175 亿美元，上年同期为增加 426 亿美元。人民币负债的减少是导致上半年货币和存款类资金减少的主要原因。

专栏 5

我国按照 SDDS 要求公布全口径外债数据

国际货币基金组织在 1996 年确立了数据公布特殊标准（Special Data Dissemination Standard, SDDS），旨在提高成员国宏观经济统计数据透明度，从而使广大数据使用者特别是金融市场参与者，能够借助充分的信息来评估各国经济形势。采纳 SDDS 的国家需遵照标准的要求，公布实体经济、财政、金融、对外和社会人口五个部门的数据，外债属于对外部门的数据类别之一。目前，国际货币基金组织制定了数据公布通用系统（GDDS）和数据公布特殊标准（SDDS）两套数据公布标准。二者总体框架基本一致，但在具体操作上，SDDS对数据覆盖范围、公布频率、公布时效、数据质量、公众可得性等方面要求更高。

从2015年起，我国外债统计从GDDS过渡到SDDS，按季对外公布全口径外债数据，以便于社会各界更全面了解我国详细的外债情况。主要有三方面变化：一是调整了债务人类型划分方法。口径调整前，我国外债债务人类型划分为国务院部委、中资金融机构、外资金融机构、中资企业、外商投资企业和其他。按照SDDS调整后的外债机构部门则分为广义政府、中央银行、其他接受存款公司、其他部门、直接投资的公司间贷款。二是调整了债务类型划分方法。口径调整前，我国外债债务类型划分为外国政府贷款、国际金融组织贷款和国际商业贷款。按照SDDS调整后的债务工具则分为贷款、债务证券、货币与存款、贸易信贷与预付款、其他债务负债、SDR分配、直接投资的公司间贷款。三是将人民币外债纳入统计范围，这只是统计方法和口径的调整，并不会引起我国外债偿还责任的变化。经过上述调整，我国外债统计实现了与国际最新标准的接轨，有利于进一步提高外债统计的数据标准和国际可比性，也为构建宏观审慎框架下的外债和跨境资本流动管理体系奠定了坚实的基础。

从公布的全口径外债数据看，目前我国人民币外债规模也较高，体现了人民币国际化发展的自然结果，凸显了我国国际地位的提升。自2009年跨境人民币业务启动以来，人民币跨境结算规模持续高速增长，结算额从2009年的36亿元扩大到2014年的近10万亿元；人民币跨境收付占我国本外币跨境收付的比例逐年攀高，从2010年的1.7%上升至2014年的23.6%。人民币国际使用的领域和范围的逐步扩大，为全球金融市场发展注入了新活力，也使人民币的国际地位得到了较大提高，人民币外债的出现和规模不断增加正是上述过程的自然结果。虽然人民币外债和外币外债同属于外债的范畴，但外币外债易受汇率波动的影响，在发生危机时可能加重债务人的偿债负担；而人民币外债不存在货币错配风险和汇率风险等。今后，随着我国对外开放程度的不断提高，尤其是"一带一路"战略的逐步落实，以非居民持有、贸易融资等形式表现出来的人民币外债仍可能继续增长，这既是国际上对中国经济发展信心的体现，也是对中国改革开放成效的肯定，本质上反映了人民币的国际影响力增强，在国际资本流动中扮演的角色越来越重要。

三、国际投资
头寸状况

　　对外资产继续体现"藏汇于民"变化。 2015 年 6 月末，我国对外资产 [①] 64 337
亿美元，较上年末增长 0.4%。其中，国际储备资产余额为 37 713 亿美元，较上年末
减少 3%，继续占据对外资产首位，占资产总值的 59%，但比重较上年末减少 2 个
百分点，为 2004 年公布国际投资头寸数据以来的最低，主要是因净交易和汇率及
价格等非交易原因导致外汇储备资产分别减少 666 亿和 826 亿美元。直接投资存
量 10 129 亿美元，占资产总值的比重升至历史最高值 16%，较上年末增加 4 个百分
点，主要是受益于国家对外直接投资政策的不断拓宽，我国企业加快"走出去"战
略的政策效果持续显现。证券投资资产 2 760 亿美元，占比为 4%，较上年末略增
0.2 个百分点。存贷款等其他投资资产 13 695 亿美元，占比为 21%，较上年末下降 2
个百分点（见图 3-1）。

　　对外负债总体呈现较快增长。 2015 年 6 月末，对外负债存量 49 697 亿美元，较
上年末增长 7%，主要是证券投资股权负债全面使用市值法进行统计，剔除统计口
径调整影响，对外负债较上年末略增 5%。其中，证券投资负债 8 997 亿美元，剔除
统计口径调整因素较上年末增长 42%，主要是受国家加大境内证券市场的对外开放

图 3-1

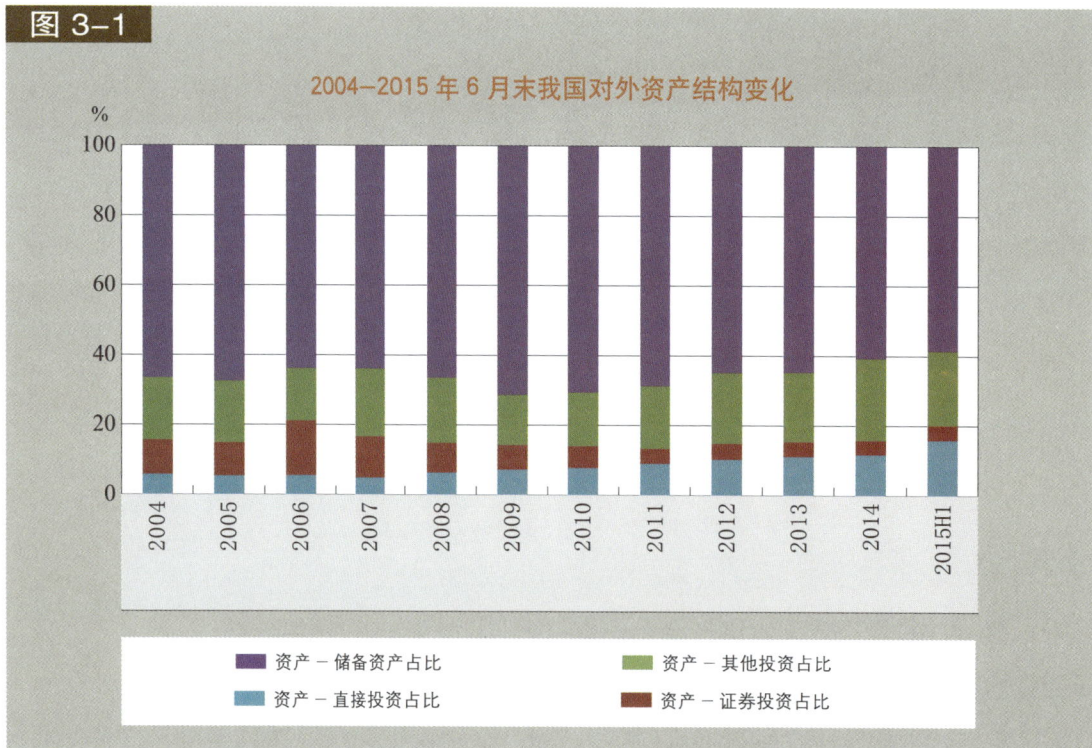

2004—2015 年 6 月末我国对外资产结构变化

图例：
- 资产－储备资产占比
- 资产－其他投资占比
- 资产－直接投资占比
- 资产－证券投资占比

数据来源：国家外汇管理局。

---

　　① 对外金融资产和负债包括直接投资、证券投资及存贷款等其他投资。之所以对外直接投资属于金融资产范畴，是
因为境内投资者持有的是境外被投资企业的股权，这与证券投资中的股权投资无本质区别，只是直接投资通常持股比例
较高，意在影响或控制企业的生产经营活动。反之，外来直接投资则属于对外金融负债范畴，也是境外投资者对外商投
资企业的权益。

图 3-2

2004—2015 年 6 月末我国对外负债结构变化

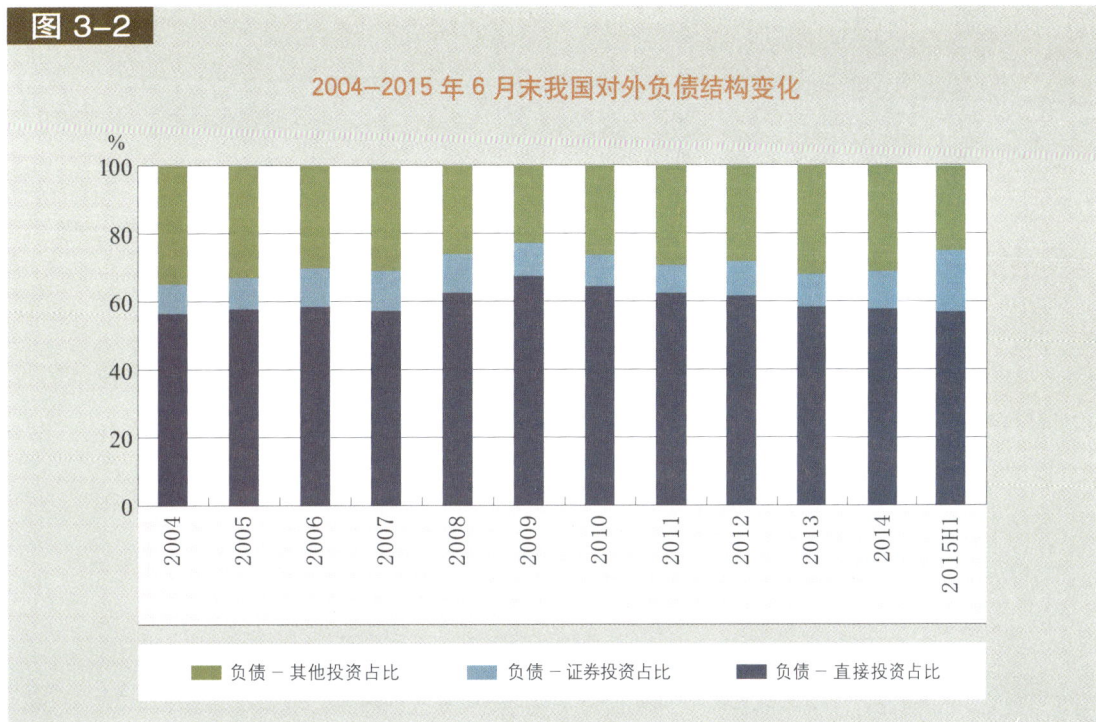

图例: ■ 负债－其他投资占比   ■ 负债－证券投资占比   ■ 负债－直接投资占比

数据来源：国家外汇管理局。

步伐等多种因素影响。证券投资负债占负债总额的比重达到 18%，剔除统计口径调整因素占比较上年末上升 5 个百分点。外国来华直接投资 28 274 亿美元[①]，增长 6%，继续位列对外负债首位，占比 57%，表明境外投资者继续看好我国经济发展的长期前景。存贷款等其他投资负债较上年末下降 14%，达到 12 318 亿美元，占负债总额的 25%（见图 3-2），主要是受境内外汇率、利率变化等因素影响，国内企业主动调整自身资产负债结构，对外债务持续去杠杆化。

对外净资产有所下降。2015 年 6 月末，我国对外净资产[②]为 14 640 亿美元，较上年末减少 3 124 亿美元（见图 3-3）。我国对外净资产集中于公共部门（包括中央银行和政府部门），而银行和企业等民间部门则为对外净负债的主体，对外资产和负债存在较明显的主体错配。截至 2015 年 6 月末，如果不包括国际储备资产 37 713 亿美元，我国对外净负债 23 073 亿美元。

对外投资收益呈现小额逆差。2015 年上半年，我国国际收支平衡表中投资收益为逆差 258 亿美元，其中，我国对外投资收益收入 1 127 亿美元，对外负债收益支

---

① 外国来华直接投资存量包括我国非金融部门和金融部门吸收来华直接投资存量，以及境内外母子公司间贷款和其他债务性往来，反映了价值重估因素影响。该口径与商务部统计的累计吸收外商直接投资不同，其数据是历年外商直接投资股本投资流量累加。

② 对外净资产变动不等于国际收支平衡表经常项目差额，具体分析参见《2013 年中国国际收支报告》专栏 3。

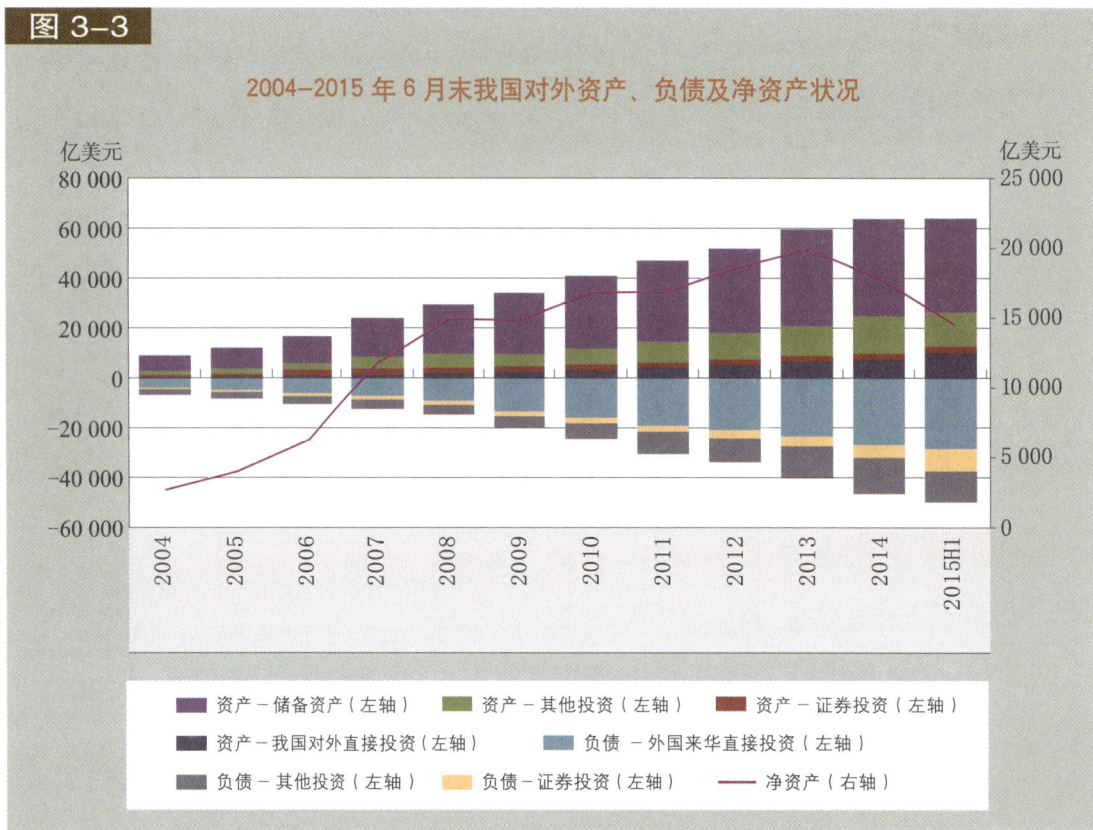

图 3-3

2004-2015 年 6 月末我国对外资产、负债及净资产状况

图例：
- 资产－储备资产（左轴）
- 资产－其他投资（左轴）
- 资产－证券投资（左轴）
- 资产－我国对外直接投资（左轴）
- 负债－外国来华直接投资（左轴）
- 负债－其他投资（左轴）
- 负债－证券投资（左轴）
- 净资产（右轴）

数据来源：国家外汇管理局。

出 1 385 亿美元，二者年化收益率差异为 –1.1 个百分点，为 2005 年以来差异最小的一年（见图 3-4）。投资收益为负原因不在于对外投资回报太低，而是利用外资成本较高，这主要与我国对外资产负债结构有关。2015 年上半年我国对外资产中约 60% 是低风险、高流动性的储备资产，按照市场规律投资回报相对其他资产较低，拉低了我国对外投资收益率；对外金融负债中约 57% 是外来直接投资，这类股权属于长期、稳定投资，流动性较差，存在经营风险，投资回报高于其他形式资产，拉高我国外来投资收益率，导致轧差后投资收益为负值（具体分析详见《2012 年中国国际收支报告》专栏 1）。不过，投资回报率仅是二者财务成本的比较，外国来华直接投资更为重要的意义在于引进外方先进技术和管理经验，创造国内就业和税收，开拓国际市场，其社会效益和经济收益远大于财务成本。此外，外方收益支出中有大比例是再投资收益，这部分收益又投回了企业，并没有实际的资金流出，扣除这一部分，我国投资收益仍为净收入。2015 年上半年对外投资收益收入与对外负债支出收益率之差创新低，表明近年通过优化对外投资资产配置，我国对外投资收益相对有所提高。

图 3-4

2005-2015 年 6 月我国对外资产负债收益率

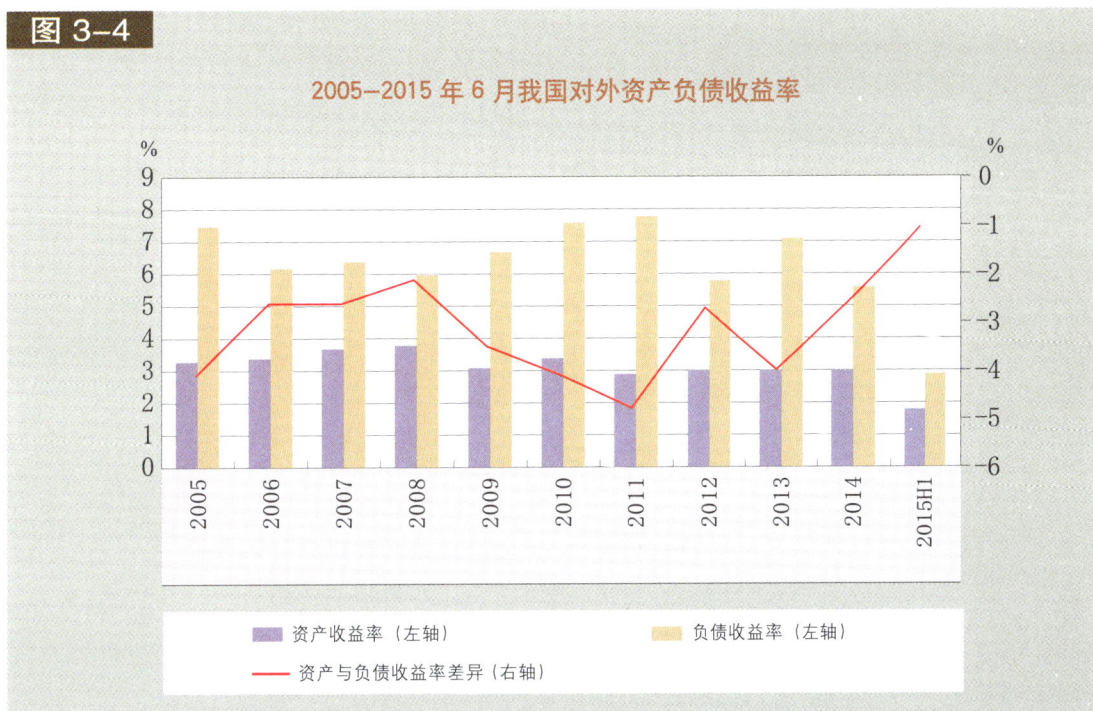

注：1. 资产（或负债）收益率 ＝ $\dfrac{\text{年度投资收益收入（或支出）}}{\text{（上年末＋本年末对外资产（或负债）存量）}/2}$ ，其中，半年度数据向前累加半年后按照整年计算。

　　2. 资产负债收益率差异 ＝ 资产收益率 － 负债收益率。

数据来源：国家外汇管理局。

表 3-1　2015 年 6 月末中国国际投资头寸表 [①]

单位：亿美元

项目	行次	2015 年 6 月末
净头寸 [②]	1	14 640
资产	2	64 337
1 直接投资	3	10 129
1.1 股权	4	8 309
1.2 关联企业债务	5	1 820
2 证券投资	6	2 760
2.1 股权	7	1 777
2.2 债券	8	983
3 金融衍生工具	9	39
4 其他投资	10	13 695

　　① 从 2015 年起，国家外汇管理局按照国际货币基金组织《国际收支和国际投资头寸手册》（第六版）编制和公布我国的国际投资头寸表（IIP）。根据手册的最新标准，全面采用市值法统计和编制我国国际投资头寸表中的各项数据，替代以往个别项目历史流量累计的方法。由于部分统计制度实施时间较短，历史数据无法获得，往期数据未能进行追溯调整，这样 2014 年前后的 IIP 数据存在不可比的情况。

　　② 净头寸是指资产减负债，"＋"表示净资产，"—"表示净负债。本表记数采用四舍五入原则。

续表

项目	行次	2015 年 6 月末
4.1 其他股权	11	1
4.2 货币和存款	12	3 125
4.3 贷款	13	4 658
4.4 保险和养老金	14	200
4.5 贸易信贷	15	4 547
4.6 其他应收款	16	1 165
5 储备资产	17	37 713
5.1 货币黄金	18	624
5.2 特别提款权	19	105
5.3 在国际货币基金组织的储备头寸	20	46
5.4 外汇储备	21	36 938
5.5 其他储备	22	0
负债	23	49 697
1 直接投资	24	28 274
1.1 股权	25	26 027
1.2 关联企业债务	26	2 247
2 证券投资	27	8 997
2.1 股权	28	6 727
2.2 债券	29	2 270
3 金融衍生工具	30	108
4 其他投资	31	12 318
4.1 其他股权	32	—
4.2 货币和存款	33	4 611
4.3 贷款	34	4 341
4.4 保险和养老金	35	85
4.5 贸易信贷	36	2 987
4.6 其他应付款	37	195
4.7 特别提款权	38	98

数据来源：国家外汇管理局。

四、外汇市场运行与人民币汇率

（一）人民币汇率走势

人民币对美元汇率保持基本稳定。 2015 年 6 月末，人民币对美元汇率中间价为 6.1136 元 / 美元，较 2014 年末小幅上涨 0.1%（见图 4-1），银行间外汇市场（CNY）和境外市场（CNH）即期交易价上半年累计分别上涨 0.05% 和 0.2%，人民币在全球范围内属于稳定货币（见图 4-2）。

人民币对一篮子货币多边汇率升值。 据国际清算银行（BIS）测算，2015 年上半年人民币名义有效汇率累计升值 3.6%，扣除通货膨胀因素的实际有效汇率累计升值 3%（见图 4-3），在 BIS 监测的 61 种货币中升值幅度分别居第 10 位和第 11 位，在全球主要货币中升值幅度居前（见图 4-4）。2005 年汇改以来，人民币名义和实际有效汇率累计分别升值 45.6% 和 55.7%，在 BIS 监测的 61 种货币中升值幅度分别居第 1 位和第 2 位。

境内外人民币汇率差价收窄。 2015 年上半年，境外 CNH 相对境内 CNY 出现由年初明显折让、价差较宽，逐渐转为双向波动、价差收窄（见图 4-5），日均价差 66 个基点，低于 2014 年全年水平（79 个基点）。第一季度国内经济下行压力较大，加之国际外汇市场风险事件迭发，引发人民币贬值预期升温，CNH 与 CNY 日均价差 98 个基点，第二季度随着国内经济缓中趋稳、强势美元放缓，市场看空人民币情绪

图 4-1

2015 年上半年境内外人民币对美元即期汇率走势

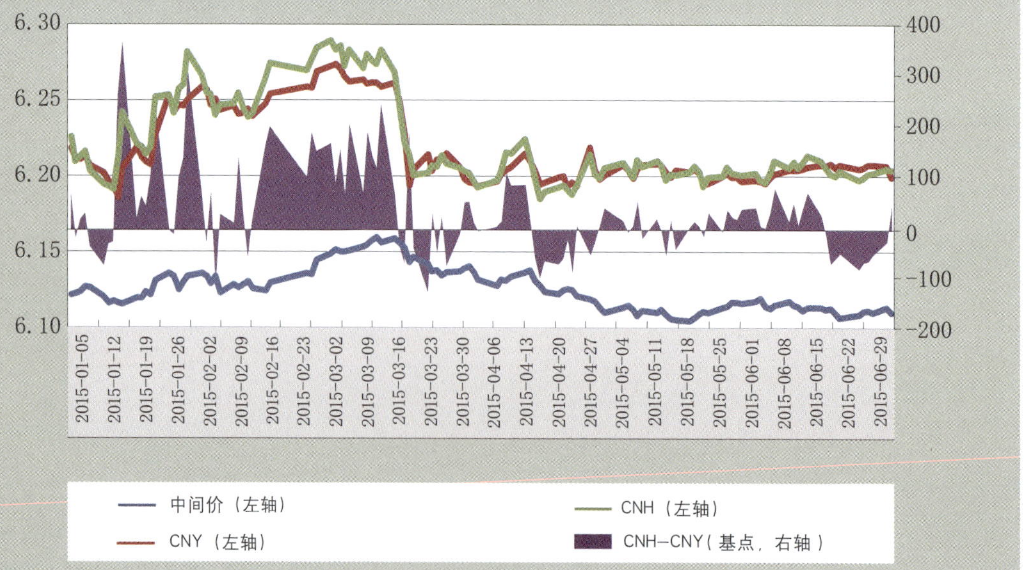

图例：
- 中间价（左轴）
- CNY（左轴）
- CNH（左轴）
- CNH-CNY（基点，右轴）

数据来源：中国外汇交易中心，路透数据库。

图 4-2

2015 年上半年全球主要发达和新兴市场货币对美元双边汇率变动

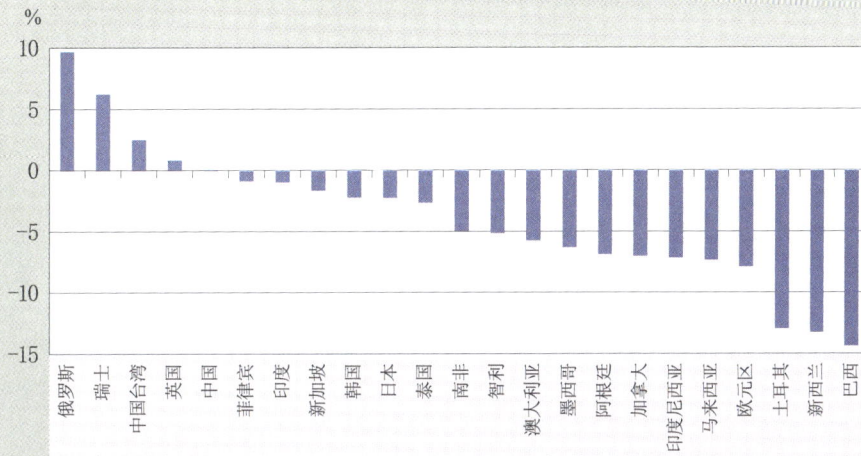

数据来源：中国外汇交易中心，彭博资讯。

图 4-3

1994 年 1 月 –2015 年 6 月人民币有效汇率走势

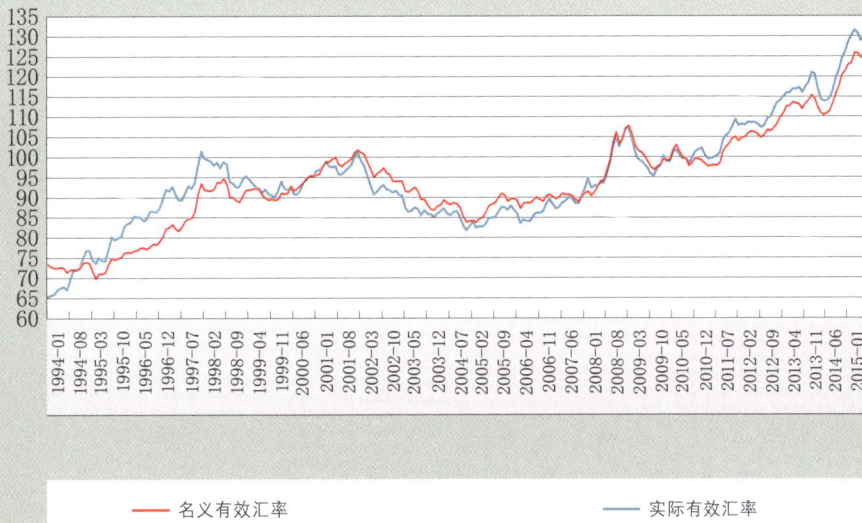

名义有效汇率　　　　实际有效汇率

数据来源：国际清算银行。

图 4-4

2015年上半年全球主要发达和新兴市场货币有效汇率变动

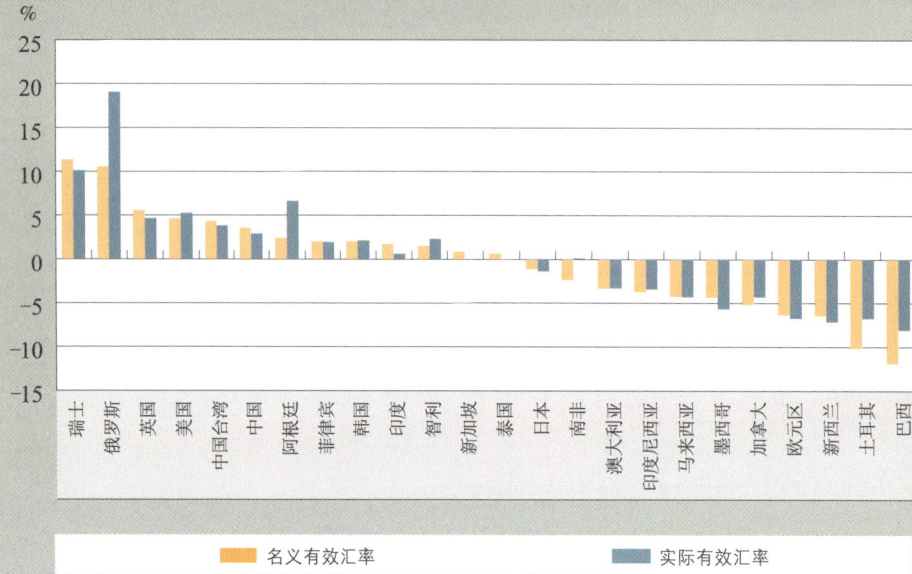

数据来源：国际清算银行。

图 4-5

境内外人民币对美元即期汇率价差

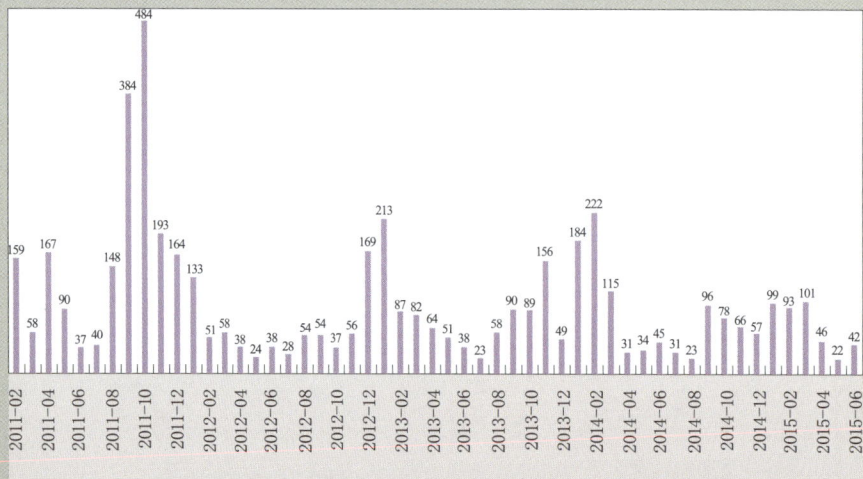

注：日均价差绝对值。
数据来源：中国外汇交易中心，路透数据库。

有所减弱，境内外价差收窄至 37 个基点，其中 5 月份日均价差仅为 22 个基点，处于历史偏低水平。

　　远期外汇市场价格大幅波动。2015 年上半年，境内外远期外汇市场美元升水幅度先升后降、大幅波动（见图 4-6），反映了预期、供求、利差等因素在市场化定价机制下的结果。第一季度，受市场看空人民币预期和外币债务去杠杆化的影响，企业大量远期净购汇推高美元升水点数。第二季度，随着人民币汇率预期趋稳，企业远期净购汇大幅回落，前期增持的外币存款也部分释放，加之本外币利差受人民币降息、降准影响逐步收窄（见图 4-7），推动美元升水点数持续回落。6 月末，境内外可交割和无本金交割远期市场 1 年期美元对人民币升水分别为 1 395 个、1 420 个和 1 314 个基点，较年初分别下降 190 个、130 个和 981 个基点。

　　人民币汇率波动率维持低位。从即期汇率走势看，2015 年上半年人民币对美元交易价始终处于中间价贬值区间窄幅波动，日间最大波幅日均 1.54%。年初，交易价维持在中间价日间 1.5% 波动水平，1 月末开始向中间价浮动区间上限靠拢并延续至 3 月初，此后短暂回调，但第二季度重新维持在中间价日间 1.5% 波动水平（见图 4-8）。从期权市场波动率走势看，上半年境内外期权市场隐含波动率先升后降，6 个月期限波动率在 2 月初最高分别触及 3.89% 和 5.63% 的 2012 年以来高点，6 月末分别为 1.88% 和 2.51%，较年初分别下降 32.4% 和 27.7%，（见图 4-9）。6 月末，24

图 4-6

2013 年以来境内外人民币对美元远期市场 1 年期美元升贴水点数

数据来源：中国外汇交易中心，路透数据库。

图 4-7

2013 年以来境内人民币与美元利差（6 个月期限）

利差 1（人民币 shibor－境内美元拆借）
利差 2（外汇掉期隐含）
利差 2－利差 1

数据来源：中国外汇交易中心，路透数据库。

图 4-8

2015 年上半年银行间外汇市场人民币对美元即期交易价波动情况

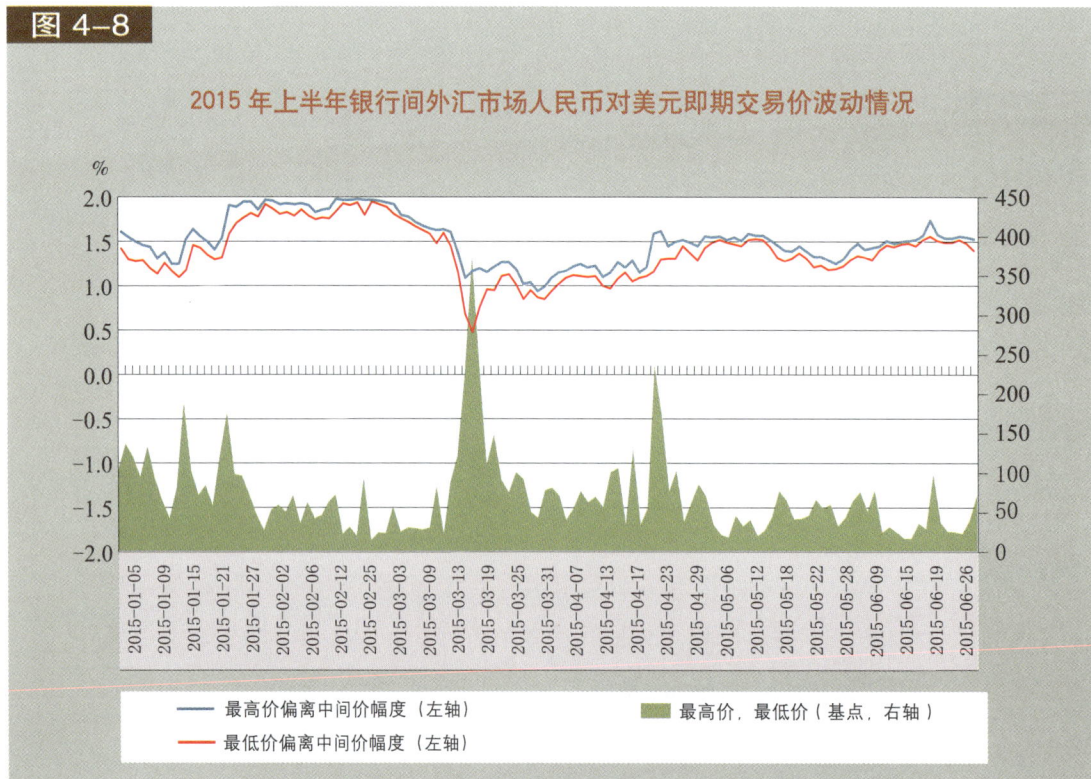

最高价偏离中间价幅度（左轴）
最低价偏离中间价幅度（左轴）
最高价，最低价（基点，右轴）

数据来源：中国外汇交易中心。

图 4-9

2012 年以来人民币对美元汇率 6 个月隐含波动率

注：平价期权隐含波动率。
数据来源：彭博资讯。

种主要发达和新兴市场货币对美元汇率 6 个月期权隐含波动率平均为 11.12%，人民币汇率弹性依然偏低。

（二）外汇市场交易

2015 年上半年，人民币外汇市场累计成交 7.35 万亿美元（日均 618 亿美元），同比增长 21.6%。其中，银行对客户市场和银行间外汇市场分别成交 2.05 万亿和 5.31 万亿美元[①]；即期和衍生产品分别成交 3.63 万亿和 3.72 万亿美元（见表 4-1），衍生产品在外汇市场交易总量中的比重升至历史新高的 50.6%，交易产品构成接近全球外汇市场状况（见图 4-10）。

即期外汇交易小幅增长。上半年，即期外汇市场累计成交 3.63 万亿美元，日均交易量同比增长 2.2%。在市场分布上，银行对客户即期结售汇（含银行自身，不含远期履约）累计 1.57 万亿美元，日均交易量同比增长 5.9%；银行间即期外汇市场累计成交 2.06 万亿美元，日均交易量同比下降 0.5%，其中美元交易份额为 93.7%。

---

① 银行对客户市场采用客户买卖外汇总额，银行间外汇市场采用单边交易量，以下同。

图 4-10

中国与全球外汇市场的交易产品构成比较

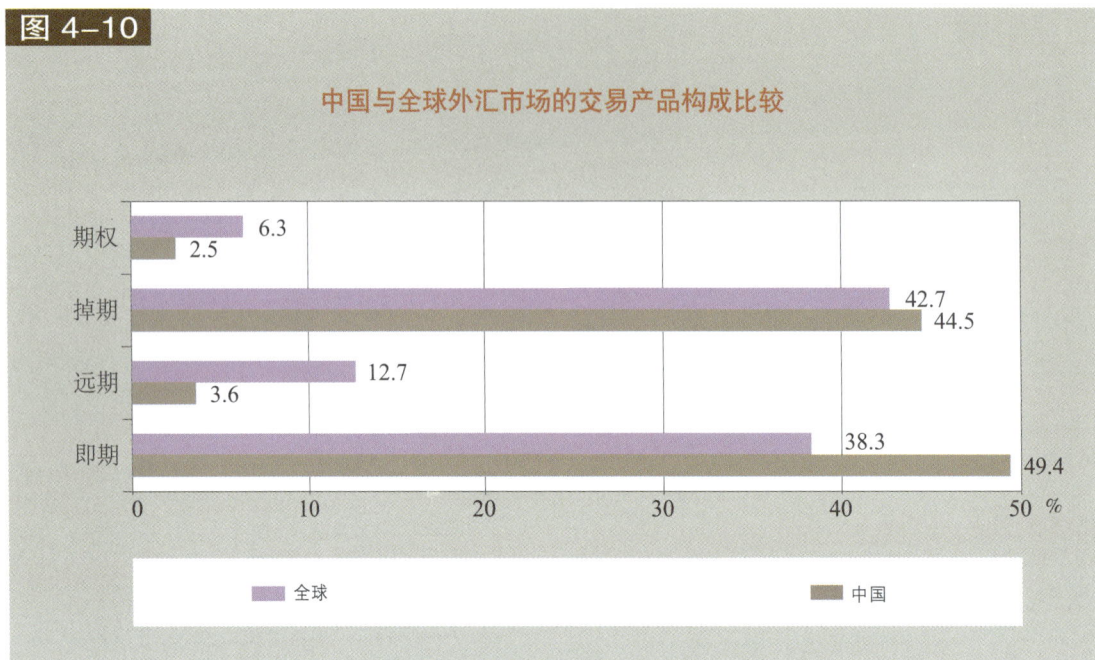

注：各产品的交易量占比，中国为 2015 年上半年数据，全球为国际清算银行 2013 年 4 月调查数据。
数据来源：国家外汇管理局，中国外汇交易中心，国际清算银行。

远期外汇交易显著下降。上半年，远期外汇市场累计成交 2 683 亿美元，日均交易量同比下降 16.3%。在市场分布上，银行对客户远期结售汇累计签约 2 511 亿美元，其中结汇和售汇分别为 912 亿和 1 598 亿美元，日均交易量分别下降 14.8%、下降 47.1% 和增长 30.8%（见图 4-11），6 个月以内的短期交易占 69.8%，较 2014 年上升 6.5 个百分点（见图 4-12）；银行间远期外汇市场累计成交 173 亿美元，日均交易量大幅下降 33.3%。企业远期购汇大幅增长，一定程度上反映了在国际经济金融复杂形势下，市场主体应对人民币汇率大幅波动的预防性交易需求上升。

掉期交易大幅增长。上半年，外汇和货币掉期市场累计成交 3.27 万亿美元，日均交易量同比增长 53%。在市场分布上，银行对客户外汇和货币掉期累计签约 1 645 亿美元，其中近端结汇/远端购汇和近端购汇/远端结汇的交易量分别为 156 亿和 1 490 亿美元，日均交易量同比分别增长 81.9%、92.3% 和 80.9%；银行间外汇和货币掉期市场累计成交 3.11 万亿美元，日均交易量同比增长 51.7%。掉期市场持续活跃，表明国内本外币资金、利率与汇率之间的市场化机制日趋紧密。

外汇期权交易大幅增长。上半年，期权市场累计成交 1 858 亿美元，日均交易量同比增长 4.1 倍。在市场分布上，银行对客户期权市场累计成交 650 亿美元，日均交易量同比增长 1.8 倍，3 个月以内的短期交易占 42.4%；银行间外汇期权市场累计成交 1 208 亿美元，日均交易量同比增长 8.2 倍。期权交易的趋向活跃，表明随着

图 4-11

2012-2015 年上半年银行对客户远期结售汇交易量

亿美元

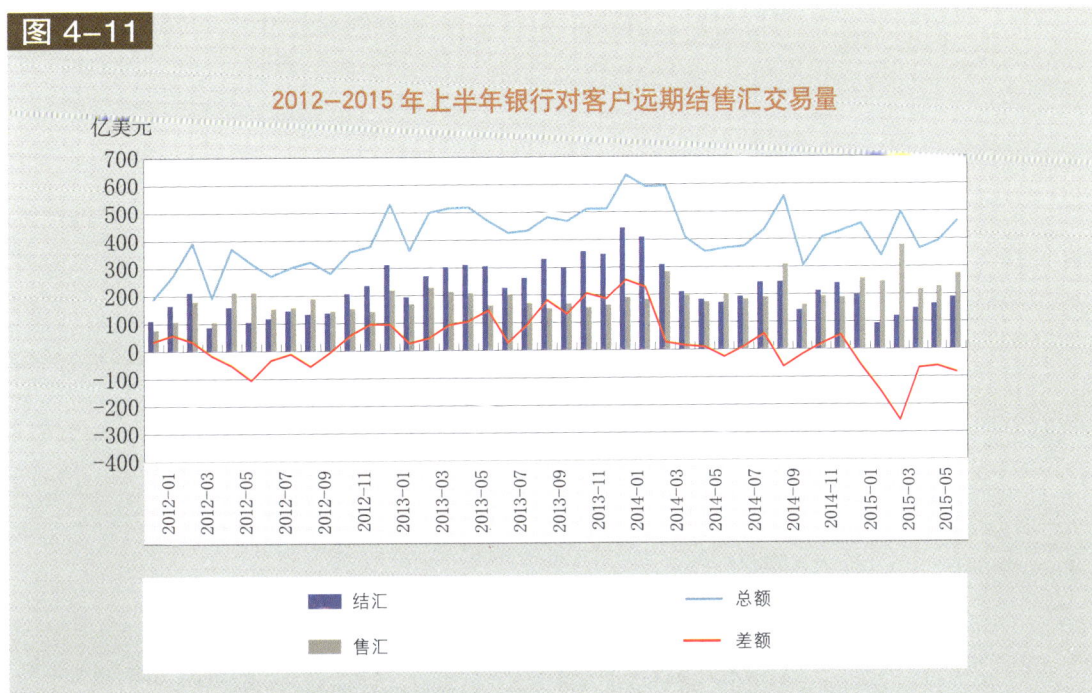

结汇   总额
售汇   差额

数据来源：国家外汇管理局。

图 4-12

2015 年上半年银行对客户远期结售汇的交易期限结构

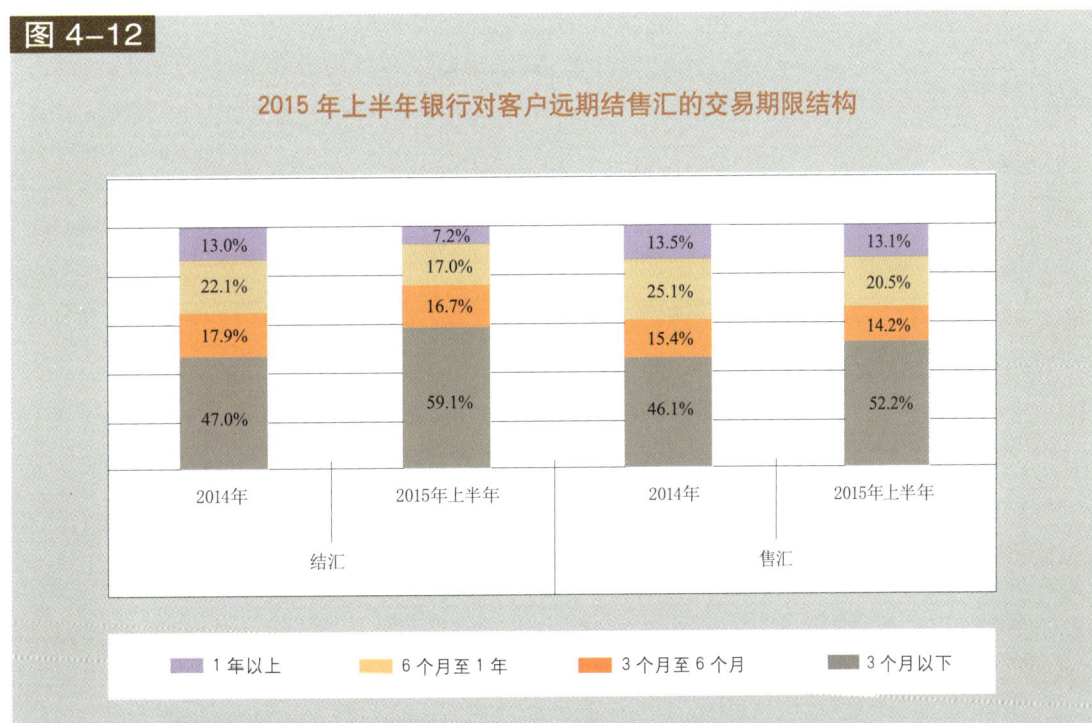

	2014年	2015年上半年	2014年	2015年上半年
1年以上	13.0%	7.2%	13.5%	13.1%
6个月至1年	22.1%	17.0%	25.1%	20.5%
3个月至6个月	17.9%	16.7%	15.4%	14.2%
3个月以下	47.0%	59.1%	46.1%	52.2%
	结汇		售汇	

1年以上   6个月至1年   3个月至6个月   3个月以下

数据来源：国家外汇管理局。

人民币汇率预期分化，期权相对于其他衍生产品所具有的多样化风险管理功能开始引起市场主体的重视和积极参与。

表 4-1　2015 年上半年人民币外汇市场交易概况

交易品种	交易量（亿美元）
即期	36 306
银行对客户市场	15 676
银行间外汇市场	20 629
远期	2 683
银行对客户市场	2 511
其中：3 个月（含）以下	1 375
3 个月至 1 年（含）	861
1 年以上	275
银行间外汇市场	173
其中：3 个月（含）以下	125
3 个月至 1 年（含）	41
1 年以上	6
外汇和货币掉期	32 702
银行对客户市场	1 645
银行间外汇市场	31 057
其中：3 个月（含）以下	27 694
3 个月至 1 年（含）	3 281
1 年以上	83
期权	1 858
银行对客户市场	650
其中：买入期权	355
卖出期权	295
其中：3 个月（含）以下	275
3 个月至 1 年（含）	257
1 年以上	117
银行间外汇市场	1 208
其中：3 个月（含）以下	958
3 个月至 1 年（含）	248
1 年以上	1
合计	73 549
其中：银行对客户市场	20 482
银行间外汇市场	53 067
其中：即期	36 306
远期	2 683
外汇和货币掉期	32 702
期权	1 858

注：数据均为单边交易额，采用四舍五入原则。
数据来源：国家外汇管理局，中国外汇交易中心。

图 4-13

中国外汇市场的参与者结构

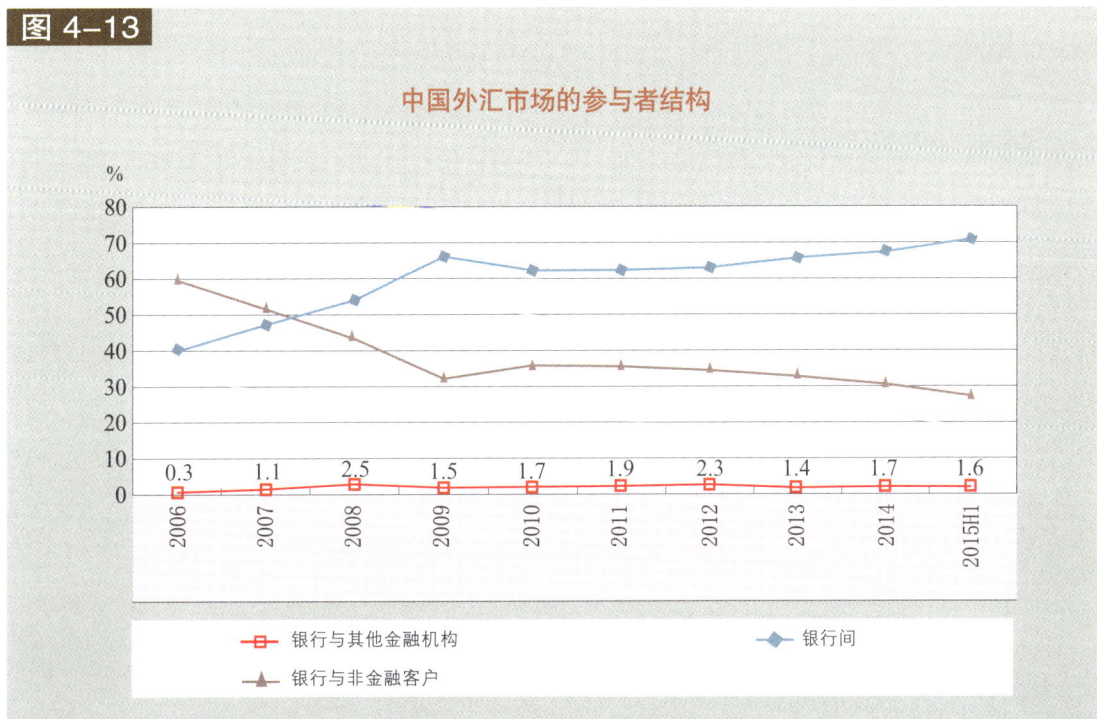

数据来源：国家外汇管理局，中国外汇交易中心。

外汇市场参与者结构保持稳定。银行自营交易延续主导地位（见图4-13），上半年银行间交易占整个外汇市场的比重从2014年的67.7%上升至71.2%，非金融客户交易的比重从30.5%下降至27.2%，非银行金融机构交易的市场份额小幅下降0.1个百分点至1.6%，非银行金融机构在我国外汇市场的参与度仍十分有限。

专栏6

汇改十年的外汇市场发展及面临的挑战

改革开放前，我国实行统收统支的外汇管理体制，没有外汇市场的基础和概念。改革开放后，我国外汇市场起步于1980年外汇调剂业务和此后的外汇调剂市场，规范于1994年银行结售汇制度和全国统一的银行间外汇市场。2005年7月21日，我国完善人民币汇率形成机制改革，外汇市场进入新的更高发展阶段。

丰富交易品种，满足多样化汇率风险管理需求。汇改以来，国内外汇市场由原先仅有即期交易和部分银行试点的远期交易两类产品，扩大至外汇掉期、货币掉期和期权产品，具有了国际市场基础产品体系。同时，为降低跨境贸易和投资的汇兑成本，支持外汇市场增加交易币种，包括美元、欧元、日元、港元、英镑、澳大利亚元、新西兰元、新加坡元、加拿大元、林吉特、俄罗斯卢布、泰铢（区域交易）和坚戈（区域交易）共十三种，基本涵盖了我国跨境收支的结算货币。

扩大市场主体，构建多元化的市场主体层次。汇改以来，银行间外汇市场开始打破原先单一银行的参与者结构，允许符合条件的非银行金融机构和非金融企业入市交易。同时，根据港澳和跨境人民币业务发展需要，一批承担境外人民币清算职能的境外银行相继进入银行间外汇市场，还有更多的境外银行在跨境贸易人民币结算业务项下与境内银行开展场外外汇交易，市场对外开放程度逐步提高。截至2015年上半年银行间外汇市场共有会员488家，包括境内银行415家、财务公司56家、基金证券2家、企业集团1家，境外清算行14家。

健全基础设施，促进市场运行提效率防风险。银行间外汇市场交易模式

图 C6-1

中国外汇市场交易量概况

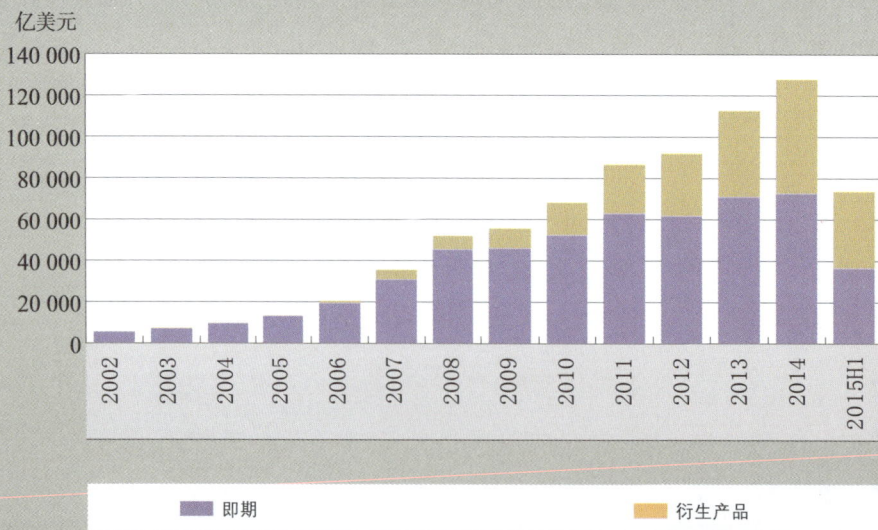

数据来源：国家外汇管理局，中国外汇交易中心。

由 2005 年汇改前电子集中撮合单一模式，扩大至集中撮合与双边询价并存、电子交易与声讯经纪互补的多样化模式，并建立分层做市商制度。同时，积极推进清算和信息设施建设，2009 年开始对场外交易尝试集中净额清算，2014 年正式启动中央对手方清算业务，并基本实现了与交易同步的信息数据全覆盖集中采集和管理，具有了较为完备的交易报告制度。此外，推动中国外汇交易中心、上海清算所作为重要市场组织的综合化和专业化发展。

2014 年，我国外汇市场人民币对外汇交易各类产品累计成交 12.8 万亿美元，较 2004 年增长 12.3 倍，其中衍生品交易量占比由 2004 年 1.8% 增长至 2014 年 43%（见图 C6-1），外汇市场深度和广度进一步扩展，为推进汇率市场化改革和支持市场主体适应汇率双向波动提供了有力保障。

过去十年外汇市场取得的发展成就是我国全面深化经济改革和对外开放、深入推进金融市场发展的必然结果，未来仍面临重大发展机遇。中国经济工业化、信息化、城镇化深入发展，经济结构转型加快，对外开放水平进一步提高，特别是人民币可兑换和国际化进程加快，将推动跨境交易规模扩大、类型增多，为外汇市场持续发展提供了基础。同时，随着人民币汇率双向浮动弹性增强，各类经济主体的风险意识不断提高，如何更有效地摆布本外币资产负债和防范利率、汇率等市场风险，为外汇市场深化发展创造了需求。但客观看，当前我国外汇市场仍存在一些新兴市场共性和中国自身特有问题，例如交易机制不灵活、市场主体类型单一、对外开放程度偏低、基础设施不健全等。

2015 年 8 月 11 日，中国人民银行完善人民币兑美元汇率中间价报价，并在下一步推进汇改安排中提出加快外汇市场发展，丰富外汇产品，推动外汇市场对外开放，延长外汇交易时间，引入合格境外主体，促进形成境内外一致的人民币汇率。展望未来，国内外汇市场发展有必要、更有条件在汇改十年基础上实现新的重大突破，为完善人民币汇率形成机制改革创造更好的市场基础。

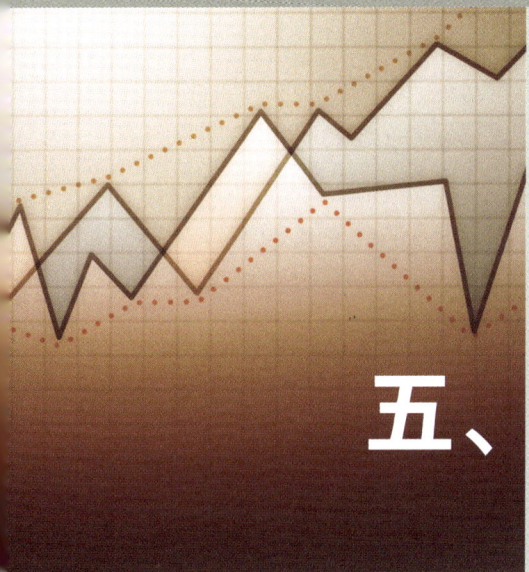

五、国际收支形势展望

2015 年下半年，我国国际收支有望延续上半年"经常账户顺差、资本和金融账户（不含储备资产变动）逆差"的格局，国际收支自主平衡能力进一步提高。

经常账户仍将保持较大顺差。 一方面，货物贸易顺差仍会维持较高水平。从出口看，下半年世界经济可能呈现美国温和扩张、欧元区和日本缓慢复苏、新兴经济体增长趋缓的格局。根据国际货币基金组织（IMF）最新预测，2015 年世界经济增长 3.3%，较 2014 年增速略低 0.1 个百分点，其中，发达经济体经济增速将由 2014 年的 1.8% 升至 2.1%，有助于稳定外需。同时，随着"一带一路"战略规划的逐步落实、上海等地自贸区的积极实践、中韩自贸协定等区域经贸合作的进一步加强，我国出口也会迎来新的机遇。从进口看，美元相对强势和商品供应过剩将继续压低国际大宗商品价格，再加上国内需求总体平稳，我国进口规模仍会明显低于出口。另一方面，服务贸易等项目将继续呈现逆差。其中，旅行项目仍是最主要的逆差来源，我国居民境外旅游、留学等消费需求依然较高，暑期旅游和年末购物旺季、秋季留学开学等季节性因素，将导致下半年旅行项目逆差高于上半年。总的来看，经常账户将在货物贸易主导下持续较大顺差，但仍会处于国际公认的合理水平之内。

跨境资本流动的波动性依然较大。 从外部环境看，目前美国经济和就业市场状况总体表现相对较好，美联储加息以及加息预期等因素将使得美元汇率易涨难跌。同时，全球经济长期不景气、欧元区部分国家债务问题、新兴市场汇率波动以及地缘政治冲突等因素，将继续影响国际金融稳定，可能推升市场避险情绪。从国内环境看，经济转型过程中的下行压力仍然存在，境内融资成本进一步降低，人民币汇率逐步趋向合理均衡水平，我国市场主体将继续调整财务运作方式，不断优化本外币资产负债结构。而且，随着我国深化改革和对外开放的稳步推进，国内企业"走出去"对外投资需求仍会较大。

我国国际收支将在适度可控的调整中逐步确立新格局。 首先，当前境内主体根据市场环境变化合理调整本外币资产负债结构，符合市场运行规律和"藏汇于民"的调控目标，有利于降低高杠杆、货币错配等相关风险。其次，我国经济仍保持中高速增长，市场发展潜力依然较大，深化改革等措施积极推进，贸易投资便利化程度进一步提升，对外资尤其是长期资本仍具有较强的吸引力。最后，我国经常账户持续顺差，外汇储备充裕，财政金融体系总体稳健，人民币汇率在合理均衡水平上保持基本稳定，均有利于国际收支平衡状况的稳步改善。今后，随着我国经济结构的优化调整，人民币汇率形成机制改革朝着市场化的方向推进，央行基本退出常态式外汇市场干预，我国国际收支将形成"经常账户顺差、资本和金融账户逆差"的新格局。

专栏 7

美联储加息周期对新兴经济体跨境资本流动的差异化影响

随着经济金融全球化的不断加深，美国货币政策的周期性变化（以联邦基金利率的变化为代表）对新兴经济体跨境资金流动产生了愈发重要的影响。20世纪90年代以来，美国大致经历了三轮加息周期：一是1994年2月份起，美联储7次上调联邦基金利率，使之从3%增至6%；二是1999年至2000年，7次上调联邦基金利率，使其从4.75%升至6.5%，并将利率水平维持到2001年1月份；三是从2004年6月起，连续17次提高利率，将联邦基金利率从1%推高至2006年6月份的5.25%，并将利率水平维持到2007年9月17日。此外，每轮加息周期前后一般都伴随着美元的走高（见图C7-1）。

美联储前两次加息周期与新兴经济体的不同表现。第一次加息周期中，拉丁美洲的墨西哥于1994年爆发危机，智利则经受住了考验；第二次加息周

图 C7-1

1990年以来美国联邦基金利率与美元指数走势

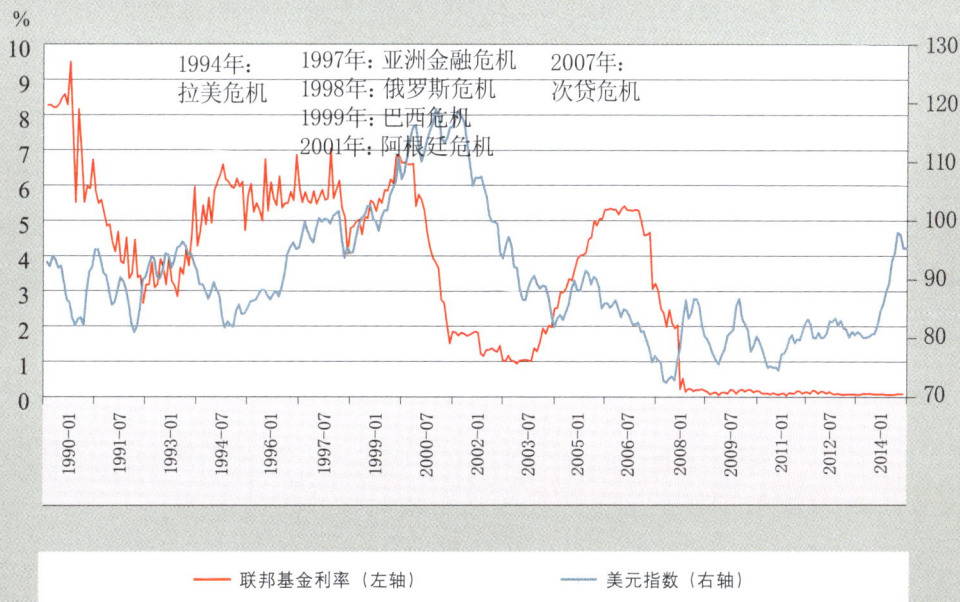

数据来源：环亚经济数据库。

期中，部分东南亚国家于 1997-1998 年爆发了金融危机，阿根廷于 2001 年爆发危机，而我国并未受到较大冲击。究其原因：一是国内经济基本面不同。如 1994 年墨西哥金融危机的重要原因之一，就是国内政局动荡等风险因素动摇了投资者对墨西哥经济发展前景的信心。再如，1998 年我国能够较好抵御亚洲金融危机的冲击，一方面是因为在市场动荡的几年前就采取了一系列改革和经济调整措施，且经济发展速度较快；另一方面外汇储备显著增加，有底气作出人民币不贬值的决定。二是汇率制度和汇率弹性不同。为控制通胀、稳定物价，上述发生危机的国家大多采取盯住美元的固定汇率制，且短期资本大量流入，随着美元升值并进入加息周期，不可避免地面临流动性收缩的困境，导致主权货币、股票市场大幅下挫，引发金融危机。而避免危机的国家如智利则稳步推进汇率市场化进程，1992 年开始实行"爬行盯住一篮子货币"的汇率制度，并于此后多次扩大汇率浮动区间。三是资本项目开放进程不同。如墨西哥采用较为激进的方式，仅用 4~5 年开放证券市场，使跨境资本出现大规模流动，金融脆弱性大大增加。智利实现证券市场国际化则经历了十余年，还制定了明晰的市场开放次序，先后进行了银行体系改革，以及贸易自由化、利率汇率市场化等改革，在做了充足的准备之后才渐进放开证券市场。此外，我国根据当时的国内经济金融状况，一直实行较为谨慎的金融开放政策，在隔离外部冲击风险方面发挥了一定作用。

美联储第三次加息周期与新兴经济体跨境资本流入。在此轮加息周期中，新兴经济体大多经历了跨境资金净流入的大幅增长，主要原因：一是 2001 年以来，新兴经济体逐渐成为全球经济增长新引擎，2004-2007 年年均 GDP 增长率为 8.0%，良好的经济发展势头吸引了大量资金流入，也更有利于抵御外部冲击。二是亚洲金融危机之后，新兴经济体吸取教训，迅速积累了大量外汇储备，经常账户逆差的状况也有所改善。三是本轮加息虽然上调幅度较大，但加息节奏较为缓慢。而且，由于发达和新兴经济体经济周期出现分化，美元仅于 2005 年短暂小幅反弹，并未出现长期大幅升值的情况。

从上述历史经验可得出以下结论：第一，良好的宏观经济基本面是抵御外部冲击的根本保障。经济增长较快更易化解其他各类经济、金融及社会问题，更有利于吸收跨境资金流动带来的冲击，这在新兴经济体面临美联储第三轮加息时表现尤为突出。第二，汇率制度灵活性及其与资本账户开放的协调十分重要。危机发生国往往由于资本账户开放但汇率制度相对僵化，难以有效管理资本流动增加后带来的风险，而在开放过程中不断增加汇率制度灵活性（如智利），则有利于实现对短期跨境资金流动的调节。第三，开放步伐应与一国的经济金融状况相适应。在经济金融状况良好的时期，各项改革措施面临的内部环境较为有利；但当国内经济基本面存在较多风险时，则应采取更加稳妥的方式，并在开放过程中加强审慎管理。

下一阶段，外汇管理部门将继续深入贯彻落实党中央、国务院的各项部署，坚持统筹兼顾、改革创新，主动适应经济发展新常态，推进简政放权、放管结合、优化服务改革，创新事中事后监管，切实履行好国家赋予外汇管理部门的职责。一是继续大力简政放权，深化外汇管理重点领域改革，推进资本项目可兑换，支持实体经济发展。二是完善跨境资金流动监测分析预警，夯实数据系统基础，严厉打击外汇领域违法违规行为，强化风险防范。三是继续加强外汇储备经营管理，确保安全、流动和保值增值。

I. Overview of the Balance of Payments

(I) The Balance-of-Payments Environment

In the first half of the year, China faced a more sophisticated economic and financial environment both domestically and internationally, and international capital flows were characterized by surging fluctuations. The Chinese economy grew at a reasonable rate and its balance of payments maintained a generally balanced situation.

The global market recovered slowly amidst diversification in the first half of 2015 (see Chart 1-1). The United States exhibited a solid growth trend in the second quarter, leading to expectations that the Fed would raise the interest rates. The Euro zone indicated signals of a recovery and the ECB's easy monetary policy relieved the downward risks in the economy, thus helping to strengthen confidence in the market. The Japanese economy returned to a growth track, and the central bank's quantitative and qualitative easy monetary policy led to a depreciation of the Japanese yen and a recovery of foreign trade. The emerging economies witnessed a descending growth momentum amid rising fluctuations in the financial markets of some economies, and more economies began to ease their monetary policies and became

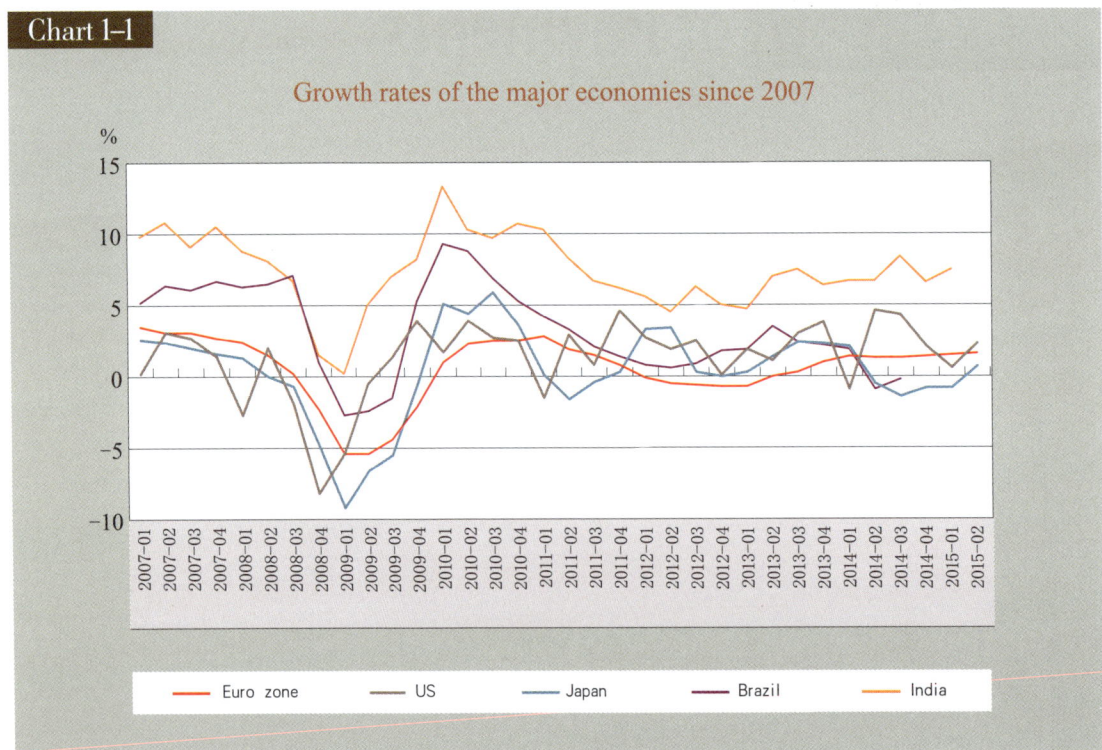

Chart 1-1 — Growth rates of the major economies since 2007

Note: The U.S. growth rate is the annualized quarterly growth; the growth rates of the other countries are the quarterly growth rates year on year.
Source:CEIC.

Chart 1–2

Fluctuations in interest rates and exchange rates in international financial markets since 2007

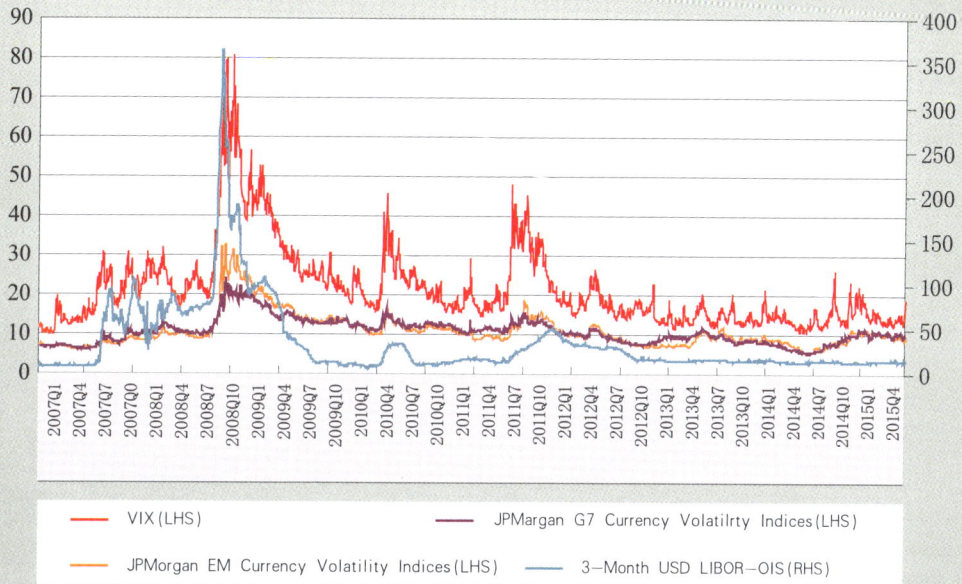

- VIX (LHS)
- JPMargan G7 Currency Volatilrty Indices (LHS)
- JPMorgan EM Currency Volatility Indices (LHS)
- 3–Month USD LIBOR–OIS (RHS)

Source: Bloomberg.

Chart 1–3

Indices of stocks, bonds, and goods since 2012

- SX5E
- BGSV
- MXEF
- SPX
- SPGSCI
- BEMS

Note: Year 2012=100.
Source: Bloomberg.

Chart 1–4

Growth rate of the quarterly GDP and the monthly CPI since 2008

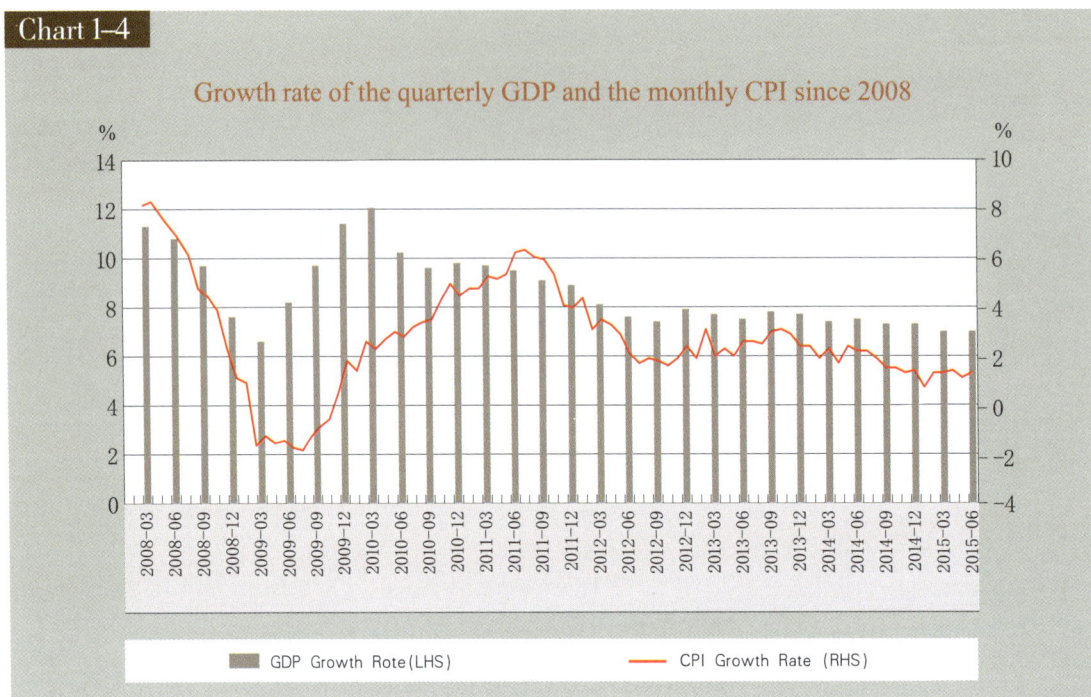

GDP Growth Rote (LHS)   CPI Growth Rate (RHS)

Sources: CEIC.

concerned about capital outflows. Moreover, the complicated global economic situation together with the monetary policy exaggerated the fluctuations in international financial markets. In the first half of the year, the US dollar appreciated with fluctuations, whereas other currencies, in both the most advanced and the emerging economies, depreciated, and the price of staple goods generally declined. In the stock and bond markets, the advanced economies outperformed the emerging economies (see Charts 1–2, 1–3).

Domestically, the Chinese economy grew according to its growth target, and the major economic indicators recovered (see Chart 1–4). In the first half of the year, the job market remained stable, with increased income and consumption by urban and suburban residents. Social financing costs declined. However, the growth of industrial products declined, and export growth slowed down due to weak external demand. Growth driven by government investment was limited. In the process of simultaneously dealing with the slowdown in economic growth, making difficult structural adjustments, and absorbing the effects of the earlier economic stimulus policies, structural adjustments may stimulate mid– and long–term growth, but downward pressures will still exist in the short term.

(II) The Main Characteristics of the Balance of Payments

In the first half of the year, China's BOP surplus[1] totaled USD 23 billion, down by 85 percent year on year (see Table 1–1). In particular, the current account surplus totaled USD 148.6 billion, up by 85 percent. The capital and financial account (excluding reserve assets) recorded a deficit of USD 125.6 billion, whereas in 2014 the capital and financial account recorded a surplus of USD 77.8 billion.

The trade-in-goods surplus grew rapidly. Based on the balance–of–payments statistics,[2] exports and imports of trade in goods amounted to USD 1 011.2 billion and USD 754.6 billion respectively, down by 2 percent and 15 percent year on year. The surplus in trade in goods totaled USD 256.6 billion, an increase of 73 percent year on year (see Chart 1–5).

Table 1-1 The structure of the BOP surplus since 2010

USD 100 million,%

Items	2010	2011	2012	2013	2014	2015H1
BOP balance	5 247	4 016	1 836	4 943	2 579	230
Current account balance	2 378	1 361	2154	1 482	2 197	1 486
As a % of the BOP balance	45	34	117	30	85	646
As a % of GDP	4.0	1.9	2.6	1.6	2.1	3.1
Capital and financial account balance	2 869	2 655	-318	3 461	382	-1 256
As a % of the BOP balance	55	66	-17	70	15	-546
As a % of GDP	4.8	3.6	-0.4	3.6	0.4	-2.6

Sources: SAFE, NBS.

Trade in services continued to expand. In the first half of the year, trade–in–services revenue and expenditures amounted to USD 112.2 billion and USD 206.7 billion respectively, up by 1 percent and 20 percent year on year. Trade in services recorded a deficit of USD 94.5 billion, increasing by 53 percent year on year. In particular, the

---

[1] BOP surplus = current account balance + capital and financial account balance (excluding reserve assets).

[2] The BOP statistics and the statistics of the General Administration of Customs with respect to trade in goods can be reconciled by the following: First, imports based on the BOP statistics equal 95 percent of the imports based on the customs statistics by quoting the CIF and assuming 5 percent to be insurance and freight. Second, the BOP statistics include goods repatriation, goods purchased at ports, and smuggled goods that are deducted from the import and export returns.

Chart 1–5

Major items under the current account since 2001

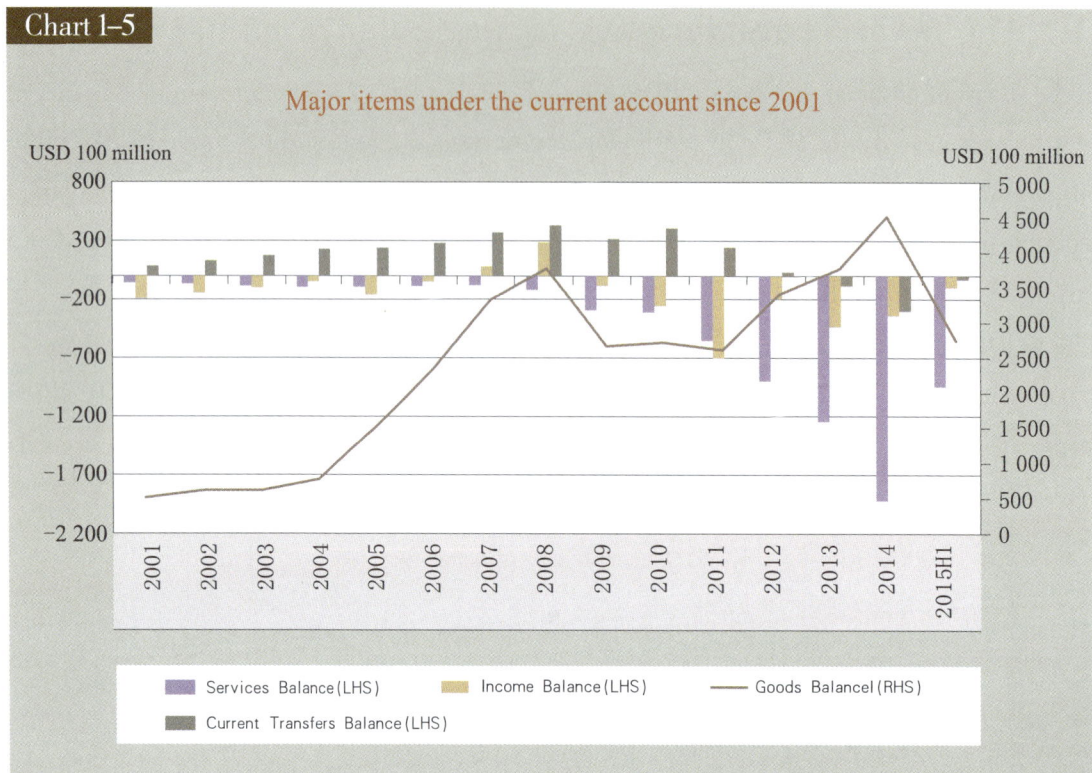

Source: SAFE.

transportation deficit decreased by 24 percent and the travel deficit continued to grow by 103 percent year on year (see Chart 1–5).

Primary income[1] turned to a deficit. In the first half of the year, primary income revenue and expenditures amounted to USD 131 billion and USD 141.4 billion, up by 20 percent and 36 percent respectively. The primary–income item recorded a deficit of USD 10.4 billion, whereas it recorded a surplus of USD 5.5 billion in the first half of 2014. In particular, employee compensation recorded a surplus of USD 15.1 billion, up 47 percent year on year; investment income recorded a deficit of USD 25.8 billion, an expansion of 4.5 times year on year (see Chart 1–5). The deficit in investment income does not indicate a loss of overseas investment by China. In the first half of the year, China's overseas investment income amounted to USD 112.7 billion, increasing by 15 percent year on year. Inward–investment income totaled USD 138.5 billion, up by 35 percent.

The deficit in secondary income declined significantly. In the first half of the year,

---

① The IMF's *Balance of Payments and International Investment Manual* (Sixth Edition) renamed the income item under the current account as primary income and renamed current transfers as secondary income.

revenue and expenditures from secondary income amounted to USD 18.4 billion and USD 21.5 billion respectively, down by 22 percent and 39 percent year on year. Secondary income recorded a deficit of USD 3.2 billion, decreasing by 73 percent year on year (see Chart 1–5). Secondary income includes social contributions, compensation, social security, taxes, fines, and lotteries. Since 2013, secondary income changed from a surplus to a deficit due to increased external contributions by domestic enterprises and by individuals with increased personal income.

The surplus in direct investments decreased slightly. Based on the BOP statistics, the surplus in direct investments[①] totaled USD 92 billion, down by 1 percent year on year (see Chart 1–6). In particular, outward direct investments (direct–investment assets) recorded a net outflow of USD 52.9 billion, up by 70 percent, and inward direct investments (direct–investment liabilities) recorded a net inflow of USD 144.9 billion, up by 17 percent year on year.

Portfolio investments changed to a deficit. In the first half of the year, portfolio investments recorded a deficit of USD 24.1 billion, whereas they recorded a surplus of USD 36.9 billion in

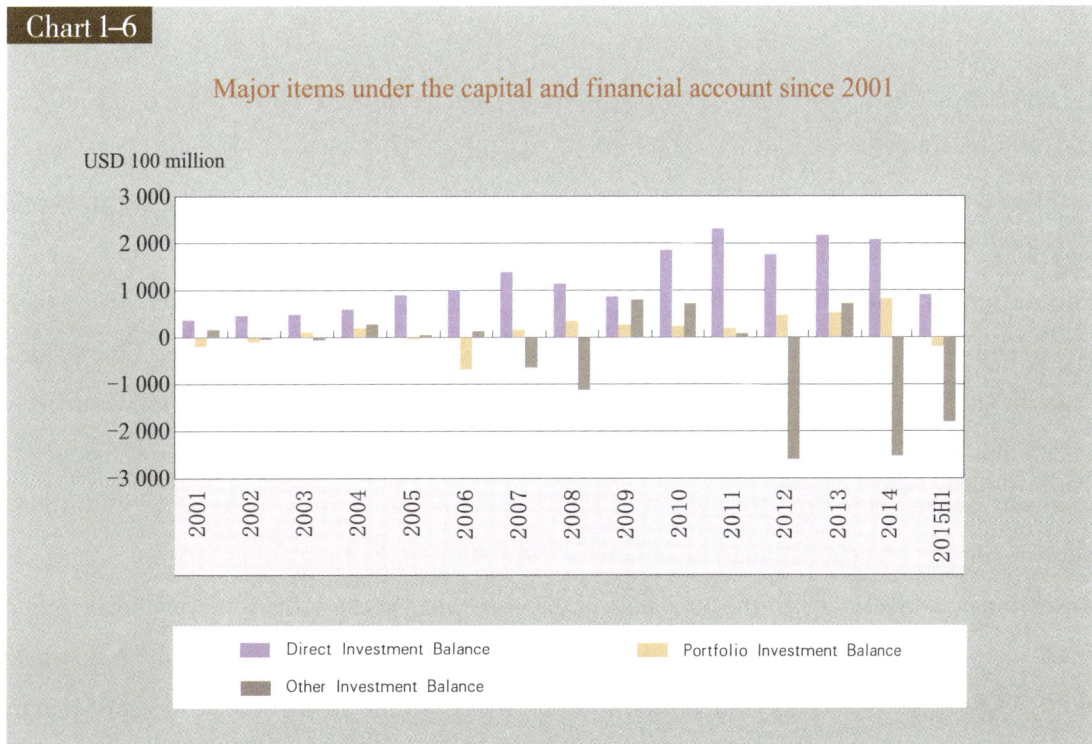

Chart 1–6

Major items under the capital and financial account since 2001

Sources: SAFE.

① Unlike the data released by the Ministry of Commerce, direct investments based on the BOP statistics also include unpaid and unremitted profits, retained earnings, shareholder loans, foreign capital utilized by financial institutions, and real estate bought by non–residents.

Chart 1-7

Foreign reserve position and growth since 2001

USD 100 million

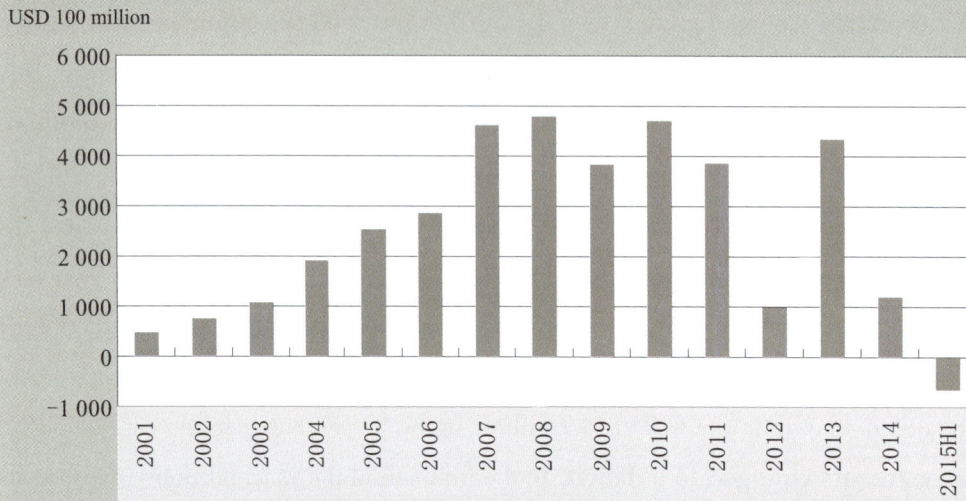

Sources: SAFE.

the first half of 2014 (see Chart 1–6). In particular, China's outward portfolio investments saw a net outflow of USD 57.2 billion, but in the first half of 2014 outward portfolio investments recorded a net inflow of USD 2.5 billion. Inward portfolio investments recorded a net inflow of USD 33.1 billion, down by 4 percent year on year.

The deficit in other investments expanded. In the first half of 2015, the deficit in other investments amounted to USD 193.1, an increase of 2.7 times year on year (see Chart 1–6). In particular, external assets, including outward loans, trade credits, and deposits recorded a net increase of USD 63.2 billion, down by 61 percent year on year. External liabilities, such as inward loans, trade credits, and deposits, recorded a net decrease of USD 129.9 billion, whereas they recorded a net increase of USD 112.4 billion in the first half of 2014.

Reserve assets declined. In the first half of 2014, China's reserve assets (excluding other flows, e.g., exchange rates and prices) decreased by USD 67.1 billion, whereas in the first half of 2014 China's reserve assets increased by USD 147.9 billion. In particular, foreign–reserve assets decreased USD 66.6 billion (see Chart 1–7), whereas they increased by USD 148.6 billion in the first half of 2014.

> **Box 1**

Statistical changes under the framework of the *Balance of Payments and International Investment Position Manual* (Sixth Edition)

Since 2015, China has begun to compile and disseminate its balance of payments and international investment position statements in line with the *Balance of Payments and International Investment Position Manual* (sixth edition, also known as BPM6). Compared with BPM5, BPM6 reinforces analysis and monitoring of the fragility and sustainability of economic performance, and emphasizes the international investment position and the balance sheet approach. The major changes include:

First, we use new terminology and names for major items. One type of change has been to change the names in Chinese translation. For instance, we now use current account to replace the previous current item in Chinese statements. We use capital and financial account to replace the previous capital and financial items. The other type of change is to change the terminology according to the English manual. This is mainly to coordinate with the concepts used in related international standards, such as national account statistics. For instance, we use *primary income* to replace the *income* item under the current account, and we use *secondary income* to replace the *current transfers* under the same account.

Second, we have reclassified items and accounts according to the new manual. First, exports and imports of goods for processing without a change of ownership were recorded as credit and debit of goods under BPM5. In BPM6, only the net value and the processing fees are recorded as services credits. Another change has been to reclassify merchanting from the services account to the goods account, and only the net exports of merchanting are recorded as a credit entry. For instance, in 2013, Chinese exports and imports of goods for processing were USD 92.5 billion and USD 82.8 billion, respectively. Under BPM5, exports and imports were recorded as goods credits and debits. But under BPM6, only net exports, USD 9.7 billion, are recorded as services credits rather than as goods credits. Another example, in 2013, the net exports of merchanting in China amounted to USD 68.6 billion, which was recorded as services credits in BPM5. However, according to BPM6, we record the figure under goods credits, not under services credits. Second, the new statement lists financial derivatives separately and no longer includes them as part of portfolio investments. Third, the new statement includes reserve assets under the financial account. However, to meet the needs of domestic users, the new financial account has two sub–accounts, namely the financial account excluding the reserve assets, and the reserve assets. The former has the same coverage as the previous Chinese financial account in BPM5. In the first half of 2015, the capital and financial account recorded a deficit of USD 58.3 billion, of which USD 125.9 billion consisted of a deficit under the financial account excluding reserve assets.

Third, we have changed the presentation of the statement. First, the new balance–of–payments statement has only one column, instead of the previous three columns, to indicate credits, debits, and the balance of each item. The new one–column presentation will facilitate time–series data analysis. Second, under the financial account, we only present net figures, and we no longer present credit and debit figures. This is mainly because financial account transactions occur with a high frequency and in a large volume and because it is more meaningful to analyze net flows of external financial assets and liabilities than the total volume. Moreover, it is more difficult to capture the inflows and outflows of every financial transaction. Under these circumstances, changes in stock are used to deduct the flows. Meanwhile, in BPM6, the financial account follows a new sign convention, with a positive sign reflecting a net increase in assets and liabilities, and a negative sign reflecting a net decrease in assets and liabilities. However, to adapt to the needs of domestic users, China's financial account still follows the BPM5 sign convention, which uses a positive sign to reflect a decrease in assets and an increase in liabilities, and uses a negative sign to reflect an increase in assets and a decrease in liabilities. For instance, in 2014, Chinese reserve assets increased by USD 117.8 billion. As a result, a negative USD 117.8 billion was recorded under reserve assets in China's 2014 BOP statement.

Fourth, we now use new statistical methodology to compile the direct investment data. The new manual adopts a new statistical methodology for direct investments. Specifically, enterprises' direct investments in overseas parent companies (known as reverse investments) follow different recording principles in BPM5 and in BPM6. In BPM5, direct–investment statistics adopted a directional principle, which divided direct investments into direct investments abroad (ODI) and direct investments in the reporting economy (FDI). For ODI, both assets and liabilities (reverse investments) were included, but ODI liabilities (reverse investments) were deducted from the ODI assets to obtain the net ODI flows. The FDI statistics followed the same principle, deducting the FDI assets (reverse investments) from the FDI liabilities to obtain the net FDI flows. According to the BPM5 principles, if a domestic direct investor invested USD 10 billion in its overseas direct-investment subsidiaries in the form of equities and loans and accepted USD 3 billion reverse investments from the overseas subsidiaries in the form of equities and loans, the USD 3 billion ODI liability would be deducted from the USD 10 billion ODI investment, which would give rise to a USD 7 billion net ODI outflow for the home country. For FDI, a similar deduction rule was applied. In BPM6, instead of deducting reverse investments from direct investments, reverse investments are recorded as direct-investment assets or liabilities on their own. For instance, overseas subsidiaries' equity and loan investments in Chinese parent companies should be recorded as Chinese direct-investment liabilities. Investments of foreign-owned companies in their foreign parent entities should be recorded as Chinese direct-investment assets. Using the same example as above, in BPM6, USD 10 billion investments from domestic investors to their foreign subsidiaries should be recorded as ODI assets, and USD 3 billion reverse investments from overseas subsidiaries to their Chinese parent companies should be recorded as FDI liabilities.

Fifth, we have improved stock statistics on certain items. In line with BPM6, China has fully adopted market-value principles when collecting and compiling the international investment position statement, and it no longer accumulates flows to calculate the stock for certain items. Meanwhile, because the new statistical methodology was only put in place recently, and because it is difficult to obtain back data, China did not revise its historic IIP data, making the data for some items before and after 2014 incompatible. For instance, before 2014 China used cumulative overseas IPO flows to obtain IPO-related equity liabilities. In 2015, China changed the methodology and used market values at the end of the reference period. Due to the changes in the valuation methodology, equity liabilities before and after 2014 cannot be compared.

Table 1-2 Balance of payments in the first half of 2015

Unit: USD 100 million

Item	Line No.	2015H1
1. Current account	**1**	**1 486**
Credit	2	12 728
Debit	3	-11 242
1.A Goods and services	4	1 621
Credit	5	11 234
Debit	6	-9 613
1.A.a Goods	7	2 566

(continued)

Item	Line No.	2015H1
Credit	8	10 112
Debit	9	-7 546
1.A.b Services	10	-945
Credit	11	1 122
Debit	12	-2 067
1.A.b.1 Manufacturing services on physical inputs owned by others	13	97
Credit	14	98
Debit	15	-1
1.A.b.2 Maintenance and repair services n.i.e	16	11
Credit	17	17
Debit	18	-6
1.A.b.3 Transport	19	-220
Credit	20	198
Debit	21	-418
1.A.b.4 Travel	22	-892
Credit	23	277
Debit	24	-1 169
1.A.b.5 Construction	25	31
Credit	26	82
Debit	27	-51
1.A.b.6 Insurance and pension services	28	-14
Credit	29	20
Debit	30	-34
1.A.b.7 Financial services	31	-4
Credit	32	11
Debit	33	-15
1.A.b.8 Charges for the use of intellectual property	34	-99
Credit	35	6
Debit	36	-105
1.A.b.9 Telecommunications, computer, and information services	37	59
Credit	38	114
Debit	39	-55
1.A.b.10 Other business services	40	100
Credit	41	290
Debit	42	-190
1.A.b.11 Personal, cultural, and recreational services	43	-4
Credit	44	4
Debit	45	-8
1.A.b.12 Government goods and services n.i.e	46	-9
Credit	47	5
Debit	48	-14
1.B Primary income	49	-104
Credit	50	1 310
Debit	51	-1 414
1.B.1 Compensation of employees	52	151
Credit	53	179
Debit	54	-28
1.B.2 Investment income	55	-258
Credit	56	1 127
Debit	57	-1 385
1.B.3 Other primary income	58	4
Credit	59	4
Debit	60	-1
1.C Secondary income	61	-32
Credit	62	184

(continued)

Item	Line No.	2015H1
Debit	63	-215
2. Capital and financial account	**64**	**-585**
2.1 Capital account	65	3
Credit	66	4
Debit	67	-1
2.2 Financial account	68	-587
Assets	69	-1 084
Liabilities	70	497
2.2.1 Financial account excluding reserve assets	71	-1 259
Financial assets excluding reserve assets	72	-1 756
Liabilities	73	497
2.2.1.1 Direct investment	74	920
2.2.1.1.1 Assets	75	-529
2.2.1.1.1.1 Equity and investment fund shares	76	-495
2.2.1.1.1.2 Debt instruments	77	-34
2.2.1.1.2 Liabilities	78	1 449
2.2.1.1.2.1 Equity and investment fund shares	79	1 233
2.2.1.1.2.2 Debt instruments	80	215
2.2.1.2 Portfolio investment	81	-241
2.2.1.2.1 Assets	82	-572
2.2.1.2.1.1 Equity and investment fund shares	83	-326
2.2.1.2.1.2 Debt securities	84	-247
2.2.1.2.2 Liabilities	85	331
2.2.1.2.2.1 Equity and investment fund shares	86	212
2.2.1.2.2.2 Debt securities	87	120
2.2.1.3 Financial derivatives (other than reserves) and employee stock options	88	-7
2.2.1.3.1 Assets	89	-23
2.2.1.3.2 Liabilities	90	16
2.2.1.4 Other investment	91	-1 931
2.2.1.4.1 Assets	92	-632
2.2.1.4.1.1 Other equity	93	0
2.2.1.4.1.2 Currency and deposits	94	-152
2.2.1.4.1.3 Loans	95	-541
2.2.1.4.1.4 Insurance, pension, and standardized guarantee schemes	96	-56
2.2.1.4.1.5 Trade credit and advances	97	130
2.2.1.4.1.6 Other accounts receivable	98	-13
2.2.1.4.2 Liabilities	99	-1 299
2.2.1.4.2.1 Other equity	100	0
2.2.1.4.2.2 Currency and deposits	101	-175
2.2.1.4.2.3 Loans	102	-759
2.2.1.4.2.4 Insurance, pension, and standardized guarantee schemes	103	14
2.2.1.4.2.5 Trade credit and advances	104	-357
2.2.1.4.2.6 Other accounts payable	105	-23
2.2.1.4.2.7 Special drawing rights	106	0
2.2.2 Reserve assets	107	671
2.2.2.1 Monetary gold	108	0
2.2.2.2 Special drawing rights	109	-4
2.2.2.3 Reserve position in the IMF	110	10
2.2.2.4 Foreign exchange reserves	111	666
2.2.2.5 Other reserve assets	112	0
3.Net errors and omissions	**113**	**-901**

Note: 1. The chart is compiled according to BPM6.

2. In the financial account, a positive value for assets represents a net decrease while a negative value represents a net increase. A positive value for liabilites reprensents a net increase while a negative value represents a net decrease.

Source: SAFE.

Box 2

A perspective on recent changes in China's gold reserves

The People's Bank of China recently published data on its gold reserves according to the IMF's SDDS requirements. At the end of June 2015, China held 1 658 tons of gold reserves, a 604–ton increase from the previous announcement of an increase in April 2009. According to the BOP statistical principles, there are two types of gold, monetary gold and non–monetary gold. Monetary gold is a type of financial asset held by the central bank. Transactions of monetary gold should be recorded under the reserve assets of the financial account. Non–monetary gold is held by sectors other than the central bank. Because non–monetary gold is regarded as a type of tangible asset, transactions of non–monetary gold should be recorded as exports and imports of goods. When the central bank increases its holdings of monetary gold, it may purchase from either domestic counterparties or foreign counterparties. If it purchases domestically, the transactions should not be included in the BOP. If it purchases internationally, the various foreign counterparties should apply their respective recording rules. Only purchases from foreign central banks and international financial organizations should be recorded as monetary gold transactions. Purchases from other foreign counterparties, such as commercial institutions, are regarded as non–monetary gold imports, which should be recorded under imports of goods. Only through monetarization (a type of non–transaction change) can non–monetary gold become the central bank's monetary gold reserves.

China's recent increase in monetary gold came from various sources, including domestic gold refining, purchases from domestic producers, and purchases from domestic and international entities. Gold refining and purchases from domestic producers and other domestic entities are domestic transactions which should not be recorded in China's balance of payments. Meanwhile, international purchases are goods imports, not monetary gold transactions, because the foreign counterparties are foreign commercial institutions, not foreign central banks or international financial organizations. As to the flows, because gold reserves have increased over the years, and because it is difficult to obtain the data sources to revise the back data, China will not revise its past balance of payments, but in the future it will record the related transactions based on the actual data. As to the stocks, the central bank's holdings of gold reserves should be recorded under reserve assets in the IIP. In the second quarter of 2015, a USD 22 billion non-transaction flow arose due to the difference between the stocks and the transaction flows of monetary gold. The non-transaction flows can be attributed to both the monetarization of gold and the price changes of gold. On June 30, 2015, China held USD 62.4 billion of monetary gold, 1.7 percent of its total reverse assets.

Although China's gold reserves are relatively small if compared with its USD 3 trillion foreign-exchange reserves and their ratio to its foreign-exchange reserves is less than 2 percent, but the absolute amount of China's gold reserves is not small. According to the WCG's July statistics, China has surpassed Russia to become the world's fifth largest gold-reserve-holding country. The top four gold-reserve-holding countries are the US, Germany, Italy, and France. However, because their currencies are freely convertible and because those countries generally hold a relatively small amount of foreign-exchange reserves, the ratios of their gold reserves to their foreign-exchange reserves are relatively high. As a developing economy whose currency is not fully convertible and a country that holds a relatively large amount of foreign-exchange reserves, the ratio of China's gold reserves to its foreign-exchange reserves naturally will be low. This is also why the ratio alone cannot justify how much gold reserves are appropriate. Take Japan, as the second largest foreign-exchange-reserves-holding country, as an example. Japan has a low gold reserve to foreign-exchange reserves ratio (2 percent).

As a unique asset, gold possesses characteristics of both a financial asset and a commodity. A combination of gold and other assets can help adjust and optimize overall risks and returns of international reserve assets. However, compared with foreign-exchange reserves, gold reserves have their own drawbacks. For instance, their price fluctuates greatly, their market is small, their holding costs are high, and they lack liquidity. As to the price, international gold prices fluctuate greatly. Since early 2009, the price of gold has increased from USD 800 per ounce to a peak of approximately USD 1 900 per ounce in 2011. But within two years, the price then dropped to USD 1 200 per ounce. The great price fluctuations make gold investments not so appealing when safety is the priority of reserve assets management. In terms of market capacity and liquidity, daily turnover in the international foreign-exchange market was more than USD 5 trillion, the balance of US bonds was USD 50 billion, but daily turnover of international gold trade was approximately USD 0.3 trillion. Under these circumstances, it is difficult to meet liquidity needs by holding a large amount of gold as reserve assets. In terms of appreciation in value, gold reserves will not incur interest income. Instead, custodian costs and storage costs are required to maintain gold reserves.

Moreover, China has become the largest gold producer in the world and a large gold consumer. In the first half of 2015, China produced 229 tons of gold and consumed 561 tons of gold. Of the gold consumed, 412 tons were used for jewelry, 102 tons were used for gold bars and coins, and 47 tons were used for industrial and other uses. It is evident that enterprises and individuals are the major consumers of gold in China. In terms of international reserves management, the country does not have to compete with the private sector for gold.

(III) Evaluation of the Balance of Payments

The current account surplus increased at a well-recognized reasonable rate. In the first half of 2015, the ratio of the current account surplus to GDP was 3.1 percent, 1.3 percentage points higher than the ratio during the first half of 2014. The main reason was rapid growth in the surplus in trade in goods, with a ratio to GDP of 5.3 percent, increasing by 2 percentage points year on year. The ratios of the deficit of trade in services and the deficit in investment

Chart 1–8

The ratio of the current account balance to GDP and its composition since 1990

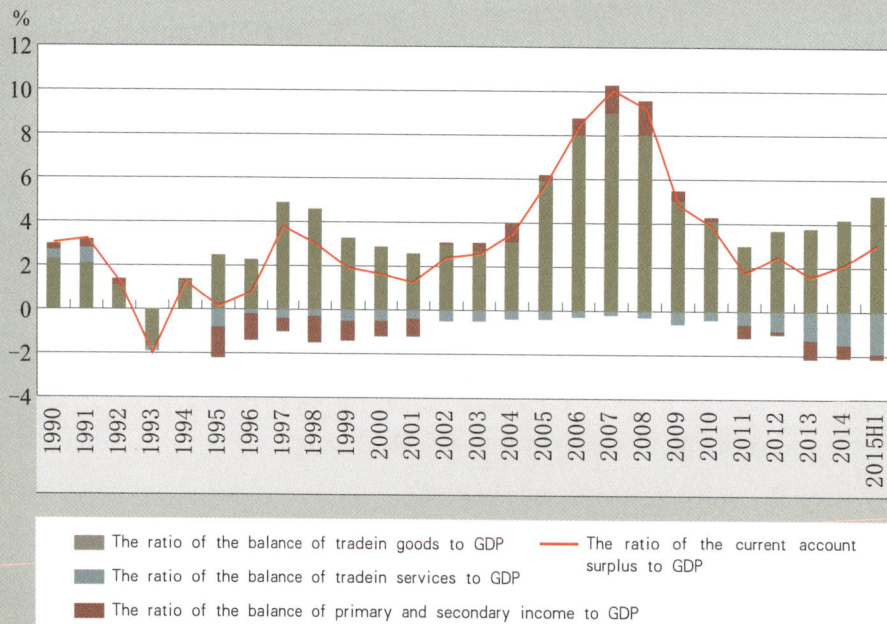

- The ratio of the balance of tradein goods to GDP
- The ratio of the balance of tradein services to GDP
- The ratio of the balance of primary and secondary income to GDP
- The ratio of the current account surplus to GDP

Sources: SAFE, NBS.

income were 2.0 percent and 0.5 percent respectively, increasing by 0.6 percentage point and 0.4 percentage point (see Chart 1–8). In addition, the total surplus of the current account and of direct investments amounted to USD 240.6 billion, increasing by 39 percent year on year and indicating a solid capability to guard against cross–border capital flows.

Cross-border capital outflows continued but slowed down to become more balanced in the second quarter. In the first quarter, the capital and financial account deficit amounted to USD 98.1 billion, an increase of USD 67.7 billion from the surplus in the fourth quarter of 2014. Foreign– reserve assets decreased by USD 79.5 billion, which was USD 50.2 billion more than the decrease during the last quarter. In the second quarter, cross–border capital outflows slowed down. The deficit in the capital and financial account was USD 27.5 billion, USD 70.7 billion less than that in the first quarter. Foreign–reserve assets increased by USD 13 billion whereas it had decreased during the first quarter (see Chart 1–9).

Structural adjustments by domestic entities in the balance sheet were the main cause of cross-border capital flows. On the one hand, the strategy to encourage foreign exchange assets held by residents achieved a significant effect of increased external assets. In the first half of the year, outflows of outward direct investments (external assets) increased by USD 52.9 billion, up by 70 percent year on year. Net outflows of outward portfolio investments (external assets) increased

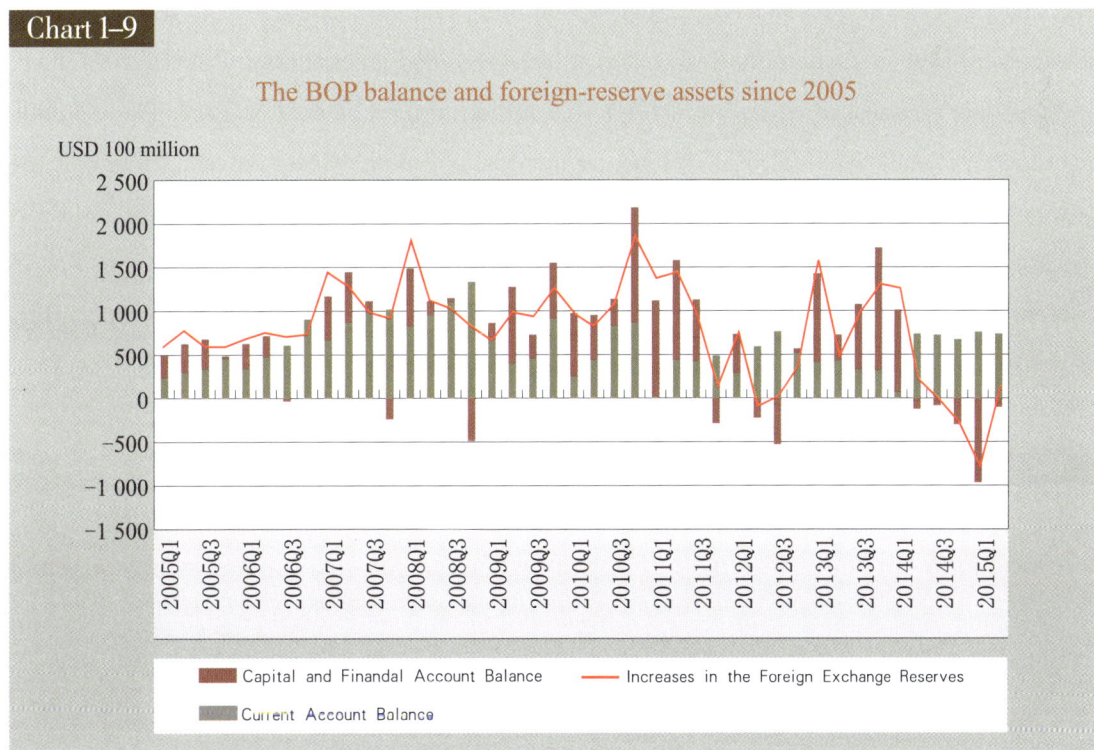

Chart 1–9

The BOP balance and foreign-reserve assets since 2005

Sources: SAFE.

Chart 1–10

Portfolio investments and other investments since 2005

USD 100 million

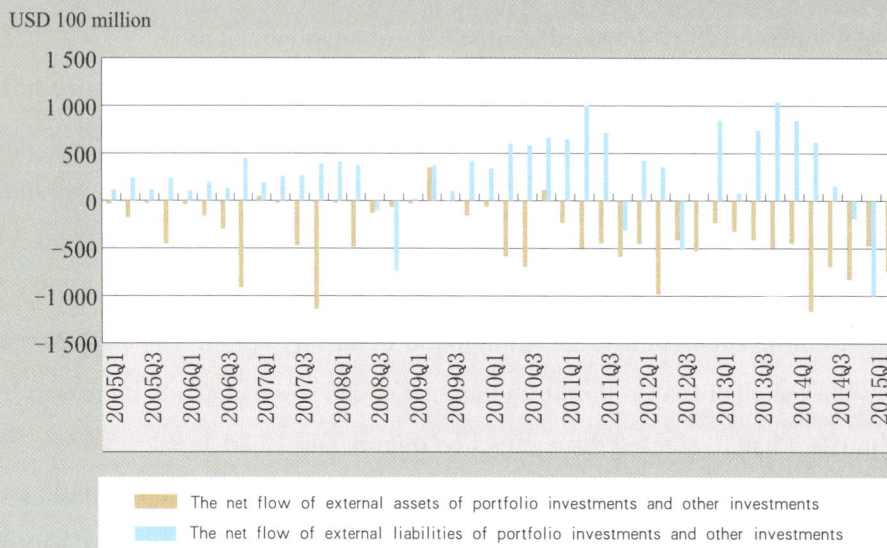

The net flow of external assets of portfolio investments and other investments

The net flow of external liabilities of portfolio investments and other investments

Sources: SAFE.

by USD 57.2 billion, whereas in the first half of 2014 there was a net inflow of USD 2.5 billion (see Chart 1–10). On the other hand, domestic entities decreased external liabilities in order to deleverage. In the first half of the year, external loans recorded a net outflow of USD 75.9 billion, whereas they recorded a net inflow of USD 76.9 billion in the first half of 2014. Trade credits recorded a net outflow of USD 35.7 billion, an increase of 3.3 times year on year. Moreover, the deleveraging process of domestic entities was adjusted due to changes in the environment and RMB exchange–rate movements were expected to gradually stabilize. In the second quarter, the outflow of external loans and trade credits decreased by USD 17.9 billion and USD 13.6 billion respectively, 69 percent and 39 percent less than the outflows in the first quarter.

Box 3

The main factors contributing to the decrease in foreign–exchange reserve assets

On June 30, 2015, China's foreign–exchange reserve assets totaled to USD 3.6938 trillion, but on June 30, 2014, China's foreign–exchange reserve assets recorded a historic high of USD 3.993 2 trillion. During this one year, foreign–exchange reserve assets decreased by USD 299.4

billion. The main contributing factors are as follows (see Chart C3–1).

First, non-transaction changes, such as foreign-exchange rate changes and price changes, contributed to a decrease of approximately USD 200 billion in foreign-exchange reserves. Because the revaluation changes were in the book value, there were no actual capital flows out of the reserves. According to China's BOP, foreign–exchange reserves decreased by USD 96.3 billion during the period from July 2014 to June 2015, a decrease reflecting actual BOP transactions (including foreign–exchange reserve income). During the same period, a decrease of USD 203.1 billion in foreign–exchange reserves was due to revaluation factors, such as exchange–rate changes and price changes. For instance, the USD index increased by 20 percent during this period, making other foreign–currency assets depreciate in value when converted to USD values.

Second, domestic enterprises and banks adjusted their RMB and foreign- currency balance sheets by increasing their foreign-currency assets and decreasing their foreign-currency liabilities. During the period from July 2014 to June 2015, domestic enterprises and individuals became more willing to hold foreign currencies. As a result, their foreign–currency deposits in domestic banks initially decreased and then increased, and finally increased by a cumulative USD 23.6 billion during the period. Meanwhile, enterprises tended to purchase foreign currencies to repay their domestic foreign–currency debts. During the same period, domestic foreign–currency loans of domestic banks decreased by a cumulative USD 32.8 billion. The largest decline occurred in the second half of 2014, but in the first half of 2015 the situation became stable. Moreover, foreign–currency forward sales to bank clients largely exceeded forward purchases, meaning that banks had to be in a net selling position with their clients. To control the risks of exchange–rate fluctuations, banks accordingly increased their foreign–exchange positions by USD 66.6 billion. The above adjustments increased domestic and international foreign–exchange supplies through channels such as banks increasing their foreign–exchange position in their own books and taking more foreign–currency deposits from their clients. The adjustments also decreased foreign–exchange demands for domestic and international loans. As a result, banks tended to invest more foreign–currency abroad. In terms of the BOP, the bank sector increased its external assets and decreased its external liabilities, thus contributing to an expanding deficit under the capital and financial account.

Third, a net foreign-currency cross-border outflow occurred among market

participants such as enterprises. From July 2014 to June 2015, net cross–border outflows of non–bank entities, such as domestic enterprises and individuals, amounted to USD 45.6 billion. Their payments were mainly for international travel, outward investments, and international loan repayments. In contrast, FDI and overseas IPOs recorded relatively large net foreign–currency inflows, indicating that long–term foreign– investment capital continued to flow into China. During the same period, banks purchased foreign currency and made foreign payments in the amount of USD 49.4 billion. This was mainly because domestic clients had strong investment and consumption demands for precious metal such as gold. As a result, this stimulated gold imports. To offset foreign– exchange exposure due to precious metal investments, banks purchased a large amount of foreign currencies. This also reflected the fact that the private sector was keen to store gold. Moreover, income from foreign–exchange reserve assets contributed to an increase in foreign– exchange reserves. From July 2014 to June 2015, investment–income credits recorded USD 197.9 billion, of which income from foreign–exchange reserve assets constituted a large contribution. In summary, the recent decreases in foreign–exchange reserves can largely be attributed to revaluation factors, such as exchange–rate changes and price changes. They also reflect the optimization and adjustment by domestic entities of their RMB and foreign–currency assets and liabilities.

Chart C3–1

The main factors contributing to changes in China's foreign-exchange reserves

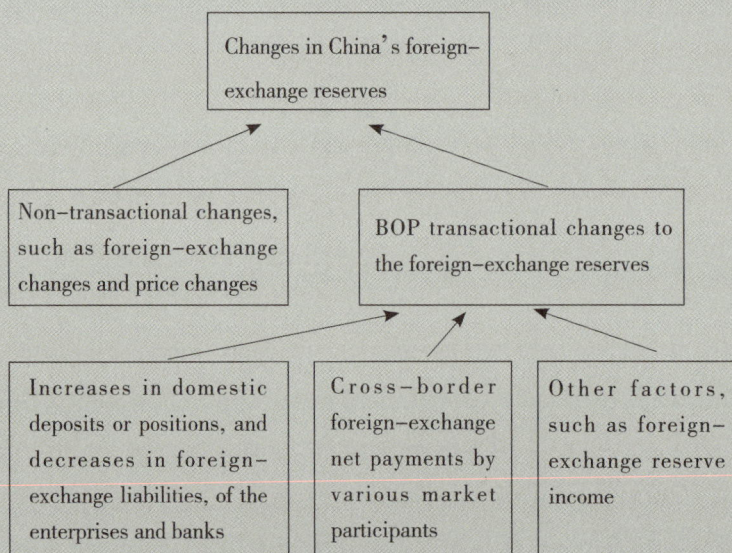

II.Analysis of the Major Items in the Balance of Payments

(I) Trade in Goods

Trade in goods was characterized by a large surplus and a decline in dependence on foreign trade. According to statistics of the General Administration of Customs, in the first half of the year China's exports increased by 0.7 percent year on year, and China's imports decreased by 15.7 percent. The surplus in trade in goods was USD 262.2 billion, up by 1.5 times, and the ratio of the surplus to GDP was 5.4 percent, 3.1 percentage points higher year on year. In the first half of the year, China's foreign trade dependence (the ratio of exports and imports to GDP) was 38.8 percent, 5.7 percentage points lower than that in the first half of 2014 (see Chart 2–1).

The ordinary trade balance changed from a deficit to a surplus due to the surging surplus of private enterprises. In the first half of 2015, China's ordinary trade surplus totaled USD 126.1 billion, whereas in the first half year of 2014 ordinary trade recorded a deficit of USD 13.6 billion. The processing trade surplus was USD 162.5 billion, down by 2.8 percent year on year (see Chart 2–2). The trade surplus of private enterprises totaled USD 272.9 billion, a significant increase of 60.8 percent year on year. The trade surplus of foreign–funded enterprises totaled USD 76.9 billion, up by 19 percent. Trade of state–owned enterprises recorded a deficit of USD 86.5 billion, down by 34.2 percent year on year. The contribution to the surplus in trade in goods by processing trade and foreign–funded

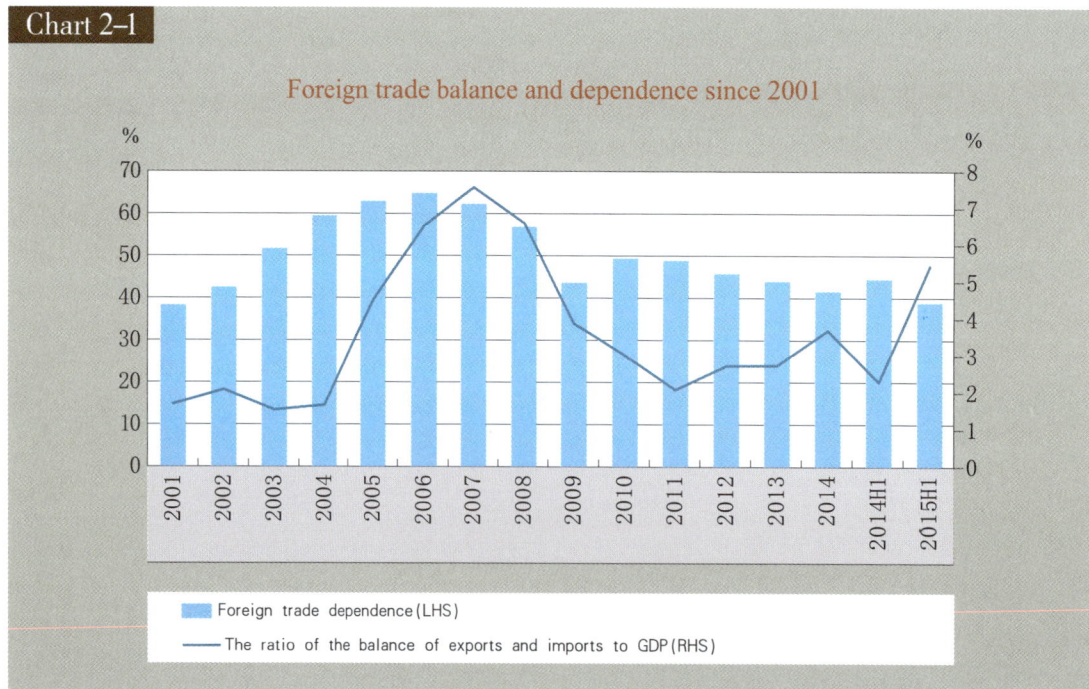

Chart 2–1

Foreign trade balance and dependence since 2001

Foreign trade dependence (LHS)

The ratio of the balance of exports and imports to GDP (RHS)

Sources: General Administration of Customs, NBS.

Chart 2–2

Composition of trade in terms of trade patterns since 2000

USD 100 million

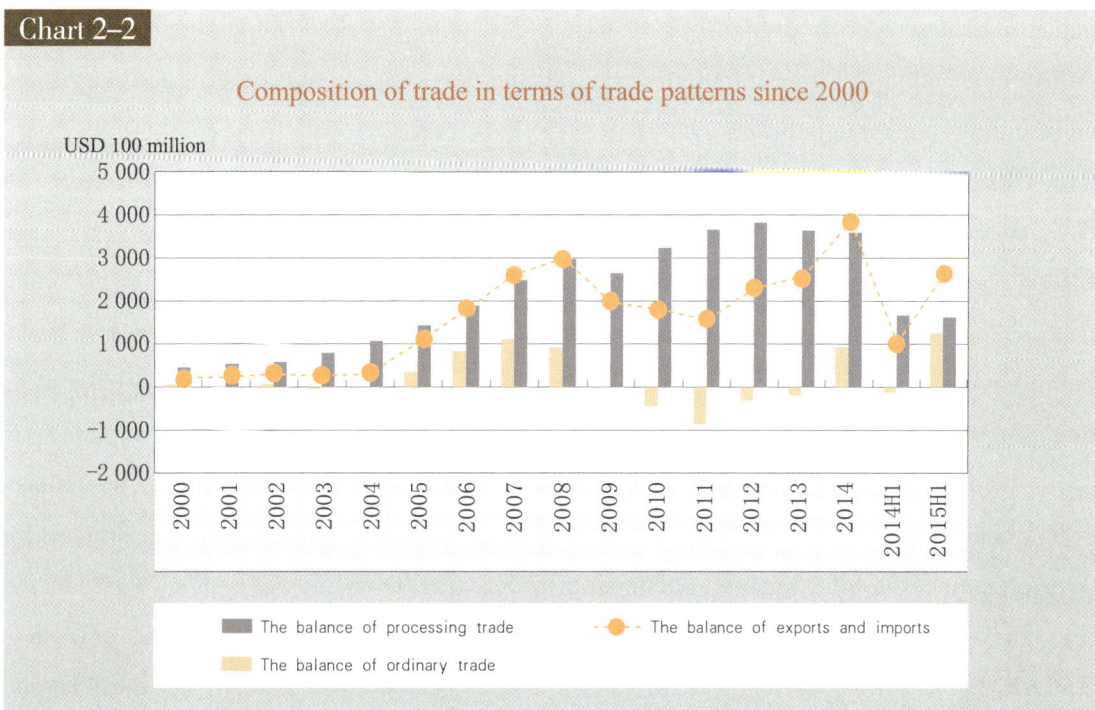

- ■ The balance of processing trade
- ● The balance of exports and imports
- ■ The balance of ordinary trade

Source: General Administration of Customs.

Chart 2–3

Composition of trade in goods in terms of trade participants since 2000

USD 100 million

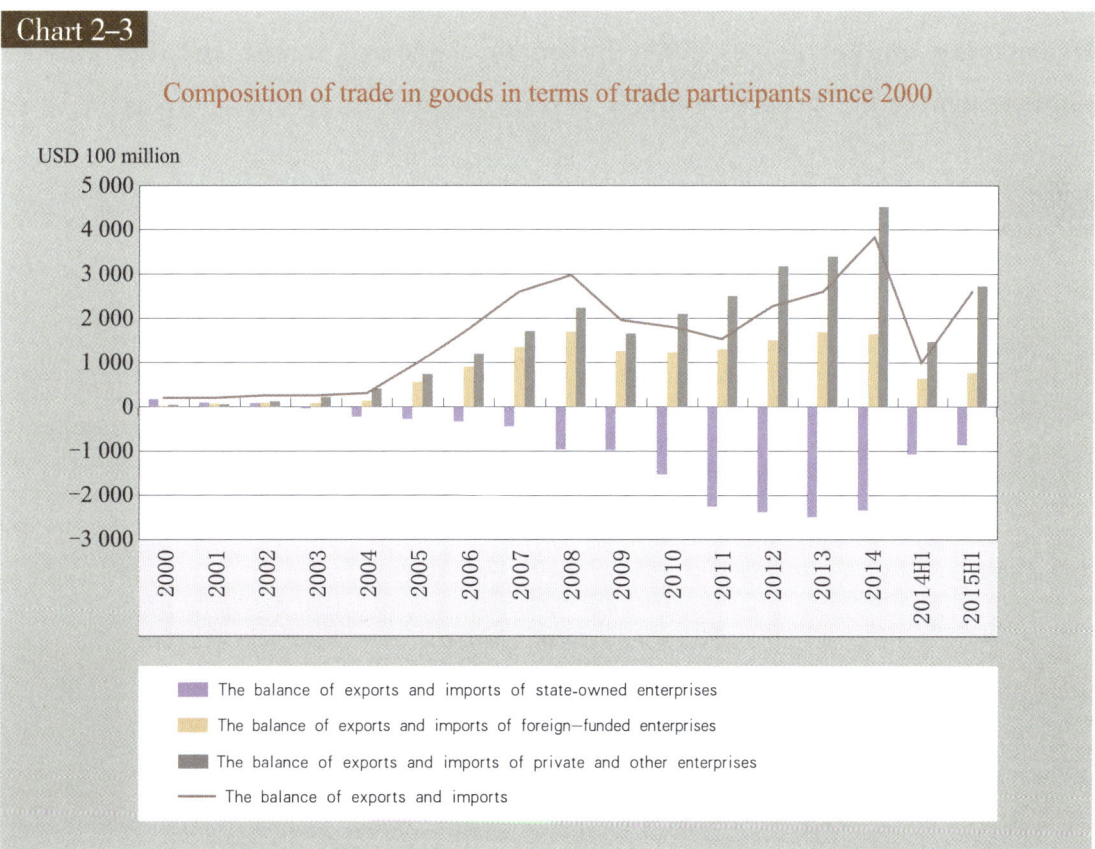

- ■ The balance of exports and imports of state-owned enterprises
- ■ The balance of exports and imports of foreign–funded enterprises
- ■ The balance of exports and imports of private and other enterprises
- — The balance of exports and imports

Source: General Administration of Customs.

enterprises has recently dropped (see Chart 2–3), reflecting the strengthened endogenous growth momentum of Chinese foreign trade and the decreased import costs of ordinary trade and Chinese–funded enterprises.

The Chinese export market share in the major developed markets grew steadily in the process of promoting market diversification. In the first half of 2015, exports to the United States grew by 9.3 percent year on year, and exports to Japan and the European Union declined by 10.6 percent and 2.5 percent respectively year on year. From the perspective of the importing countries, imports from China by the United States accounted for 20.4 percent of its total imports, 1.8 percentage points higher than the ratio in the first half of 2014. Imports from China by the European Union accounted for 19.3 percent of its total imports, 2.5 percentage points higher than that in the first half of 2014. Imports from China by Japan accounted for 23.9 percent of its total imports, increasing by 2.2 percentage points year on year. In the first half of the year, China's exports to the emerging markets rose rapidly, and its exports to ASEAN, India, Latin America, and Africa grew by 9.7 percent, 10.7 percent, 3.7 percent, and 12.8 percent respectively. Total exports to the emerging markets accounted for 26.1 percent of China's total exports, 2 percentage points higher year on year.

Decreasing import prices contributed to a growth in the surplus and an improvement in the terms of trade. In the first half of 2015, the trade surplus increased

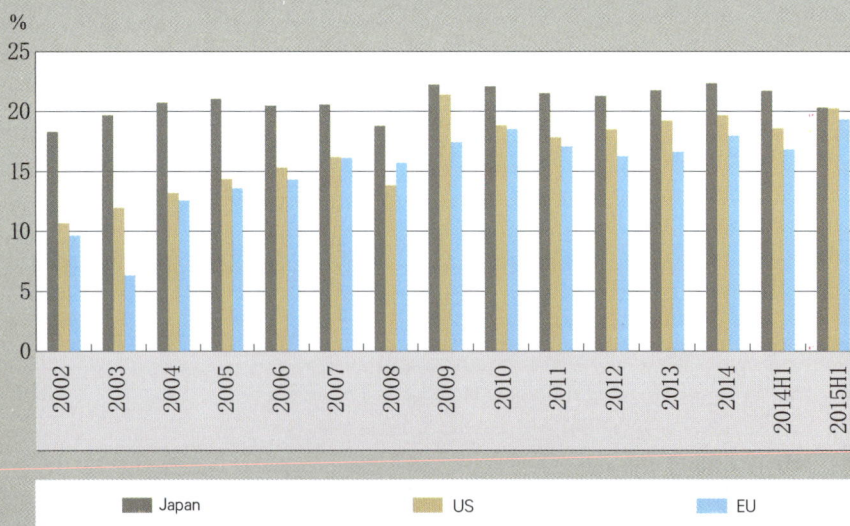

Chart 2–4

Market shares in the advanced economies since 2002

Source: General Administration of Customs.

Chart 2–5

The influence of volume and price on the trade balance

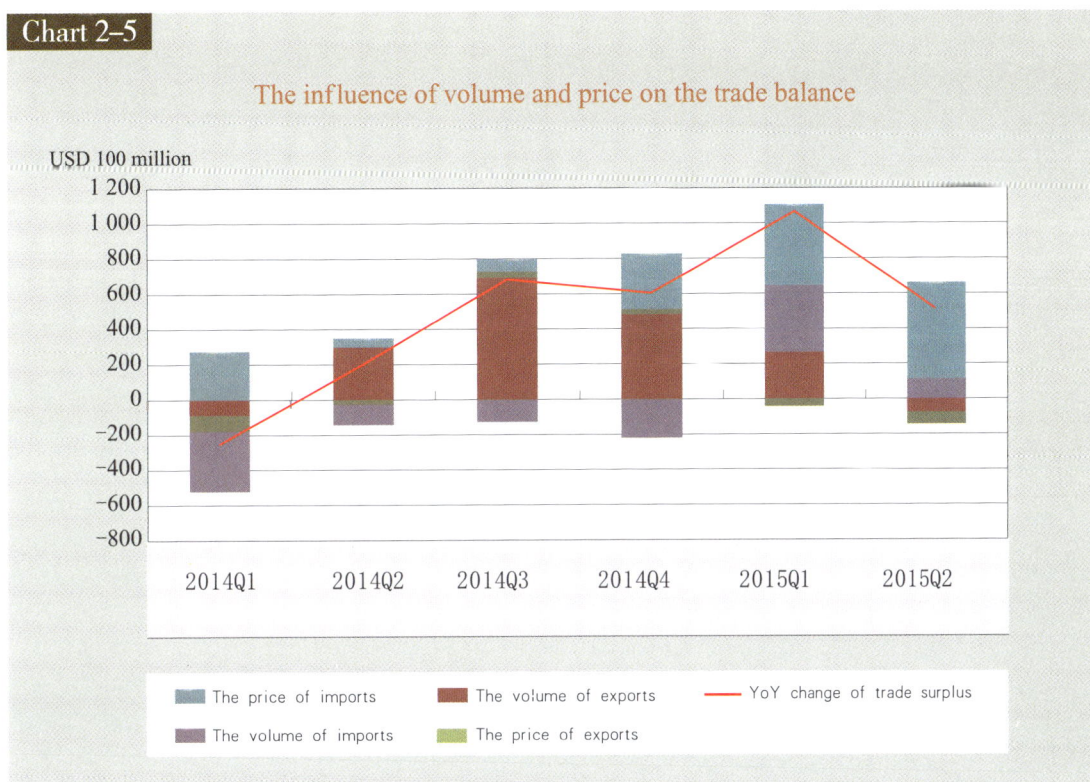

Source: CEIC.

by USD 157.9 billion. In particular, due to the significant decline in the price of staple goods, including oil and iron, the import price index dropped by 10.7 percent monthly, contributing 64 percent to the total increase in the surplus, that is, USD 101.1 billion (see Chart 2–5). In the first half of the year, China's export price index declined by 1.1 percent monthly. The terms of trade improved to 110.8 percent on an average monthly basis compared with that in the first half of 2014.

(II) Trade in Services[①]

Trade in services grew steadily due to the development of both high value-added trade in services and traditional trade in services. Against the background of decelerated economic growth and weak foreign–trade development, China's trade in services continued to grow rapidly. In the first half of the year, trade in services amounted to USD 318.8 billion, up

---

① BPM6 adjusted the concept of trade in services by moving processing trade from trade in goods to trade in services, and moving merchanting from trade in services to trade in goods. Moreover, the classifications and sub–items under trade in services changed as well.

Chart 2-6

Trade in goods and trade in services since 2004

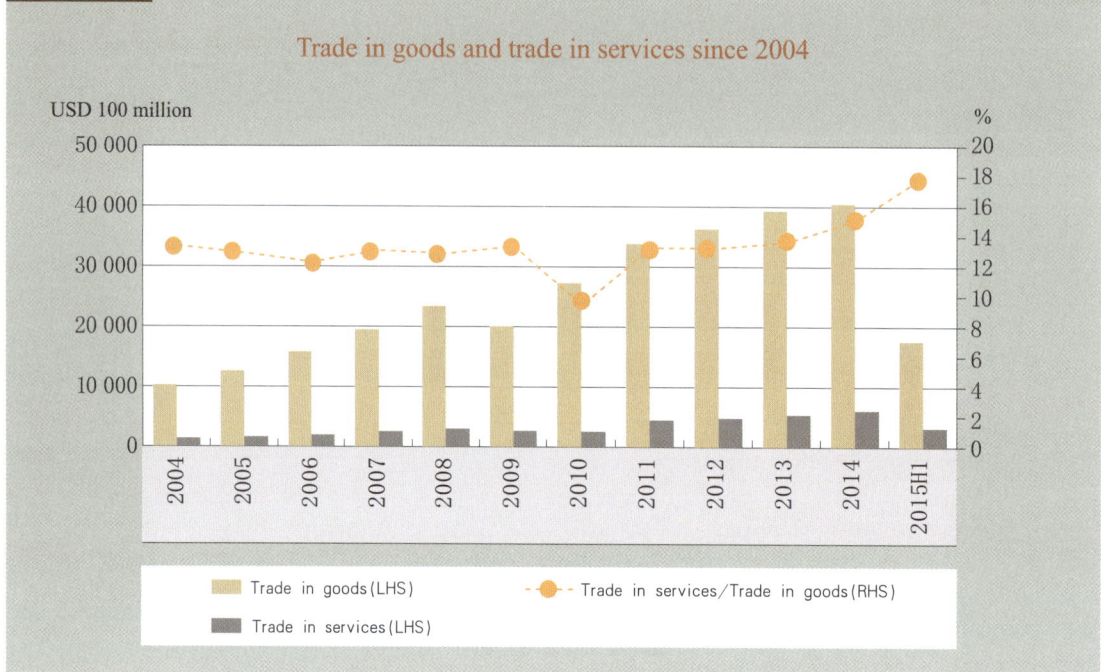

Source: SAFE.

by 12 percent year on year, whereas trade in goods dropped by 8 percent. The ratio of trade in services to trade in goods was 18 percent, 3 percentage points higher year on year (see Chart 2–6). Promoted by the strategy to improve the structure of trade in services and to support high value–added services, trade in services was further upgraded. In the first half of 2015, telecommunications, computer and information services, and construction and entertainment grew by 19 percent, 79 percent, and 1.3 times respectively.

Revenue from trade in services grew at a decreasing rate. In the first half of the year, revenue from trade in services totaled USD 112.2 billion, up by 1 percent year on year (see Chart 2–7), and its growth rate declined by 13 percentage points year on year. In the first half of the year, major items under the performance of trade in services were diversified, causing the growth of total revenue from trade in services to decelerate. In particular, transportation, travel, construction, telecommunications, computer and information services increased by USD 9.7 billion, and other commercial services (including research and development, management consultancies, technical services, and operational leasing) decreased by USD 9.7 billion year on year.

Expenditures for trade in services maintained rapid growth, with an increased contribution from travel. In the first half of 2015, trade–in– services expenditures amounted to USD 206.7 billion (see Chart 2–7), up 20 percent year on year. In particular, travel

| Chart 2–7 |

Trade in services since 2004

USD 100 million

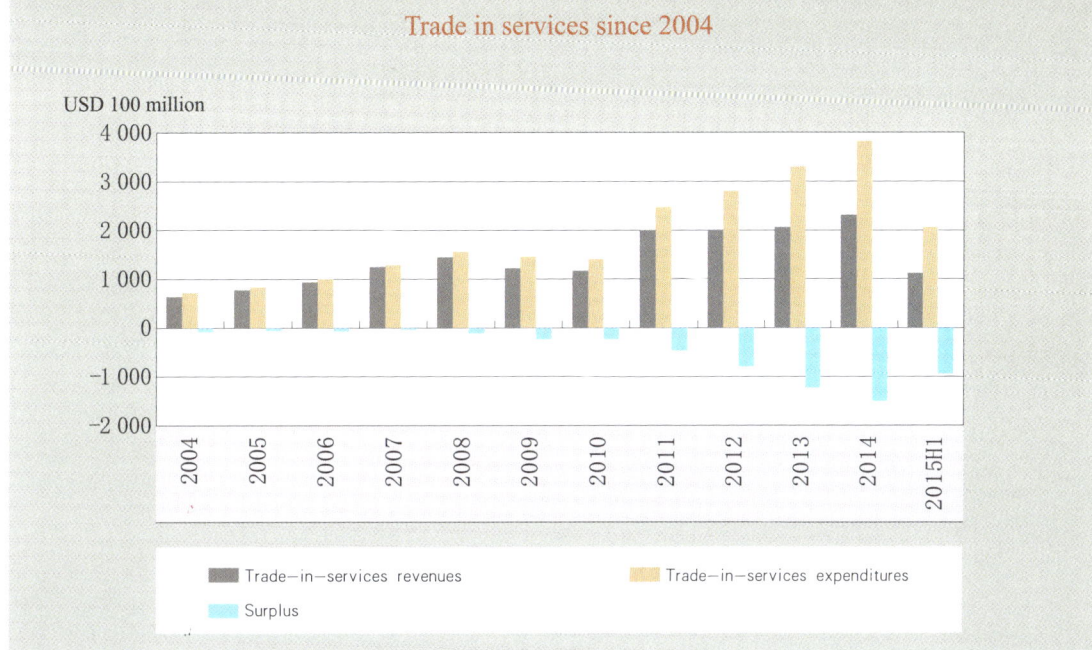

Legend:
- Trade-in-services revenues
- Trade-in-services expenditures
- Surplus

Source: SAFE.

expenditures totaled USD 116.9 billion, accounting for 57 percent of total trade–in–services expenditures and ranking as the number–one source of trade–in–services expenditures. Moreover, the contribution by travel has been increasing in recent years. Transportation and other business services ranked as the second and the third largest sources, with expenditures of USD 41.8 billion and USD 19 billion respectively.

The rapid growth in travel expenditures was the main source of the expanded deficit in trade in services. In the first half of 2015, the deficit in trade in services was USD 94.5 billion, an increase of 53 percent year on year. Travel, which accounted for nearly one–half of the trade in services, was the major source of the expanded deficit in trade in services (see Chart 2–8). Increased dispensable income, easier visa application policies, increases in overseas study, and currency depreciations in some countries all resulted in more attractive overseas shopping, travel, and study. In the first half of 2015, outbound visitors totaled USD 61.9 million, up by 14 percent year on year. In the first half of the year, travel expenditures totaled USD 116.9 billion, up by 70 percent, and travel revenue totaled USD 27.7 billion, up by 12 percent. The travel deficit was USD 89.2 billion, twice the deficit in the first half of 2014 and contributing to 94 percent of the deficit in total trade in services.

The deficit was concentrated in particular countries and regions. In the first half of the

Chart 2–8

Contribution of travel to the deficit of trade in services since 2009

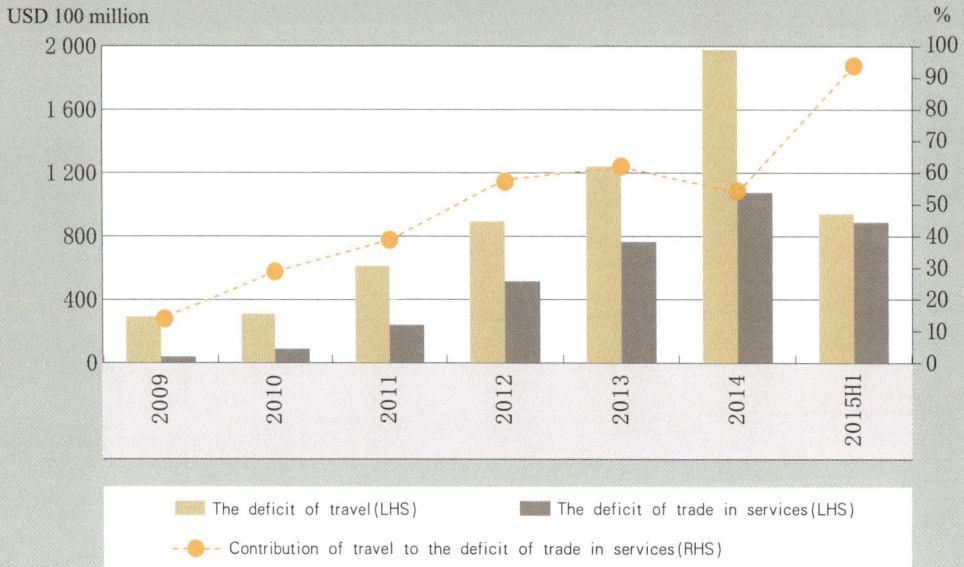

USD 100 million

%

- The deficit of travel (LHS)
- The deficit of trade in services (LHS)
- Contribution of travel to the deficit of trade in services (RHS)

Source: SAFE.

Chart 2–9

Trade in services in terms of trading partners during the first half of 2015

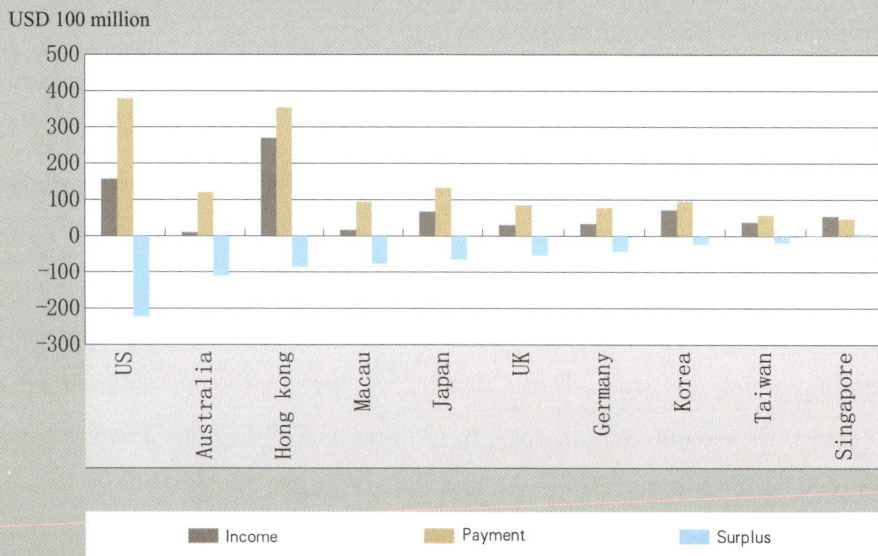

USD 100 million

- Income
- Payment
- Surplus

Source: SAFE.

year, among its ten major trading partners, China posted deficits with nine partners, accounting for 75 percent of its deficit in its total trade in services. In particular, the deficits in trade in services with the United States, Australia, Hong Kong SAR, Macau SAR, Japan, the United Kingdom, Germany, Korea, and Taiwan of China were USD 22.3 billion, USD 11.1 billion, USD 8.6 billion, USD 7.8 billion, USD 6.6 billion, USD 5.5 billion, USD 4.4 billion, USD 2.4 billion, and USD 2 billion respectively (see Chart 2–9). Trade in services had formerly posted a surplus with the Hong Kong SAR. However, when merchandise was moved from trade in services to trade in goods after BPM6, China's trade in services with the Hong Kong SAR posted a deficit of USD 8.6 billion, whereas in the first half year of 2014 it posted a surplus of USD 30.6 billion. In the first half of 2015, China's trade in services with Singapore recorded a small surplus of USD 0.7 billion.

(III) Direct Investments

Direct investments continued to record a net inflow.[1] In the first half of the year, based on the BOP statistics direct investments posted a net inflow of USD 92 billion, down by 1 percent year on year. In 2014, global direct investments decreased by 16 percent. China replaced the United States as the country attracting the most direct investments. In 2015, direct investments continued a significant net inflow, indicating that China was competitive in terms of direct investments. In the first half of 2015, the growth of net inflows of direct investments decreased due to the increased outward investments over the decreased inward direct investments (see Chart 2–10).

The surge in outward direct investments reflected increased investments in overseas markets. In the first half of 2015, the net increase in outward direct investments amounted to USD 52.9 billion, up by 70 percent year on year (see Chart 2–11). In particular, new investment totaled USD 77.4 billion, growth of 41 percent year on year, and investment repatriations totaled USD 24.5 billion, up by 3 percent.

From the perspective of the investments, over 90 percent was a net increase in equity investments (USD 49.5 billion). Both new equity investments and profit reinvestments grew at a rate of over 10 percent, reflecting that domestic enterprises were positive about overseas investments. Moreover, sound performance also led to expanded overseas investments. Outward bond investments recorded a net increase of USD 3.4 billion, whereas in the first half

---

[1] Direct investment net flows = net increase in outward direct investments–the net increase in inward direct investments. When the net increase in outward direct investments exceeds the net increase in inward direct investments, direct investments record a net outflow. When the net increase in inward direct investments exceeds the net increase in outward direct investments, direct investments record a net inflow.

Chart 2-10

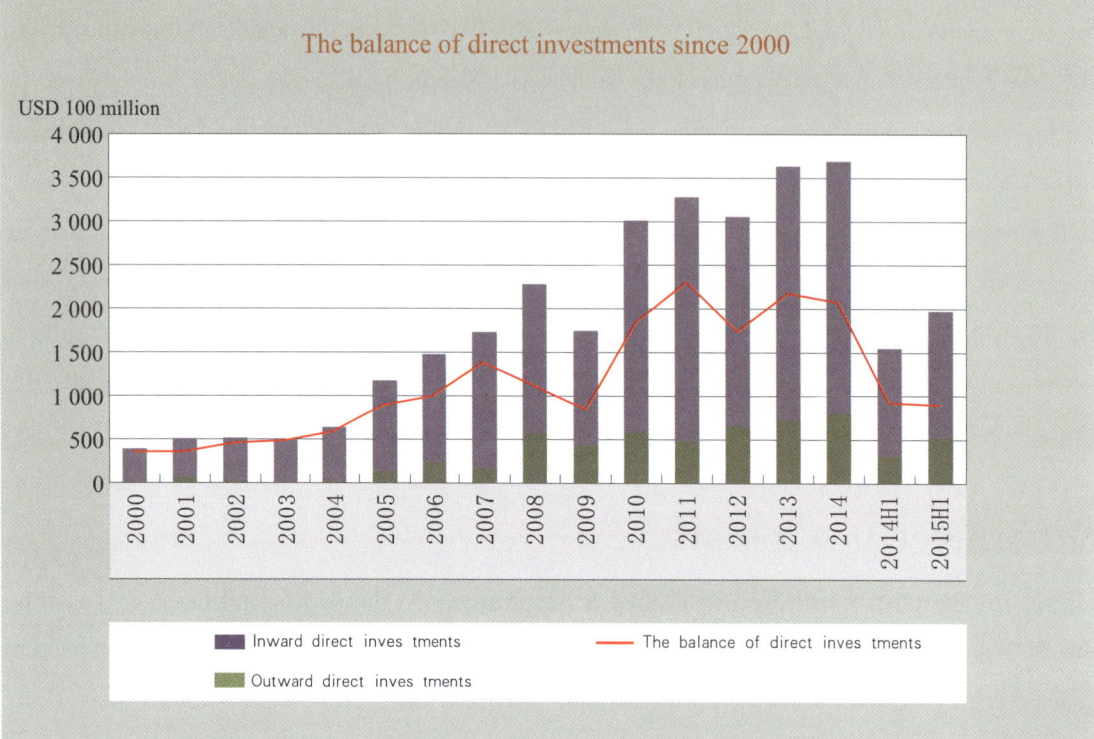

The balance of direct investments since 2000

USD 100 million

Legend:
- Inward direct investments
- Outward direct investments
- The balance of direct investments

Source: SAFE.

Chart 2-11

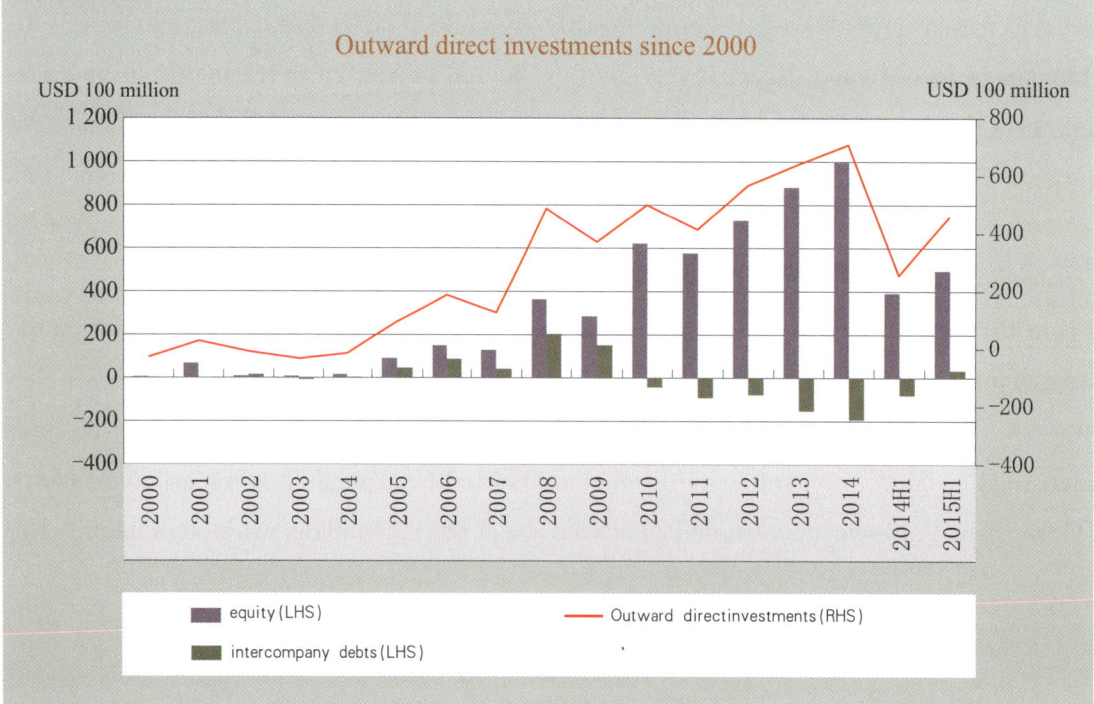

Outward direct investments since 2000

USD 100 million   USD 100 million

Legend:
- equity (LHS)
- intercompany debts (LHS)
- Outward direct investments (RHS)

Source: SAFE.

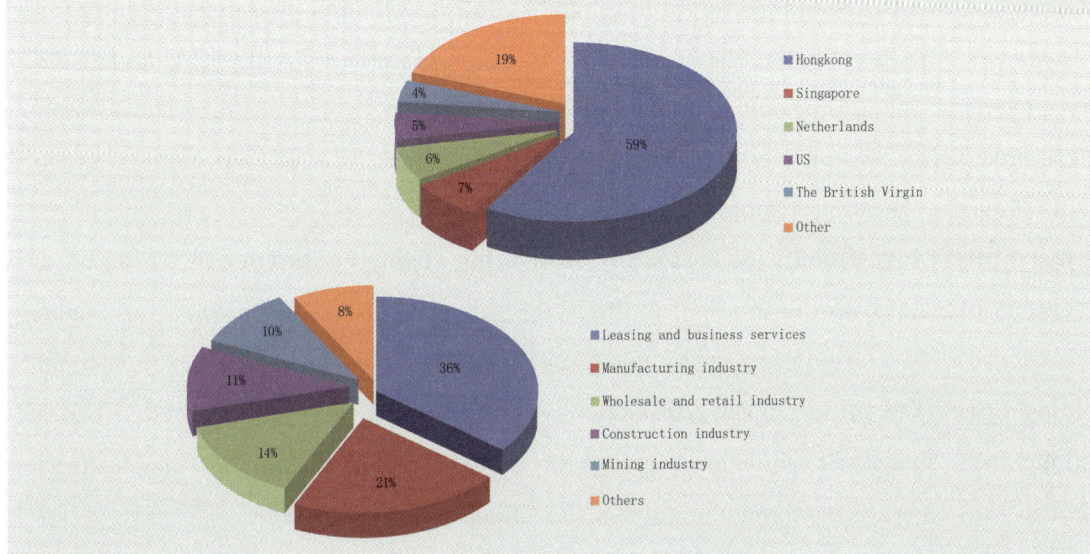

Chart 2-12

The distribution of outward direct investments by the non-financial sector in the first half of 2015
(in terms of industries and destinations)

Source: SAFE.

of 2014 net outward bond investments decreased by USD 8.1 billion. Bond investments are more flexible and are easily affected by short-term factors.

In terms of sectors, net increases in outward investments of the non-financial sector totaled USD 39.9 billion, up by 57 percent. In the first half of 2015, small and medium investments became active and investments of private enterprises grew rapidly. Outward investments were relatively concentrated in terms of industries and destinations (see Chart 2-12). The advanced economies, including the European countries and the United States, were already recovering and became more attractive to foreign investors. The net increase in outward direct investments of the financial sector totaled USD 13.4 billion, a growth of 1.3 times year on year, among which 70 percent was by banking sector. The main source was profit reinvestments and the major destination was the Hong Kong SAR. The financial sector followed their clients as more domestic enterprises pursued the going-out strategy.

In terms of direct-investment relations,[1] a major part of outward direct investments was

---

① According to BPM6, direct-investment relations are divided into three categories, investment by direct investors in direct-investment enterprises, investment by direct-investment enterprises in direct investors (reverse investments), and investments among affiliated enterprises. With regard to direct-investment assets (outward direct investments), they are categorized as investment by domestic direct investors in overseas direct-investment enterprises (ODI enterprises), investments by domestic direct enterprises (FDI enterprises) in overseas direct investors (reverse investments), and investments by domestic enterprises in overseas parent enterprises.

conducted by domestic investors in overseas investment enterprises, recording a net increase of USD 49.2 billion or up by 58 percent and accounting for 93 percent of the net increase in the total outward direct investments. Moreover, investments by foreign–funded enterprises in overseas direct investors (reverse investments) and investments by domestic enterprises in overseas affiliates together recorded a net increase of USD 3.7 billion. Although those investments accounted for only 7 percent of the net increase in outward direct investments, these enterprises were gradually playing a more important role as fund centers as more multinational corporations centralized fund settlements.

Inward direct investments grew steadily, indicating strong confidence in China among overseas investors. In the first half of 2015, the net increase in inward direct investments totaled USD 144.9 billion, up by 17 percent year on year. In particular, new investments totaled USD 200.8 billion, up by 26 percent, and investment repatriations totaled USD 56 billion, up by 56 percent. China has replaced the United States as the number–one destination for direct investments and foreign investments in China continued to grow.

In terms of sectors, the net increase in inward direct investments in the non-financial sector totaled USD 131.5 billion, up by 11 percent year on year and accounting for 90 percent of the total. The transformation of the economic structure, the adjustment of the output, and the industrial upgrading encouraged overseas investors to adjust their strategies. In the first half of the year, manufacturing accounted for 29 percent of the total, down by 4 percentage points year on year. Tertiary industry, such as business services, accounted for a larger part of the FDI. The net increase in FDI by the financial sector totaled USD 13.4 billion, an increase of 1.2 times, among which over 50 percent was invested in the banking sector and insurance. Most of this consisted of profit reinvestments, indicating that domestic institutions were performing well and there were no signs of a large repatriation of investments.

In terms of instruments, 85 percent consisted of equity investments (USD 123.3 billion), up by 11 percent (see Chart 2-13). Against the background of the decelerated economic growth in China, new equity investments and profit reinvestments of FDI rose by 8 percent and 14 percent respectively, reflecting long–term confidence in China by foreign investors. The other 15 percent of the total consisted of bond investments (USD 21.5 billion), up by 68 percent, which was mainly conducted by multinational corporations for flexible fiscal arrangements according to the different situations in both the domestic and overseas markets. Moreover, cross–border investments with RMB grew continuously; 52 percent of the net inflows of FDI was in RMB, and net inflows in USD accounted for only 41 percent of the total.

Chart 2-13

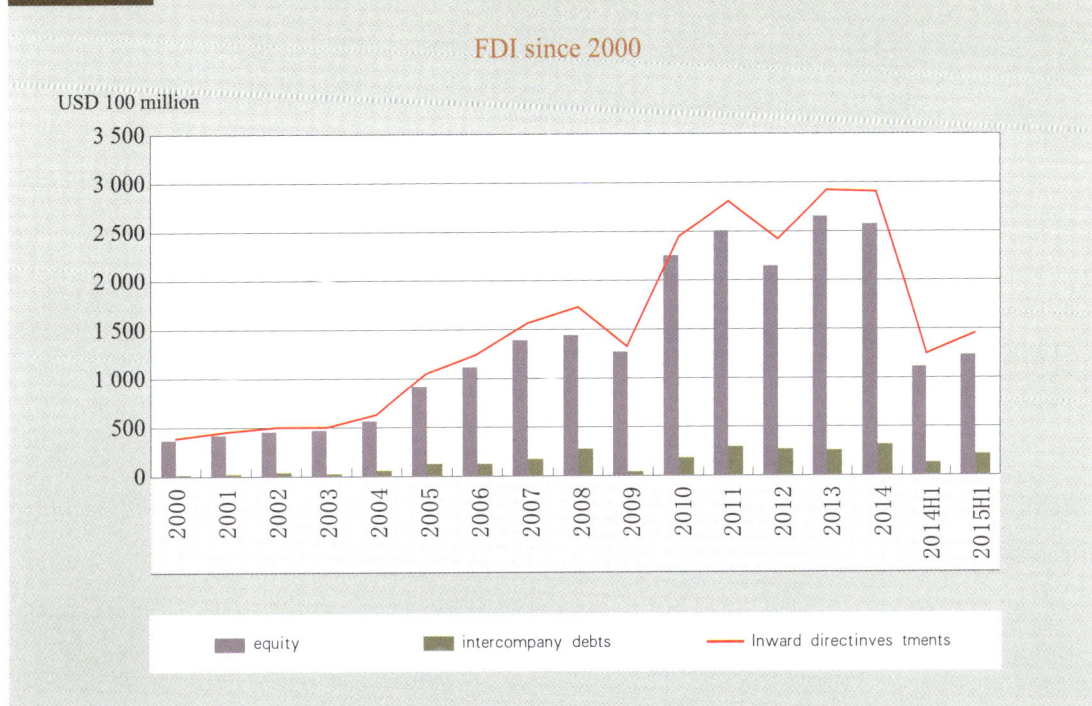

FDI since 2000

USD 100 million

Source: SAFE.

In terms of investment relations,[1] investments in foreign-funded enterprises by foreign investors were the major component of FDI, which recorded a net increase of USD 135.9 billion in the first half of 2015 and a growth rate of 9 percent year on year, accounting for 94 percent of the total. Foreign investors expressed confidence in China over the long term. Domestic direct investments by ODI investors (reverse investments) and investments by overseas affiliates together totaled USD 9 billion, accounting for only 6 percent of the total.

Box 4

Procyclicality of ODI investments

During the past ten years, more Chinese enterprises have invested overseas due to encouragement by the government's going-out strategy. Such overseas investments

---

① For direct-investment liabilities (FDI), investment relations are grouped in three categories: investments in foreign-funded enterprises by foreign investors, investments in domestic investors by ODI investors (reverse investments), and investments in domestic enterprises by overseas affiliates.

consisted mainly of staple goods. Since March 2011, the price of staple goods experienced a downward cycle, which, more or less, influenced the previous investment projects. Outward investments in staple goods decreased due to this procyclicality. Outward–investment enterprises have to focus not only on project analysis but also on cyclicality studies. Investment schemes as well as stress tests under unfavorable situations are important for outward investments, which should be conducted cautiously based on market principles.

Staple goods were the major area of outward investments. During the past ten years, staple goods were the major source of the increased outward investments. According to Dealogic's statistics, from 2000 to 2014 overseas M&As totaled USD 439.9 billion for 213 transactions, among which M&As of staple goods amounted to USD 243.3 billion for 696 transactions and accounted for 55 percent of the total. M&As of staple goods focused on energy and mines. In particular, M&As by CNPC, SINOPEC, and CNOOC totaled USD 120 billion, accounting for nearly 50 percent of the total.

Staple-goods investments are characterized by procyclicality. From 2005 to 2011,

Chart C4–1

Prices of staple goods and overseas M&As since 2005

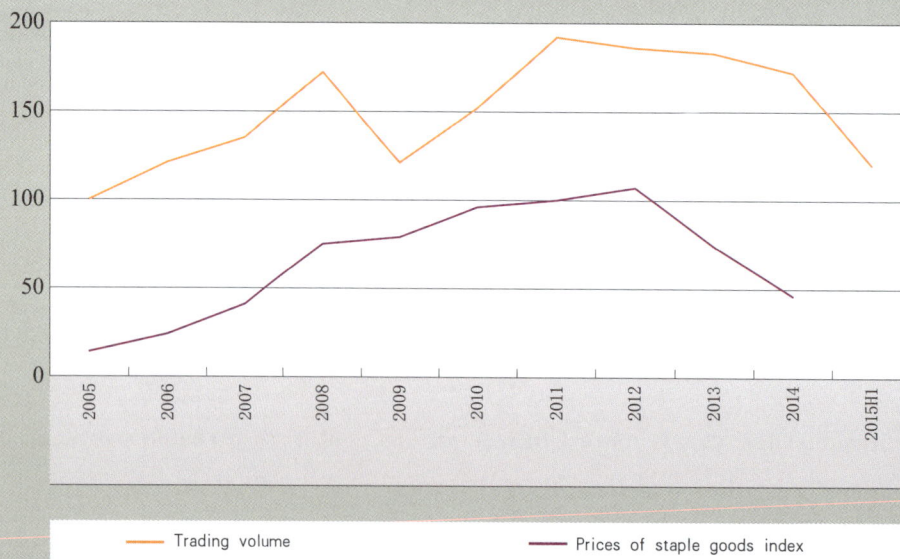

Sources: IMF, Dealogic.

overseas M&As transactions by Chinese enterprises surged significantly with the rising price of staple goods. Since March 2011, the price of staple goods has experienced a global downturn, and the prices of crude oil, iron, and soybeans dropped by over one-half from their previous highs. Overseas M&As by Chinese enterprises slowed down. During the last ten years, M&As of staple goods were positively correlated with their prices (see Chart C4-1).

An unfavorable influence of procyclicality began to emerge. The desire of Chinese enterprises for overseas M&As was strengthened during the process of the rise in prices. But those enterprises suffered big investment losses as the prices declines. In addition, they lost a precious opportunity for low value investments. For instance, in 2012, a state-owned enterprise acquired 8 percent of the equity in Sunshine Oils Sands Ltd., a Canadian company, with HKD 1.2 billion. Sunshine Oil Sands went through a difficult period against the background of the drop in oil prices and was forced to sell its assets at a low price to pay back its liabilities. By the end of June 2015, the market price of the M&A had declined by over 80 percent, with a market-to market loss of HKD 1 billion.

Research on business cycles for overseas investments should be strengthened. First, investors should follow factors such as supply and demand, the international environment, and the geopolitical situation, and should strengthen their study of the business cycle to make counter-cyclical investment decisions. Second, budgets should be carefully designed to ensure reasonable profits over the mid- and long term. Third, risks and difficulties should be adequately considered and related emergency plans should be made in the case of downturn risks.

Overseas investments should adhere to market-oriented principles. As an investor, an enterprise should respect market rules, accept regulation by the market, and assume the related responsibilities. First, property and responsibility for a project, as well as its capital funding, should be clarified. Investments should be made under clear within the framework of property rights and related responsibilities. Those who invest should be those who assume the responsibility, and those who take the risks should reap the related profits. Second, investors should be constrained by their capital and should undertake reasonable financing costs to ensure a sufficient cash flow to cover their capital costs, thus investors should receive economic returns and control risks with respect to their investments and financing. Third, strategic projects should be implemented to maximize market-oriented operations, with positive incentives and restraint mechanisms to prevent moral hazard and to realize national strategic interests.

Overseas investments require cooperation among different agencies. Chinese enterprises engaged in overseas direct investments for staple goods until recent years when they were constrained by insufficient experience and were unfamiliar with local markets. Thus, cooperation with other agencies in terms of flexible tactics, such as stock holding, joint ventures, and funds, should be strengthened. The government should improve coordination of domestic demand and pay attention to the extension and convergence of industrial chains. For example, several mine enterprises may co–invest in a mine project and also coordinate in advance with transportation enterprises and to construct infrastructure. In addition, multilateral development organizations, overseas peer companies, and local enterprises should play their respective comparative advantages.

(IV) Portfolio Investments

Net assets of portfolio investments increased. In the first half of the year, the net assets of portfolio investments increased by USD 24.1 billion, whereas in the first half of 2014 the net

Chart 2–14

Net portfolio investments since 2001

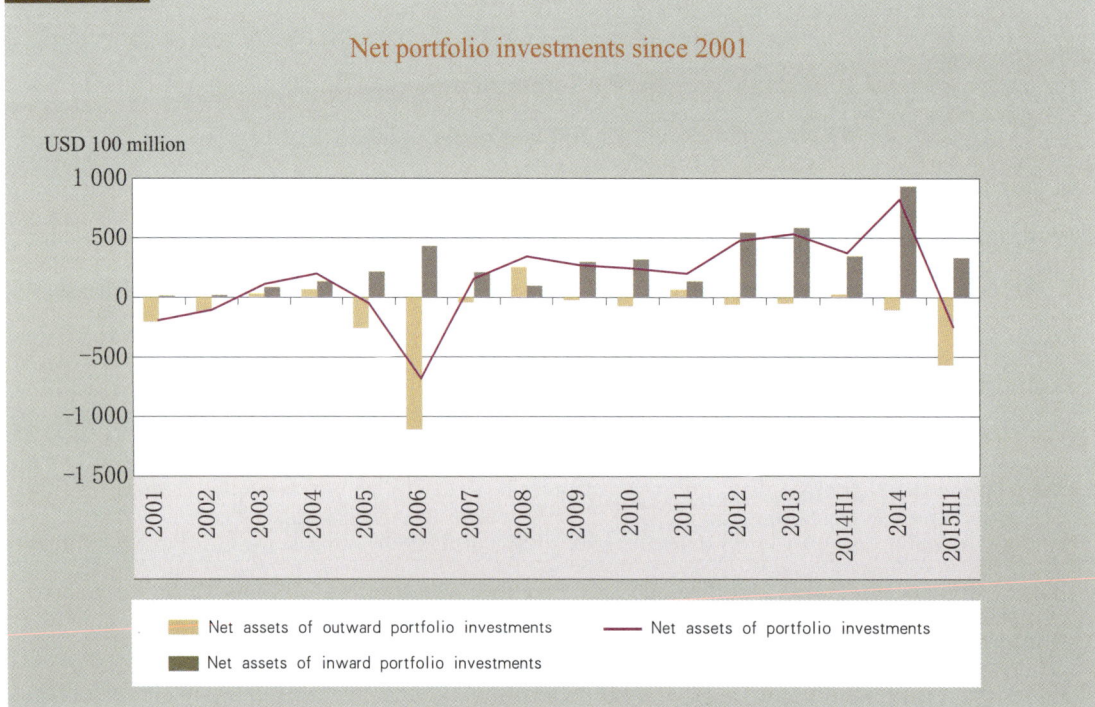

Source: SAFE.

assets decreased by USD 36.9 billion (see Chart 2–14). Driven by the opening of the capital market and the stable international securities market, both outward and inward portfolio investments were active, with frequent and a larger scale of capital flows. In particular, outward portfolio investments rose significantly and were the main source of the increase in net assets.

Outward portfolio investments grew significantly. In the first half of 2015, outward portfolio investments increased by USD 57.2 billion, whereas in the first half of 2014 they decreased by USD 2.5 billion. In particular, equity investments and bond investments increased by USD 32.6 billion and USD 24.7 billion respectively. The further opening of the capital market and the evolution of the international market environment were the main reasons encouraging outward portfolio investments. On the one hand, the Shanghai – Hong Kong Connect provided a more convenient channel for RMB cross–border portfolio investments. In the first half of the year, outward portfolio investments via the Shanghai – Hong Kong Connect increased by USD 10.7 billion, accounting for 33 percent of the total increase in equity investments. On the other hand, the stock and bond markets in the United States and the major European countries recorded good performance during the first half of the year due to the US economic recovery and the strengthened expectations of a rise in interest rates by the FED. Domestic entities showed a growing interest in outward investments. Financial institutions, including banks, increased outward investments via QDIIs or other channels by USD 20.7 billion in terms of equities and by USD 24.1 billion in terms of bonds.

Inward portfolio investments continued to increase. In the first half of the year, inward portfolio investments increased by USD 33.1 billion, down by 4 percent year on year, among which equity investments and bond investments increased by USD 21.2 billion and USD 12 billion respectively. Among the equity investments, with the steady improvement of the competitiveness of our companies in the overseas IPO market, an increasing number of domestic enterprises were listed overseas. In the first half of the year, domestic institutions raised funds in the amount of USD 23.5 billion. Financial corporations, such as GF Securities, Haitong Securities and other large financial companies, were among the major issuers. Moreover, China accelerated its opening up by introducing the Shanghai – Hong Kong Connect. In the first half of the year, inward investments via the Shanghai – Hong Kong Connect increased by USD 8.6 billion. In the first half of the year, the domestic stock market experienced a remarkable boom. The rising index of futures pushed up stock valuations and some foreign investors chose to cash–out their investment earnings. In the first half of the year, equity investments of QFIIs and RQFIIs decreased by USD 8.8 billion. In particular, they decreased by USD 4.7 billion in April, increased by USD 1.3 billion in May, and decreased by USD 4.2 billion in June. In the second half of June, they recorded an increase of USD 1.1 billion. Among the bond investments, bond investment liabilities in the banking sector increased. In the first half of the year, bond investments issued by the domestic banking sector in foreign banks and the monetary authorities increased by USD 6.1 billion, bond investments issued by the domestic banking sector by QFIIs and RQFIIs decreased by USD 0.6 billion, and related drafts accepted by domestic banks increased by USD 5.7 billion.

(V) Other Investments

Net assets of other investments increased. Capital flows under other investments are an important factor impacting China's balance of payments. In the first half of the year, net assets of other investments increased by USD 193.1 billion, 2.7 times the growth in the first half of 2014 and 3.3 times the increased net assets in the capital and financial account. In the first half of 2015, all items under other investments recorded an increase in net assets, reflecting changing expectations among domestic entities about the exchange rate, the interest

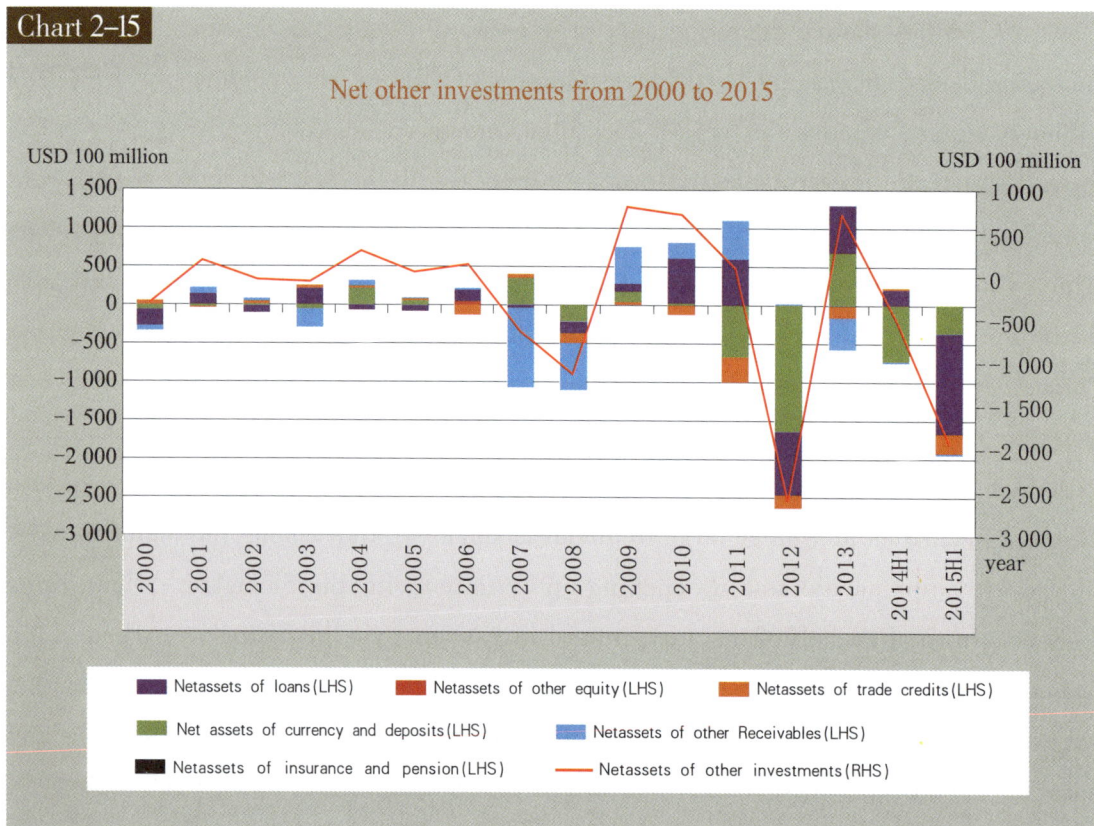

Chart 2-15

Net other investments from 2000 to 2015

Legend:
- Netassets of loans (LHS)
- Netassets of other equity (LHS)
- Netassets of trade credits (LHS)
- Net assets of currency and deposits (LHS)
- Netassets of other Receivables (LHS)
- Netassets of insurance and pension (LHS)
- Netassets of other investments (RHS)

Source: SAFE.

rate, and market risks. In particular, net assets of loans increased by USD 129.9 billion and accounted for 67 percent of the growth of total net assets of other investments, whereas in the first half year of 2014 they recorded a decrease of USD 20.3 billion. Net assets of trade credits and currency and deposits increased by USD 22.6 billion and USD 32.7 billion respectively (see Chart 2–15).

Capital outflows of other investments continued to grow. In the first half of 2015, net capital outflows under other investments increased by USD 63.2 billion, which was 61 percent less than the growth in the first half of 2014. The decrease indicated that the banking sector was expanding in overseas markets at a decelerated growth rate. The increase in overseas currency and deposits amounted to USD 15.2 billion, which represented an annual decrease of 87 percent. The increase in external loans totaled USD 54.1 billion, down by 4 percent year on year. In addition, trade–credit assets decreased by USD 13 billion, which meant a decline in receivables and advance payments. Trade–credit assets decreased USD 2.5 billion more than in the first half of 2014.

External liabilities of other investments dropped substantially. In the first half of the year, the net outflow of inward other investments (decreases in external liabilities) amounted to USD 129.9 billion, while in the first half of 2014 there was a net inflow of USD 112.4 billion. Loans from abroad recorded a decrease of USD 75.9 billion, as opposed to an increase of USD 76.9 billion in the first half of 2014, because banks intensified their risk control over trade financing due to the exposed L/C risks, and the liabilities of L/Cs decreased by USD 74 billion. Trade–credit liabilities decreased by USD 35.7 billion (advance payables and revenue), USD 27.4 billion more than the decrease in the first half of 2014. Currency and deposits decreased by USD 17.5 billion, in comparison to an increase of USD 42.6 billion in the first half of 2014. The decreased RMB liabilities were the main source of the decreased currency and deposits.

> **Box 5**
>
> ### China dissemination of its external debt data according to the SDDS
>
> The IMF introduced its Special Data Dissemination Standard (SDDS) in 1996 to improve the transparency of member countries' macroeconomic statistical data and to facilitate the use of the data, especially among financial market participants, so as to analyze the economic situation with sufficient information. The SDDS countries should follow the

requirements of the SDDS by disseminating five categories of data concerning the economy, the fiscal situation, finance, the external sector, and the society and the population. External debt data are included in the category of the external sector. Thus far, the IMF has established two sets of data–dissemination standards, The General Data Dissemination System (GDDS) and the Special Data Dissemination Standard (SDDS). The two standards are generally consistent, but the SDDS requires higher standards as compared to the GDDS with respect to the data coverage, and the dissemination frequency, timeliness, quality, and accessibility by the public.

Since 2015, China has improved its external debt statistics according to the SDDS instead of the GDDS, and has disseminated its external debt data on a quarterly basis so that the public may have a comprehensive understanding of China's external debt situation. There have been three major adjustments. The first adjustment concerns the types of debtors. Before the adjustment, the debtor types were the central government, Chinese–funded financial institutions, foreign–funded institutions, Chinese–funded enterprises, foreign–funded enterprises, and others. According to the SDDS, debtors are now categorized as the general government, the central bank, other deposit–taking companies, other sectors, and direct investments, i.e., inter–company loans. The second adjustment affects the debt instrument. China used to attribute the external debt to loans from foreign governments, loans from international financial organizations, and international commercial loans. According to the SDDS, the debt instrument include loans, debt securities, currency and deposits, trade credits and advances, other debt liabilities, SDR allocations, and direct investments, i.e., inter–company loans. The third adjustment includes the RMB external debt as part of the total. This only affects the statistical method and coverage, and will not result in the payment of any increased liabilities. After these adjustments, China's external debt statistics are now consistent with international standards. This has helped improve statistical standards and international comparability. In addition, the adjustments have established a solid foundation for the external debt as well as for the management of cross–border capital flows under a macro prudential framework.

Based on the newly released data, China recorded a high level of external debt denominated in RMB, which was driven by the internationalization of the RMB and China's rising international role. Since China launched RMB cross–border transactions in 2009, RMB cross–border settlements have maintained rapid growth, totaling nearly

CNY 10 trillion in 2014, as opposed to CNY 3.6 billion in 2009. The ratio of cross–border receipts and payments in RMB to the total increased from 1.7 percent in 2010 to 23.6 percent in 2014. The international use of RMB witnessed a regional expansion as well, which stimulated global financial markets and improved the global importance of the RMB. The result has been an increase in the RMB external debt. Although both the RMB external debt and the external debt denominated in foreign currencies are both external debt, external debt in foreign currencies is easily impacted by exchange–rate fluctuations and may intensify the repayment burdens of debtors during periods of crisis. With respect to the external debt in RMB, there is no risk of a currency mismatch with the exchange rate. In the future, with a more open economy and further implementation of the one belt, one road strategy, the RMB external debt held by nonresidents and trade financing will continue to grow. This growth is indicative of the confidence in Chinese economic development as well as acknowledgment of China's reform and opening achievements. In addition, it indicates the growing international importance of the RMB, which is playing a more important role in international capital flows.

III. International Investment Position

External assets were increasingly held by residents. By the end of June 2015, China's external assets[①] totaled USD 6 433.7 billion, a growth of 0.4 percent compared to the end of 2014. In particular, foreign–reserve assets totaled USD 3 771.3 billion, a decrease of 3 percent compared to the end of 2014. Foreign–reserve assets were still the most important portion of external assets and accounted for 59 percent of the total, a drop by 2 percentage points from the ratio at the end of 2014 and reaching the lowest level since 2004 when China released its IIP data for the first time. The main sources of the decrease were net transactions and non–transactional factors, such as exchange rates and prices, which posted a decrease of USD 66.6 billion and USD 82.6 billion respectively. Outstanding direct investments amounted to USD 1 012.9 billion and accounted for 16 percent of total external assets, recording a historical high and increasing by 4 percentage points compared to the ratio in 2014. Direct investments benefited from a better overseas direct–investment policy and implementation of the going–out strategy.

External liabilities grew rapidly. By the end of June 2015, outstanding external liabilities

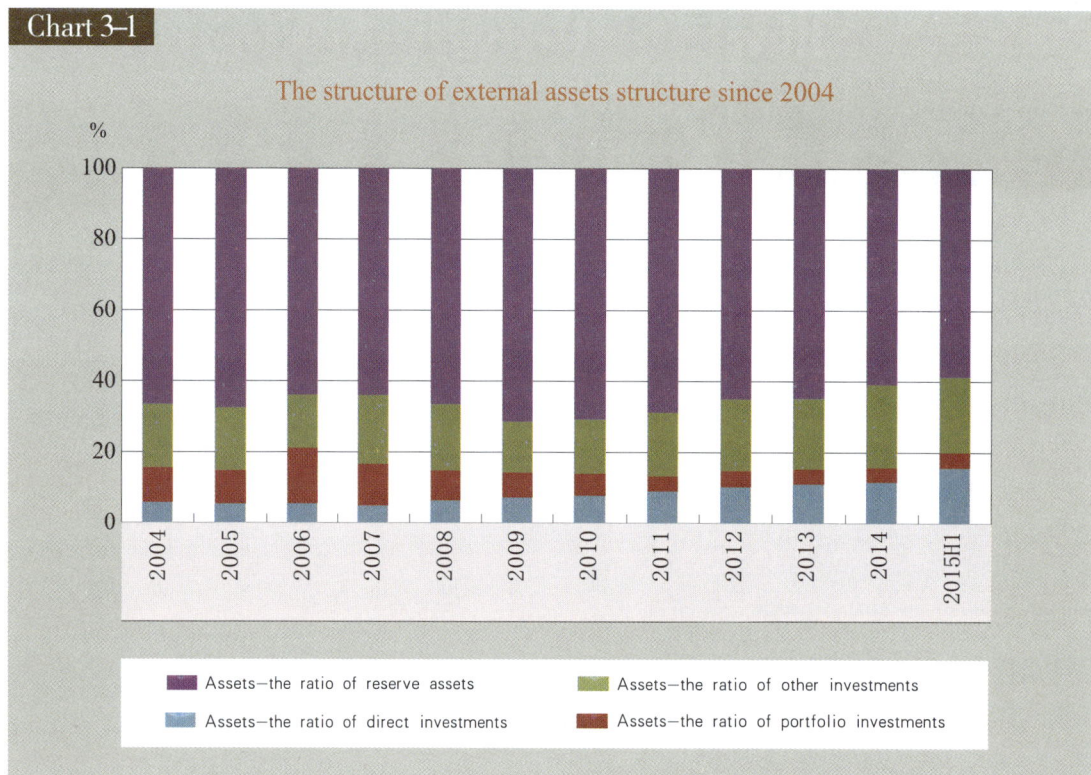

Chart 3–1

The structure of external assets structure since 2004

Legend:
- Assets—the ratio of reserve assets
- Assets—the ratio of direct investments
- Assets—the ratio of other investments
- Assets—the ratio of portfolio investments

Source: SAFE.

---

① External assets and liabilities include direct investments, portfolio investments and deposits, and loans. Outward direct investments are categorized as external financial assets because the shares held by domestic investors in overseas enterprises have the same nature as equity investments of portfolio investments, with the exception that their influence on the operations of the target enterprises may be different, and vice versa, for inward direct investments.

amounted to USD 4 969.7 billion, up by 7 percent compared with the outstanding external liabilities at the end of 2014. Equity liabilities of portfolio investments are now calculated by the market value. By excluding the above adjustment, external liabilities increased by 5 percent compared to the end of 2014. In particular, portfolio investment liabilities totaled USD 899.7 billion, an increase of 42 percent excluding the statistical adjustment, and the increase was driven by multiple factors such as the improved opening up of the domestic securities market. Portfolio investment liabilities accounted for 18 percent of the total outstanding liabilities, which was 5 percentage points higher than the ratio at the end of 2014 after excluding the statistical adjustment. Outstanding inward direct investments[①] totaled USD 2 827.4 billion, growing by 6 percent and continuing to constitute the largest part of the external liabilities, accounting for 57 percent of the total. This indicated that foreign investors were positive China's economic development over the long term. Other investment liabilities, including deposits and loans, dropped by 14 percent to USD 1 231.8 billion, accounting for 25

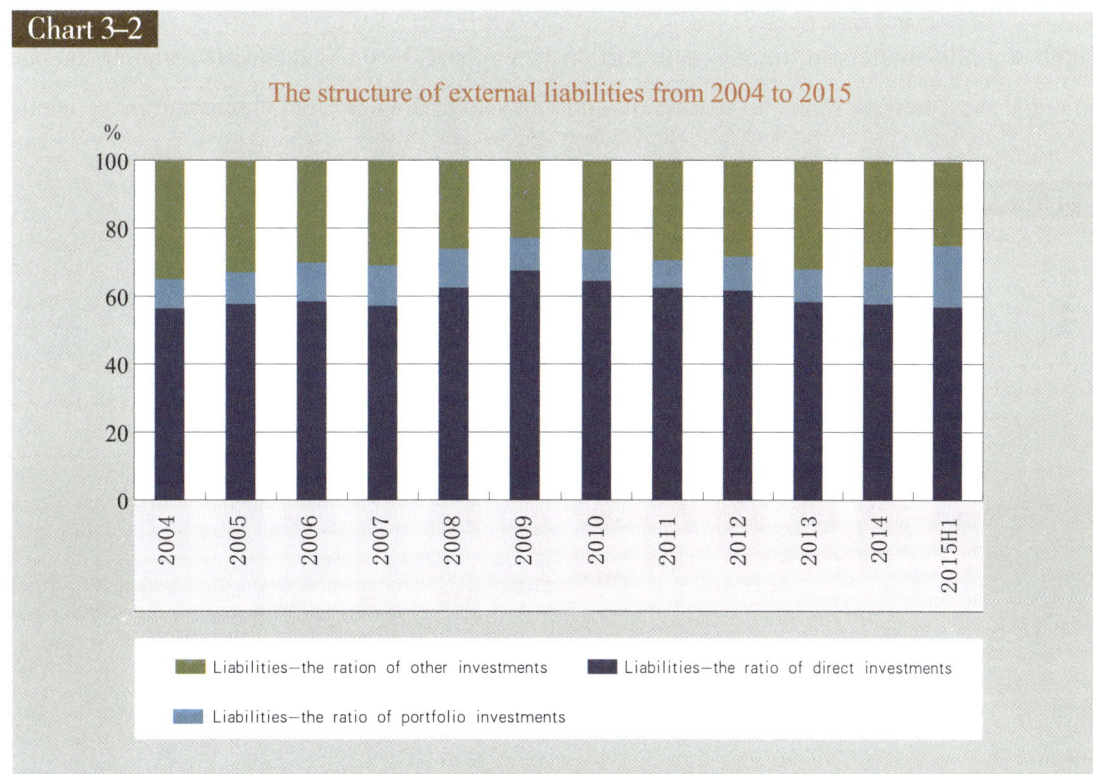

Chart 3–2

The structure of external liabilities from 2004 to 2015

Source: SAFE.

① The inward direct-investment position includes the non-financial sector's and the financial sector's inward direct-investment positions and the loan and debt positions extended by foreign direct investors, foreign affiliates, and foreign-related companies. It also reflects the valuation effects. The inward direct-investment position in the IIP is different from the cumulative MOFCOM FDI statistics by the MOFCOM, which are equal to the sum of the past FDI equity inflows.

percent of the total (see Chart 3–2). This was due to fluctuations in the exchange rate and the interest rate in both the domestic and international markets, which led domestic enterprises to adjust their balance sheets and to deleverage their external liabilities.

Net external assets decreased. By the end of June 2015, China's net external assets totaled USD 1 464 billion, a decrease of USD 312.4 billion compared to the net assets at the end of 2014 (see Chart 3–3). China's net external assets were mainly held by the public sector (including the central bank and the government), and net external liabilities were held by the private sector, banks, and corporations. External assets and liabilities were mismatched with respect to the holding entities. By the end of June 2015, when excluding the foreign–reserve assets (USD 3 771.3 billion), China posted net liabilities of USD 2 307.3 billion.

External investment income recorded a small deficit. In the first half of the year, investment income posted a deficit of USD 25.8 billion in the balance of payments. In particular, outward investment income and expenditures totaled USD 112.7 billion and USD 138.5 billion respectively, and the annualized yield difference was −1.1 percentage points, which was the smallest difference since 2005 (see Chart 3–4). Negative investment income reflected the relatively high cost of foreign funds instead of the low yield of outward investments

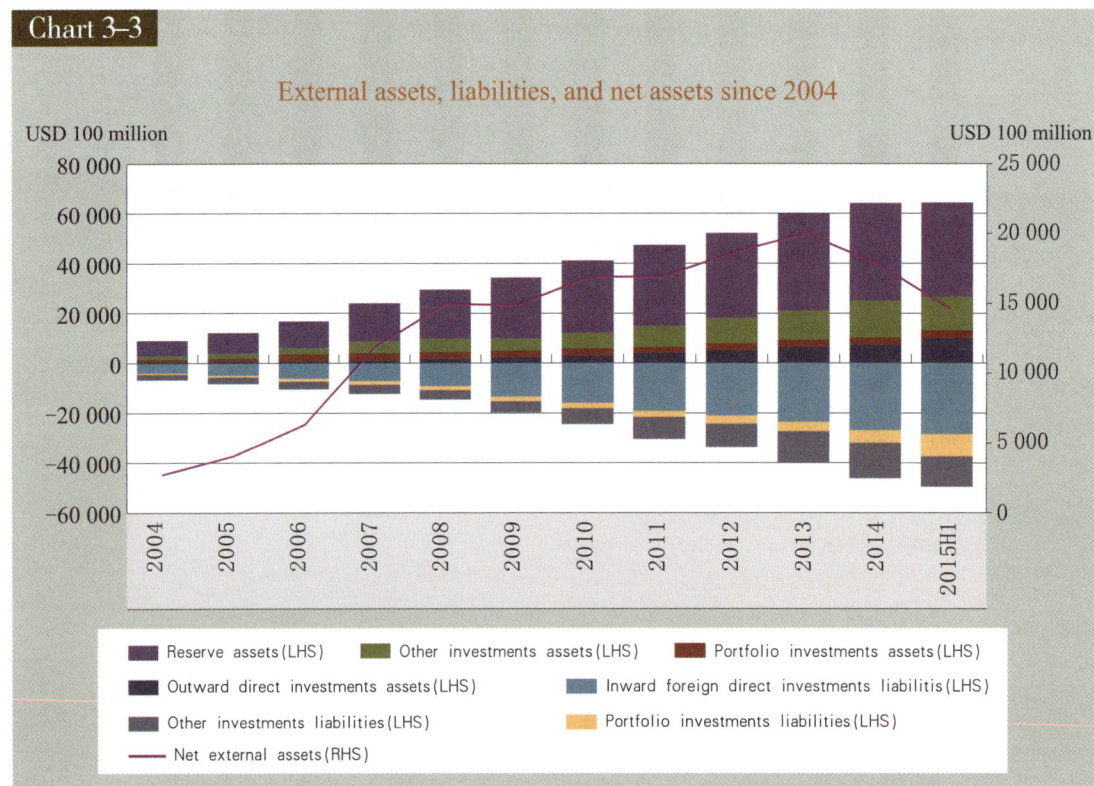

Chart 3–3

External assets, liabilities, and net assets since 2004

Source: SAFE.

Chart 3–4

The yields of external assets and liabilities since 2005

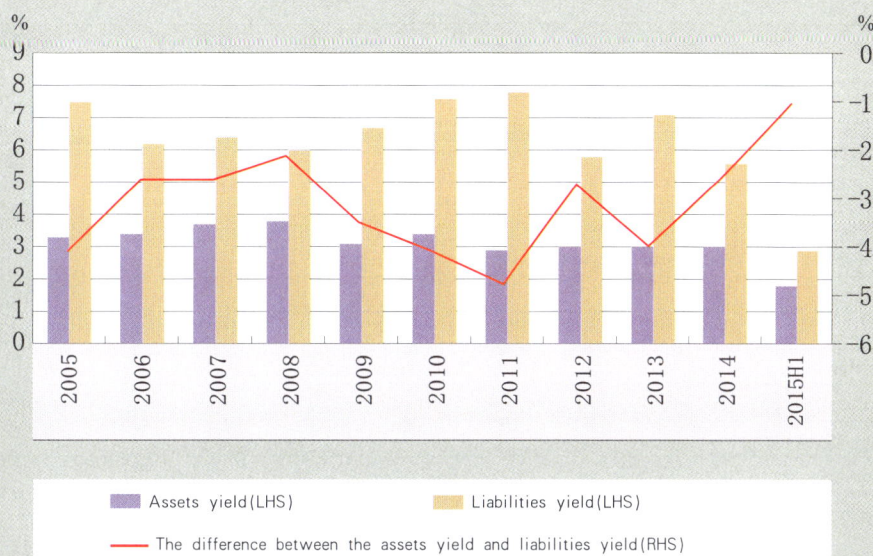

Assets yield(LHS) ▪ Liabilities yield(LHS)
—— The difference between the assets yield and liabilities yield(RHS)

Notes: 1. Assets (liabilities) yield rate = investment income (payments)/[asset (liability) position by the end of this year + the asset (liability) position by the end of the last year]/2.

　　　2. The spread = the asset yield rate + the liabilities yield rate.

Source: SAFE.

and was related to the external asset and liability structure. During the first half of 2015, 60 percent of external assets were reserve assets with low risk and high liquidity, whose relatively low yields contributed to the low yield of total assets; 57 percent of the external liabilities were direct investments, which were long–term investments with low liquidity and relatively high risks, and they contributed to a higher inward investment yield. Thus, the total yield after netting was negative (see the detailed analysis in the *Balance of Payments Report 2012*, Box 1). However, the investment yield only represents the financial cost of assets and liabilities. The more important contribution of FDI is to introduce advanced technology and management experience, to create job opportunities and taxes, and to develop the international market, whose social and economic income exceeds the financial costs. Moreover, a large portion of the investment income was reinvested and there were no real capital outflows. By excluding this part, China recorded a net investment income. In the first half of the year, the difference between the outward investment yield and the inward investment yield recorded a historical low level, indicating that China's outward investment yield had improved by improving its external asset allocations in recent years.

Table 3-1 The IIP at the end of June 2015 [1]

Unit: USD 100 million

Item	Line No.	2015.06
Net International Investment Position	1	14 640
Assets	2	64 337
1 Direct investment	3	10 129
1.1 Equity and investment fund shares	4	8 309
1.2 Debt instruments	5	1 820
2 Portfolio investment	6	2 760
2.1 Equity and investment fund shares	7	1 777
2.2 Debt securities	8	983
3 Financial derivatives (other than reserves) and employee stock options	9	39
4 Other investment	10	13 695
4.1 Other equity	11	1
4.2 Currency and deposits	12	3 125
4.3 Loans	13	4 658
4.4 Insurance, pension, and standardized guarantee schemes	14	200
4.5 Trade credit and advances	15	4 547
4.6 Other accounts receivable	16	1 165
5 Reserve assets	17	37 713
5.1 Monetary gold	18	624
5.2 Special drawing rights	19	105
5.3 Reserve position in the IMF	20	46
5.4 Foreign currency reserves	21	36 938
5.5 Other reserve assets	22	0
Liabilities	23	49 697
1 Direct investment	24	28 274
1.1 Equity and investment fund shares	25	26 027
1.2 Debt instruments	26	2 247
2 Portfolio investment	27	8 997
2.1 Equity and investment fund shares	28	6 727
2.2 Debt securities	29	2 270
3 Financial derivatives (other than reserves) and employee stock options	30	108
4 Other investment	31	12 318
4.1 Other equity	32	-
4.2 Currency and deposits	33	4 611
4.3 Loans	34	4 341
4.4 Insurance, pension, and standardized guarantee schemes	35	85
4.5 Trade credit and advances	36	2 987
4.6 Other accounts payable	37	195
4.7 Special drawing rights	38	98

---

[1] Since 2015, the SAFE has compiled and disseminated China's BOP and IIP according to BPM6. According to the new standards, the market price is employed to compile all the IIP data instead of the former accumulation of historical flows for particular items. Because the historical data are not available for some newly introduced statistical items, the historical IIP adjusted with the market price cannot be traced, and the IIP data before and after 2014 are incompatible.

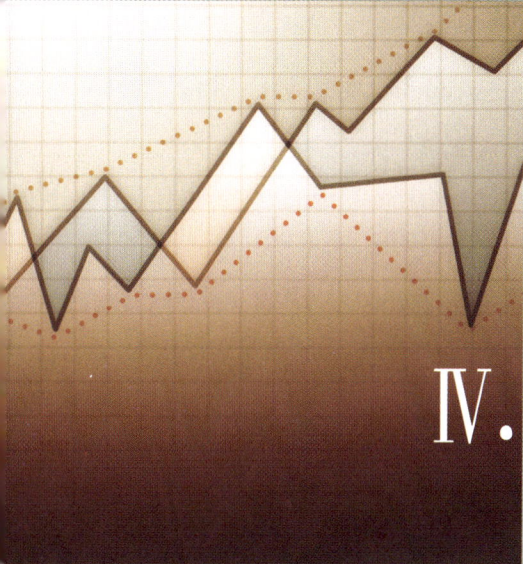

IV. Operation of the Foreign-exchange Market and the RMB Exchange Rate

(I) Trends in the RMB Exchange Rate

The RMB exchange rate against the USD was basically stable. At the end of July 2013, the mid–price of the RMB exchange rate against the USD was 6.113 6, a slight appreciation of 0.1 percent from the end of 2014 (see Chart 4–1). The RMB spot exchange rates against the USD in the inter–bank foreign–exchange market (CNY) and in the offshore market (CNH) appreciated by 0.05 percent and 0.2 percent respectively. Globally, the RMB was a stable currency (see Chart 4–2).

The RMB exchange rate appreciated against the basket of currencies. According to the BIS, the nominal effective exchange rate of the RMB appreciated by 3.6 percent in the first half of 2015. Deducting for inflation, the real effective exchange rate of the RMB appreciated by 3 percent (see Chart 4–3). Among the 61 currencies observed by the BIS, the RMB ranked 10th in terms of the extent of the appreciation in its nominal effective exchange rate and ranked 11th in terms of the extent of the appreciation in its real effective exchange rate. In terms of the extent of the appreciation, the RMB had a high ranking among the major global currencies (see Chart 4–4). Since the regime reform in 2005, the nominal and real effective exchange rates of the RMB appreciated by 45.6 percent and 55.7 percent respectively. The extent of their appreciations ranked first and second respectively among the 61 currencies observed by the

Chart 4–1

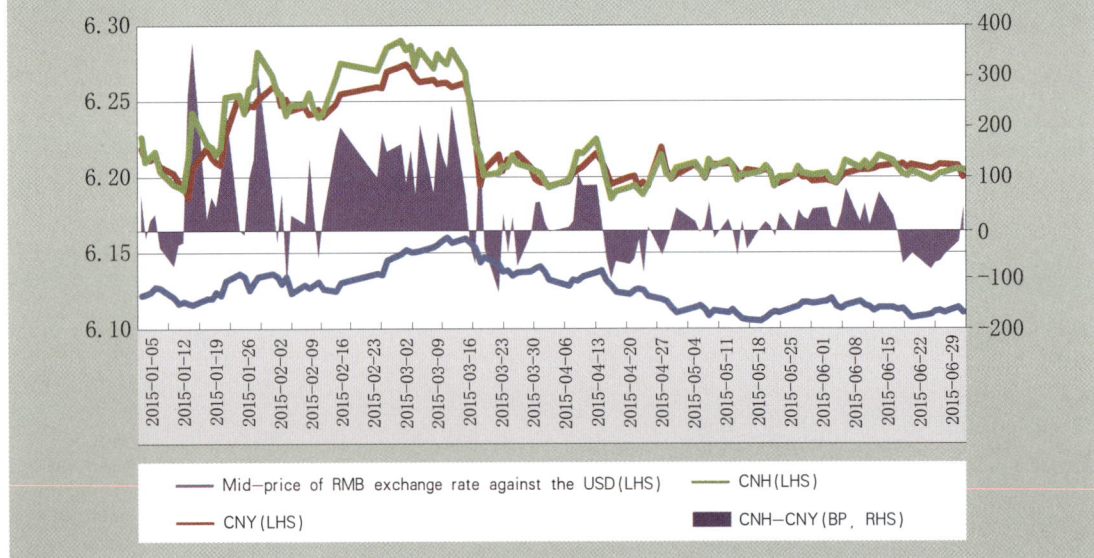

Trends in the spot RMB exchange rate against the USD in the domestic and offshore markets, first half of 2015

Sources: CFETS, Reuters.

Operation of the Foreign-exchange Market and the RMB Exchange Rate | China's Balance of Payments Report
First Half of 2015

113

Chart 4-2

Changes in the exchange rates of the major developed economies and the emerging markets against the USD, first half of 2015

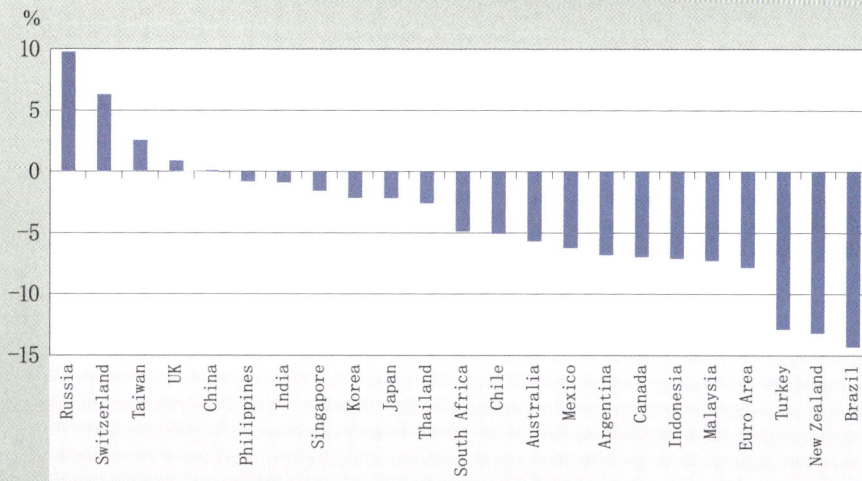

Sources: CFETS, Bloomberg.

Chart 4-3

Trends in the RMB effective exchange rate, January 1994 to June 2015

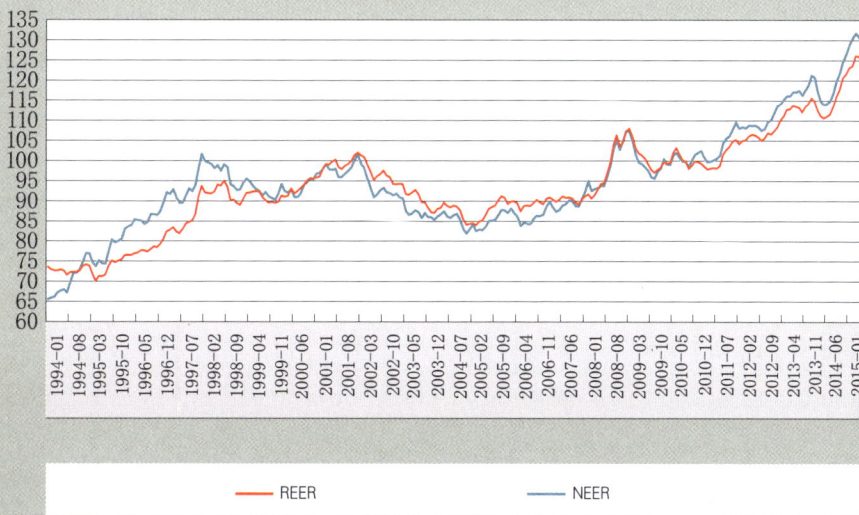

REER   NEER

Sources: BIS.

Chart 4–4

Changes in the effective exchange rates of the major developed economies and the emerging markets, first half of 2015

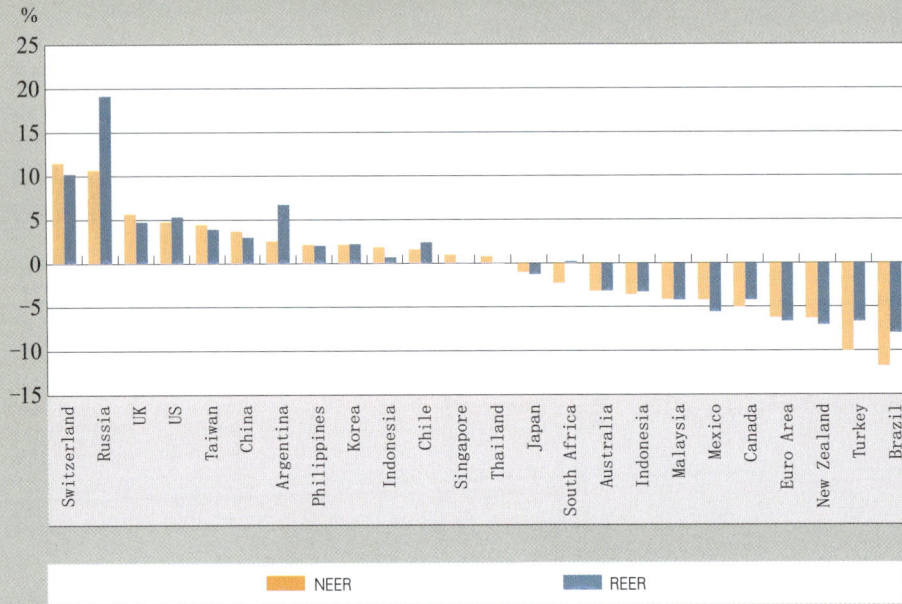

Sources: BIS.

Chart 4–5

Spread of the spot RMB exchange rates against the USD in the domestic and offshore markets, first half of 2015

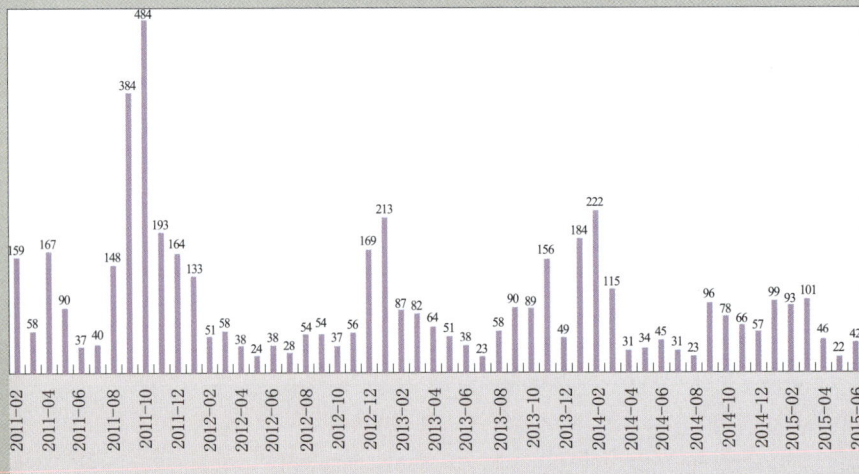

Note: The absoute value of the average daily spread.
Sources: CFETS, Reuters.

Operation of the Foreign-exchange Market and the RMB Exchange Rate | China's Balance of Payments Report
First Half of 2015

115

BIS.

A smaller spread of the RMB exchange rates in the domestic and offshore markets. The CNH showed an obvious depreciation and a wide spread against the CNY at the beginning of 2005. Thereafter, it fluctuated in two directions and the spread declined (see Chart 4–5). The daily average spread was 66 bps, smaller than the 79 bps in 2014. In the first quarter of 2015, due to downward pressures on the economy and a series of risks in the global foreign–exchange market, expectations of an RMB depreciation grew stronger. The daily average spread of the CNH and the CNY was 98 bps. In the second quarter, as the domestic economy steadily stabilized and the appreciation of the USD slowed down, expectations of an RMB depreciation weakened. The spread declined to 37 bps. In May, the daily average spread was at a historical low level of 22 bps.

The foreign-exchange forward market showed large volatility. In the first half of 2015, the USD premiums in the domestic and offshore foreign exchange forwards market changed from increasing at the beginning of the year to declining thereafter, exhibiting large volatility (see Charts 4–6). The situation was mainly an outcome of the market pricing impacted by expectation factors, supply and demand, and the interest rate spreads. In the first quarter, due to expectations of shorting the RMB and the deleveraging process of debts denominated in foreign currencies, enterprises carried out a large number of net purchases of forwards and pushed up the USD premium. In the second quarter, as expectations about the RMB exchange rate stabilized, the number of net purchases of forwards by enterprises declined and foreign–currency deposits that had accumulated in the previous period also declined. Meanwhile, as a result of the reduction in the RMB interest rate and the deposit reserve rate, the interest rate spread declined (see Chart 4–7) and the USD premium also gradually declined. At the end of June 2015, the one–year USD premiums of the domestic delivered forward rate, the offshore delivered forward rate, and the offshore delivered forward rate without principals were 1 395 bps, 1 420 bps, and 1 314 bps respectively, down by 190 percent, 130 percent, and 981 percent from the beginning of 2015.

The volatility of the RMB exchange rate remained at a low level. In the first half of 2015, the spot RMB exchange rate against the USD fluctuated to a small extent at the mid–price of the depreciation band, with the largest daily average fluctuation standing at 1.54 percent. At the beginning of 2015, the RMB exchange rate moved within 1.5 percent of the mid–price. From the end of January, the RMB exchange rate started to move toward the upper limit of the floating band of the mid–price and this trend continued until the end of March. Thereafter, it

Chart 4–6

The premium and discount of the 1-year RMB forward rate against the USD in the domestic and offshore markets since 2013

— In the offshore DF markets — In the domestic markets — In the offshore NDF markets

Sources: CFETS, Reuters.

Chart 4–7

The 6-month interest-rate spread of the domestic RMB and the USD since 2013

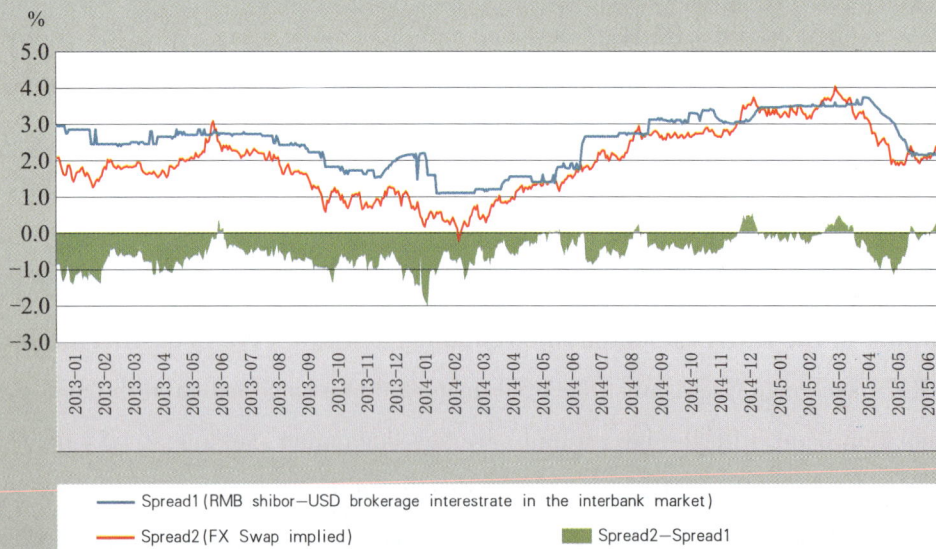

— Spread1 (RMB shibor—USD brokerage interestrate in the interbank market)
— Spread2 (FX Swap implied)   ▮ Spread2—Spread1

Sources: CFETS, Reuters.

Operation of the Foreign-exchange Market and the RMB Exchange Rate | China's Balance of Payments Report
First Half of 2015

117

gradually moved away from the upper limit, and in the second quarter it returned within about 1.5 percent around the mid–price (see Chart 4–8). From the perspective of the volatility trend in the options market, the implied volatilities in the domestic and offshore options markets went up at the beginning of 2015 and thereafter fell. At the beginning of February, the 6–month volatilities in the domestic and offshore markets reached 3.89 percent and 5.63 percent respectively, which were both at historic high levels since 2012. At the end of June, the 6–month volatilities in the domestic and offshore markets stood at 1.88 percent and 2.51 percent, down by 32.4 percent and 27.7 percent from the beginning of 2015 respectively (see Chart 4–9). At the end of June, the 6–month implied volatility of options in the 24 currencies in the major developed countries and the emerging markets stood at 11.12 percent. The elasticity of the RMB exchange rate remained low.

(II) Transactions in the Foreign–exchange Market

In the first half of 2015, the cumulative trading volume of the RMB/foreign–currency market totaled USD 7.35 trillion, an increase of 21.6 percent from the first half of 2014, with a daily average trading

Chart 4–8

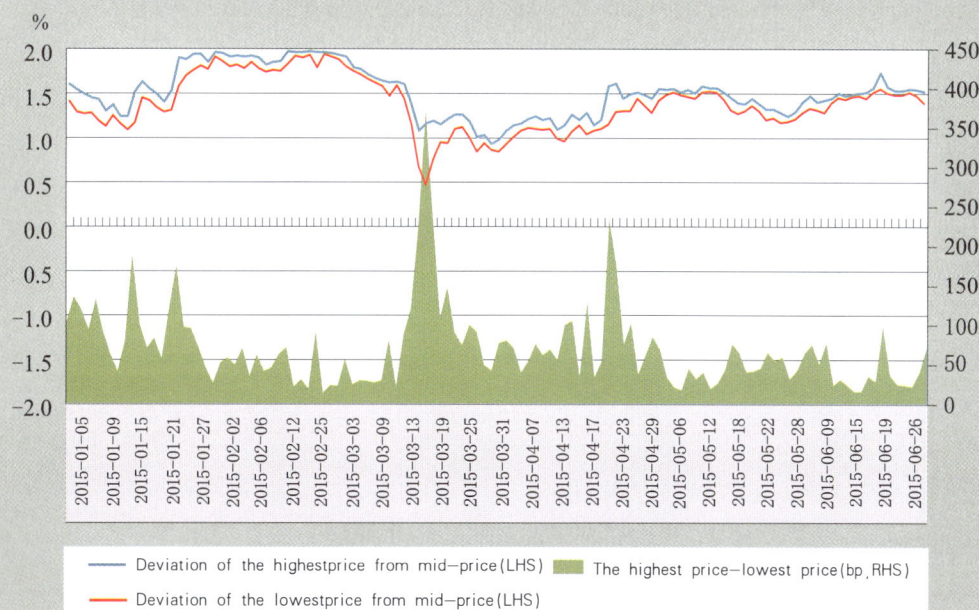

The volatility of the spot RMB exchange rate against the USD in the inter-bank foreign-exchange market, first half of 2015

Sources: CFETS.

Chart 4–9

The 6-month implied volatility of the RMB exchange rate against the USD since 2012

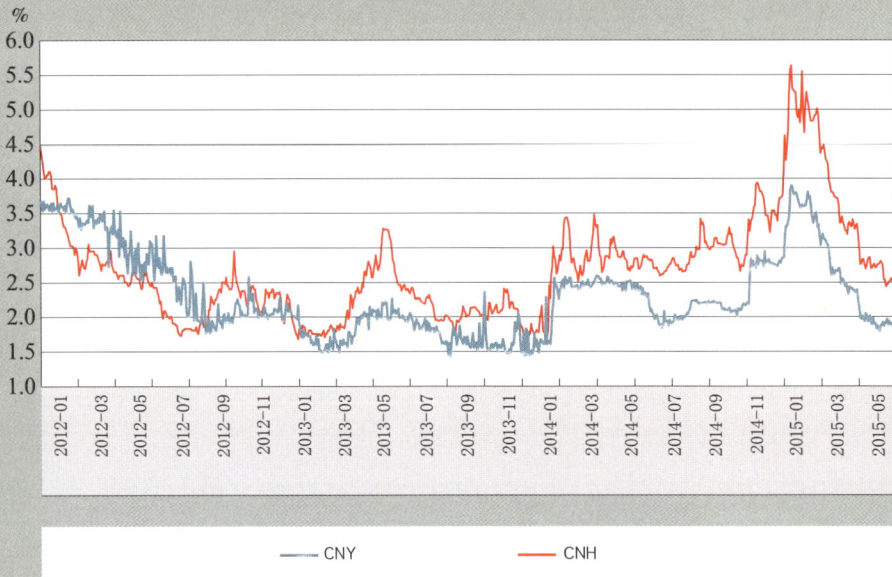

CNY
CNH

Note: The implied volatility of the flat option.
Source: Bloomberg.

Chart 4–10

A comparison of the structure of products in the domestic and global foreign-exchange markets

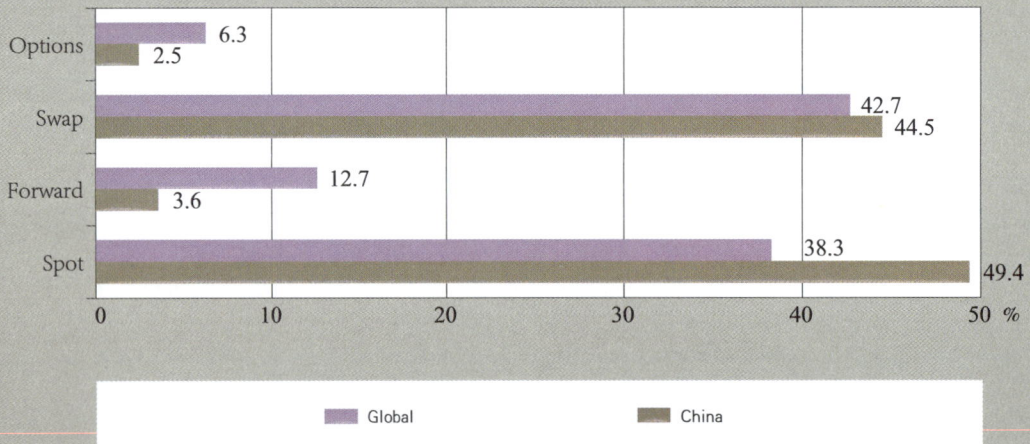

Product	Global	China
Options	6.3	2.5
Swap	42.7	44.5
Forward	12.7	3.6
Spot	38.3	49.4

Global
China

Note: The data of China is 2015H1 data; the global data is from the survey conducted by BIS in Apr. 2013.
Source: SAFE, CFETS, BIS.

Operation of the Foreign-exchange Market and the RMB Exchange Rate | China's Balance of Payments Report
First Half of 2015

119

volume of USD 61.8 billion. The total trading volume in the client market and the inter–bank market was USD 2.05 trillion and USD 5.31 trillion respectively (see Table 4–1). [1] The derivatives, at 50.6 percent, accounted for a historic high share of the total transactions in the foreign–exchange market. The structure was close to that of the global foreign–exchange market (see Chart 4–10).

Foreign-exchange spot transactions grew slightly. In the first half of 2015, the spot foreign–exchange market saw a trading volume of USD 3.63 trillion and its daily average trading volume went up by 15.3 percent from the first half of the previous year. Spot purchases and sales of foreign exchange in the client market totaled USD 1.57 trillion (including the banks themselves, but excluding implementation of forwards) and the daily average trading volume went up by 5.9 percent from the first half of the previous year. The spot inter–bank foreign–exchange market saw a trading volume of USD 2.06 trillion and its daily average trading volume went down by 0.5 percent from the first half of the previous year. The share of USD transactions was 93.7 percent.

A large decrease in foreign exchange forwards transactions. In the first half of 2015, the forwards markets saw a trading volume of USD 268.3 billion and its daily average trading volume went down by 16.3 percent from the previous year. In the client market, forwards purchases and sales of foreign exchange totaled USD 251.1 billion and the daily average trading volume went down by 14.8 percent. Forwards purchases were USD 91.2 billion, forwards sales were USD159.8 billion, and their daily average trading volume went down by 47.1 percent and went up by 30.8 percent respectively (see Chart 4–11). Short–term 6–month transactions accounted for 69.8 percent of the total transactions (see Chart 4–12). In the inter–bank market, foreign exchange forwards totaled USD 17.3 billion, and their daily average trading volume went down by as much as 33.3 percent. The big increase of forwards purchases of foreign exchange by enterprises reflected the fact that market participants had a growing demand for transactions in order to prevent the risks of a strong RMB exchange rate appreciation against the backdrop of the complicated international financial situations.

A large increase in swap transactions. In the first half of 2015, cumulative foreign exchange and currency swap transactions totaled USD 3.27 billion, and the daily average trading volume went up by 53 percent from the first half of the previous year. Cumulative foreign exchange and currency swap transactions in the client market reached USD 164.5 billion, and their daily average trading volume went up by 81.9 percent from the first half of the previous year.

---

[1] The amount of transactions in the client market is the total amount of transactions including purchases and sales of foreign exchange by clients. The amount of transactions in the inter–bank market is the amount of unilateral transactions. The same as below.

Spot purchases/forward sales and spot sales/forward purchases stood at USD 15.6 billion and USD 149 billion respectively, and their daily average trading volumes went up by 92.3 percent and 80.9 percent respectively from the first half of the previous year. The cumulative foreign exchange and currency swap transactions in the inter-bank market reached USD 3.11 trillion and their daily average trading volume went up by 51.7 percent from the first half of the previous year. The spot market continued to witness active transactions. This reflected the fact that the market-oriented mechanism between the domestic RMB and foreign currencies and between the interest rate and foreign-exchange rates were closer.

A large increase in foreign-exchange options. In the first half of 2015, the trading volume of options totaled USD 185.8 billion, and its daily average trading volume went up by 4.1 times from the first half of the previous year. The client market saw a total trading volume of USD 65 billion, and its daily average trading volume went up by 1.8 times from the first half of the previous year. The inter-bank market saw a total trading volume of USD 120.8 billion, and its daily average trading volume went up by 8.2 times from the first half of the previous year. As expectations regarding the RMB exchange rate diversified, the growing active options market showed that market participants put more emphasis on and took a more active part in options that had diversified functions to manage risks, as compared with other derivatives.

Chart 4-11

The trading volume of forward foreign-exchange transactions in the client market, 2012 to the first half of 2015

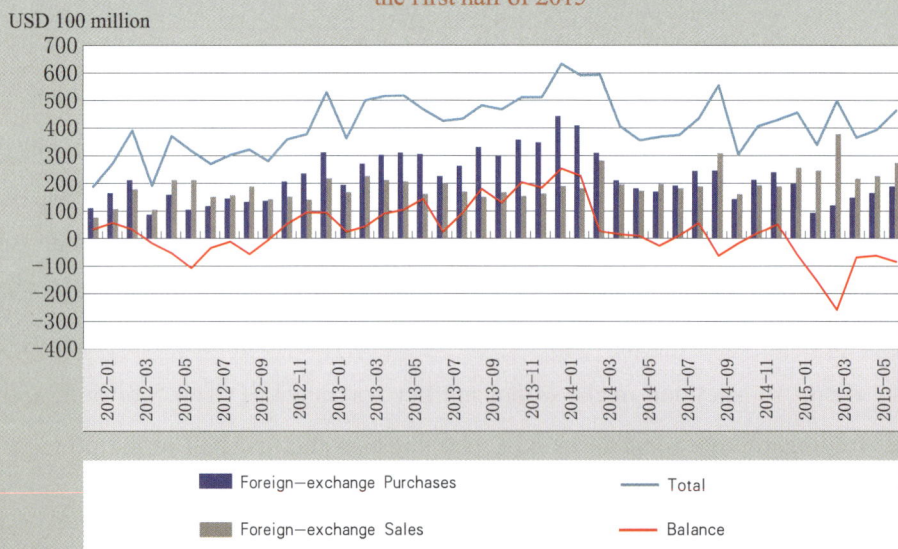

Source: SAFE.

Operation of the Foreign-exchange Market and the RMB Exchange Rate | China's Balance of Payments Report
First Half of 2015

121

Chart 4–12

The term structure of forward transactions of foreign-exchange purchases and sales in the client market, first half of 2015

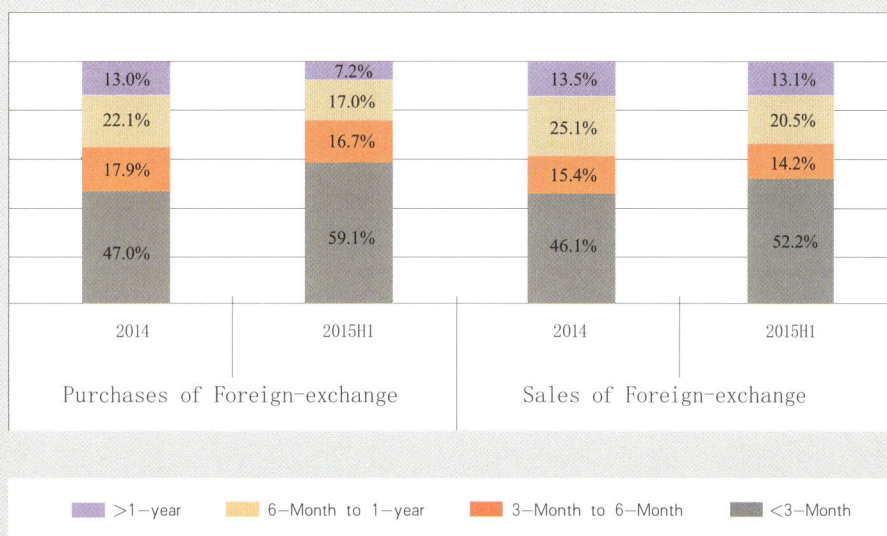

Source: SAFE.

Table 4-1 Transactions in the RMB/foreign-exchange market, first half of 2015

Products	Trading Volume (100 million USD)
Spot	36 306
Client Market	15 676
Interbank Foreign Exchange Market	20 629
Forward	2 683
Client Market	2 511
Less than 3 months (including 3 months)	1 375
3 months to 1 year (including 1 year)	861
More than 1 year	275
Interbank Foreign Exchange Market	173
Less than 3 months (including 3 months)	125
3 months to 1 year (including 1 year)	41
More than 1 year	6
Foreign Exchange and Currency Swaps	32 702
Client Market	1 645

(continued)

Products	Trading Volume (100 million USD)
Interbank Foreign Exchange Market	31 057
Less than 3 months (including 3 months)	27 694
3 months to 1 year (including 1 year)	3 281
More than 1 year	83
Options	1 858
Client Market	650
Foreign Exchange Call Options/RMB Put Options	355
Foreign Exchange Put Options/RMB Call Options	295
Less than 3 months (including 3 months)	275
3 months to 1 year (including 1 year)	257
More than 1 year	117
Interbank Foreign Exchange Market	1 208
Less than 3 months (including 3 months)	958
3 months to 1 year (including 1 year)	248
More than 1 year	1
Total	73 549
Client Market	20 482
Interbank Foreign Exchange Market	53 067
Including: Spots	36 306
Forwards	2 683
Foreign Exchange and Currency Swaps	32 702
Options	1 858

Note: The trading volumes used here are all unilateral transactions and the data employ rounded-off numbers.
Sources: SAFE, CFETS.

Continued stability in the structure of participants in foreign- exchange markets.
Proprietary transactions by banks continued to dominate (see Chart 4–13). The share of inter–bank transactions among all foreign–exchange transactions rose from 67.7 percent in 2014 to 71.2 percent in the first half of 2015. The share of bank transactions with non–financial customers fell from 30.5 percent to 27.2 percent. The share of non–banking financial institutions was 1.6 percent, down 0.1 percent. Participation in the foreign–exchange market by non–banking financial institutions remained quite limited.

Operation of the Foreign-exchange Market and the RMB Exchange Rate | China's Balance of Payments Report
First Half of 2015

123

Chart 4–13

The structure of participants in China's foreign-exchange markets

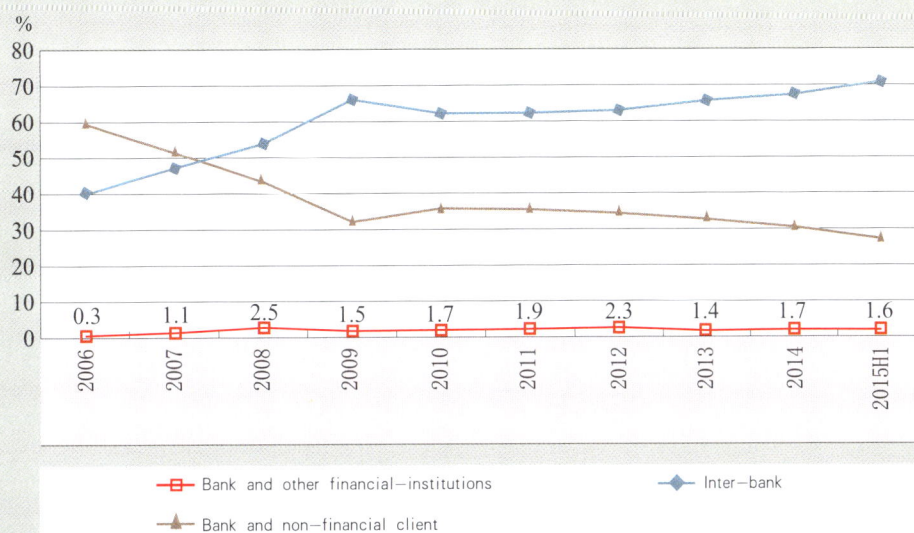

Sources: SAFE, CFETS.

Box 6

The ten-year development of foreign-exchange markets since the regime reform and Future Challenges

Before the reform and opening, China adopted a centralized foreign-exchange management system which unified receipts and payments. At that time, there was no foundation for or recognition of foreign-exchange markets. After the reform and opening, China's foreign-exchange market began with adjustment transactions of foreign exchange in 1980 and swap operations to carry out foreign-exchange adjustment transactions thereafter. The foreign-exchange market became more regulated after 1994 when regulations for foreign exchange purchases and sales by banks were formulated and a unified domestic inter-bank foreign-exchange market was established. In July 2005, China optimized the RMB exchange-rate formation mechanism and the foreign-exchange market began to move to a new and higher stage.

Products were more diversified to meet the different demands for foreign- exchange

risk management. Before the regime reform, there were only spot transactions and pilot forwards by some banks in the domestic foreign–exchange market. After the regime reform, the domestic foreign–exchange market had the basic products of international foreign–exchange markets, including foreign–exchange swaps, currency swaps, and options products. In order to reduce the exchange costs of cross–border trade and investment, we introduced more trading currencies to the market. There are now 13 foreign currencies in the market, including the USD, EUR, JPY, HKD, GBP, AUD, NZD, CAD, MYR, RUB, THB (regional transactions), and KZT (regional transactions), which basically cover all the settlement currencies for cross–border receipts and payments.

Enlarged market participants and the construction of a diversified structure of market participants. After the regime reform, the inter–bank foreign–exchange market transformed its simple structure, which only had banking participants and allowed only qualified non–banking financial institutions and non–financial institutions to join. In response to demands from Hong Kong and Macao, and the cross–border RMB development, a group of foreign banks that assumed responsibility for settlement of the off shore RMB successively joined the inter–bank market. More foreign banks carried out OTC foreign–exchange transactions with domestic banks for cross–border trade RMB settlements. The market gradually became more open to the outside. By the first half of 2015, there were 488 members in the inter–bank foreign–exchange market, including 415 domestic banks, 56 financial corporations, 2 funds and securities, 1 enterprise group, and 14 off shore settlement banks.

Improvement in the fundamental infrastructure and promotion of market operations to improve efficiency and to prevent risks. Before the regime reform in 2005, the electronic centralized matching mode was the only trading mode in the inter–bank foreign–exchange market. Now we have diversified modes in the market, with the co–existence of centralized matching and bilateral enquiries, and the electronic trading and voice brokerage complement each other. A classified market–making system has also been established. Meanwhile, we have actively promoted construction of facilities for settlements and information. In 2009, we began to implement centralized netting settlements for OTC transactions. In 2014, we formally launched central counterparty settlements and basically achieved centralized collection of information and management of all transactions in real time. We also formed a complete transaction reporting system. Moreover, we encouraged

Chart C6-1

An overview of the trading volume of China's foreign-exchange market

USD 100 million

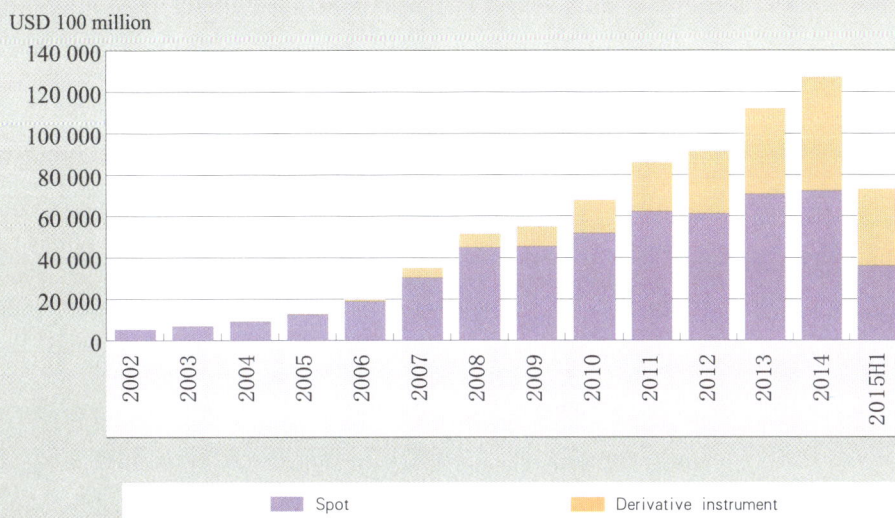

Sources: SAFE, CFETS.

the CFETS and the Shanghai Settlement Center to develop as important market organizers in a comprehensive and specialized way.

In 2014, the RMB/foreign-currency transactions of different products in China's foreign-exchange market totaled 12.8 trillion, up 12.3 times since 2004. The share of derivative transactions grew from 1.8 percent in 2004 to 43 percent in 2014 (see Chart C 6–1). The depth and breadth of the foreign-exchange market were further expanded, offering sound guarantees to promote the market-oriented reform of exchange rates and to support market participants to adapt to two-way movements in the exchange rates.

The achievements of the foreign-exchange market during the past ten years have been a natural outcome of the comprehensive economic reform and opening and the deep promotion of financial-market development. The market will still have significant development opportunities in the future. China's economic industrialization, informatization, and urbanization are improving. Structural adjustments in the economy are accelerating. China has improved its conditions for opening. Against such a background, and especially due to the accelerated process of the RMB convertibility and internationalization, the volume of cross-border transactions will be enlarged and the types of cross-border transactions will become diversified, thus offering a foundation for the sustainable development of the financial market. Meanwhile, as the elasticity of the RMB exchange rate is strengthened, the understanding of risks by different types of market participants continues to improve. Their assets and liabilities denominated in RMB and foreign currencies must be allocated more efficiently to better guard against interest and exchange rate market risks. Thus, the foreign—exchange market needs to be further developed. However, China's foreign—exchange markets still have some objective problems, some of which bear the characteristics of emerging markets and some of which are situations specific to China. These problems include the lack of elasticity in the trading mechanisms, the simplicity of the market participants, the small extent of the opening, and the imperfections in the infrastructure.

On August 11, 2015, the People's Bank of China optimized the quoting measure for the mid—price of the RMB exchange rate against the USD. In future reform arrangements, the PBOC has proposed to accelerate development of the foreign—exchange market, extend the trading time for foreign—exchange transactions, and introduce qualified offshore participants. In the future, the domestic foreign—exchange market will have conditions to achieve further important breakthroughs on the basis of the 10—year regime reform and to create a better market foundation for the further development of the reform of the RMB exchange—rate formation mechanism.

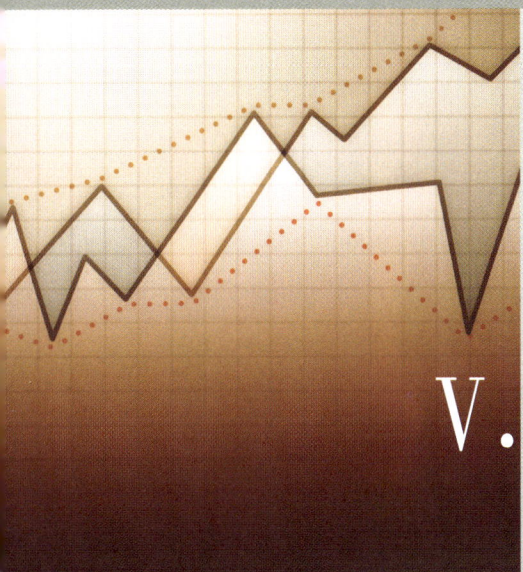

V. Outlook for the Balance of Payments

In the second half of 2015, China's balance of payments will maintain a surplus in the current account and a deficit in the capital and financial account (excluding changes in the reserve assets). China is strengthening its ability to maintain a more balanced BOP situation.

The current account will maintain a relatively large surplus. On the one hand, trade in goods will record a large surplus. As to exports, the mild expansion of the US economy, the recovery of the economies in the Euro area and Japan, and the slowing economic growth in the emerging-market economies will dominate global economic performance in the second half of 2015. According to the IMF's latest forecasts, the growth rate of the world economy will reach 3.3 percent in 2015, 0.1 percentage point lower than that in 2014. Meanwhile, the growth rate of the advanced economies will reach 2.1 percent, as opposed to a rate of 1.8 percent in 2014. External demand for Chinese goods will be stable. In addition, implementation of the "one belt, one road" strategy, the active performance of the free trade zone in Shanghai and other areas, and the strengthening of regional cooperation, such as the China-Korea Free Trade Zone, will create new opportunities for Chinese exports. As to imports, the relatively strong USD and the excess supply of commodities will continue to lower international commodity prices. Meanwhile, domestic demand will remain stable. In this context, China will export more than it will import. On the other hand, trade in services will maintain a deficit, and travel will continue to be the largest deficit sub-item. Due to surging expenditures for Chinese outbound travel and overseas study, higher consumption due to summer school holidays, and end-of-year and beginning of new semester shopping, travel will record a larger deficit in the second half of the year than in the first half of 2015. In summary, the current account will remain in surplus largely due to the surplus of trade in goods, but the surplus will remain within a reasonable range according to international standards.

Cross-border capital flows will fluctuate greatly. Internationally, because the US economic performance and employment situation will be relatively good, and there are expectations of a rise in the Fed rates, it is more likely that the USD will appreciate rather than depreciate. Meanwhile, sluggish long-term economic performance, unsettled Euro sovereign debts, fluctuations in the exchange rates of the emerging-market economies, and a possible outbreak of geopolitical conflicts will affect international financial stability and foster a market risk aversion. Domestically, due to pressures arising from the economic transition, the decline in domestic financing costs, and the RMB exchange rates progressively approaching equilibrium, market participants will continue to adjust their financial operations and to optimize their RMB and foreign-exchange balance sheets. Moreover, domestic enterprises will have a stronger demand for investments abroad due to the deepening of the reforms and the stabilization of the opening policies.

The balance of payments will gradually approach a new status quo if the adjustments are controllable and adaptive. First, domestic entities will adjust their RMB and foreign-exchange balance sheets to accommodate the changes in the market. The adjustments will be in accord with market principles and will enable the private sector to hold more foreign-exchange assets. They also will help to decrease the risks related to high leveraging and currency mismatches. Second, the medium-to-high growth rate, the great potential for market development, the active progress in deepening the reforms, and the upgrading of trade and investment facilitation will continue to make China a desirable destination for foreign investments, especially for long-term investments. Third, the persistent current account surplus, the abundant foreign-exchange reserve assets, the overall soundness of the fiscal and financial systems, and the basically stable RMB exchange rates approaching a reasonable equilibrium will contribute to a steady improvement in the balance-of-payments situation. In the future, as China progressively optimizes its economic structure, the RMB exchange-rate formation mechanism will become more market-oriented and the central bank will end its foreign-exchange market interventions, China's balance of payments will approach a new status quo, with a surplus in the current account and a deficit in the capital and financial account.

Box 7

The differentiated impact of the rising cycle in interest rates by the FED on cross-border capital flows of the emerging economies

As economic and financial globalization continues to deepen, the cyclical adjustment of the monetary policies of the US will have a more important impact on the cross-border capital flows of the emerging economies. We can look at the change in the federal funds rate as an example. In the 1990s, the US experienced 3 rounds of hikes in the interest rate. The first round was from February 1994 when the Fed raised the federal funds rate on 7 occasions and the rate grew from 4.75 percent to 6.5 percent. The second round was from 1999 to 2000. The federal funds rate was increased on 7 occasions, rising from 4.75 percent to 6.5

percent. This interest–rate level was maintained until January 2001. The third round began in June 2004 and the rate was increased on 17 occasions. The federal funds rate grew from 1 percent to 5.25 percent in June 2006. The interest–rate level was maintained until September 17, 2007. Nearly every round of hikes in the interest rate was accompanied by an appreciation of the USD. (see Chart 7–1) .

The differing performances of the emerging economies during the first two rounds of interest-rates hikes by the Fed. In the first round of interest–rate hikes, a crisis erupted in Mexico and Latin America in 1994; however, Chile stood the test of the crisis. In the second round of the interest–rates hikes, some Southeast Asian countries faced a crisis from 1997 to 1998 and Argentina faced a crisis in 2001, but China was not seriously affected.

There are three reasons to explain these differences. First, the economic fundamentals were different. For example, one of the important reasons for Mexico's crisis in 1994 was that investor confidence in Mexico's economic prospects was shaken by risk factors, such as the volatility in the domestic political conditions. China was better protected from the Asian Financial Crisis because we had implemented a series of reforms and measures to adjust the economy before the market volatility and we enjoyed rapid economic growth. In addition, we had accumulated foreign–exchange reserves, thus giving China confidence in making the decision not to devalue the RMB. Second, the regimes and the elasticity of the exchange rates varied. In order to control inflation and stabilize prices, the above countries that faced a crisis had mainly adopted a fixed interest–rate regime pegged to the USD and had large capital inflows. As the USD appreciated and its interest rate increased, it was inevitable that these countries would fall into the trap of a liquidity crunch, thereby causing sovereign currencies and equity markets to fall sharply and inducing the financial crisis. However, the countries that avoided the crisis, such as Chile, had steadily developed a market–oriented exchange rate. Chile had adopted an exchange–rate mechanism that was pegged to a basket of currencies and on several occasions it had enlarged the floating band of its exchange rate. Third, there were differences in these countries in terms of their capital account liberalization processes. For example, Mexico dramatically opened its securities market within four to five years and had a large volume of capital flows. The vulnerability of its financial sector increased greatly. However, Chile spent more than ten years to internationalize its securities market and to establish a clear sequencing for its market liberalization. Before preparing to open the securities market, it carried out reforms of its banking system, trade liberalization, and market—oriented interest rates and exchange rates in sequence. Based on the domestic economic and financial conditions during that period, China maintained prudential policies with regard to financial liberalization that played a certain role in isolating the external shocks.

The connection between the third round of interest-rate hikes and the cross-border capital inflows in the emerging economies. In the third round of the interest—rate hikes, most of the emerging economies experienced a big increase in cross—border inflows. There are three major reasons for this. First, since 2001, the emerging economies had gradually become the engine behind global economic growth. Their yearly average GDP growth rate from 2004 to 2007 reached 8.0 percent. Their good economic prospects attracted a large amount of capital inflows and also helped to guard against external shocks. Second, after the Asian Financial Crisis, the emerging markets had learned some lessons and rapidly accumulated a large amount of foreign—exchange reserves. Their current account deficit also improved. Third, though interest rates went up substantially, the pace of the increase was slow. Since the economic cycles of the developed and emerging economies diverged, the USD rebounded only by a small extent in 2005 and did not appreciate to a large extent for a long time.

We can draw some conclusions from these historical experiences. First, sound economic fundamentals are a radical safeguard against external shocks. The rapid economic growth was helpful to address the economic, financial, and social problems. It also helped to absorb the turbulence derived from the cross—border capital flows. This philosophy was very obvious during the third round of the interest—rate hikes. Second, the flexibility of the exchange—rate regime in accordance with the liberalization of the capital account was very important. The countries where a crisis erupted had an open capital account but their exchange—rate regimes were rigid. Under such circumstances, it was very difficult to manage the risks induced by the surge in capital flows. The continuously increasing flexibility of the exchange—rate regime during the opening process was helpful to adjust the short—term cross—border capital flows. Chile is a typical example. Third, the opening process should be in accordance with the domestic economic and financial conditions. Sound economic and financial conditions provided a helpful domestic environment for the reform measures. However, when the domestic fundamentals faced many risks, it was appropriate to adopt more cautious measures and to strengthen prudential management.

Chart C7-1

Trends in the federal funds rate and the USD index, from 1990

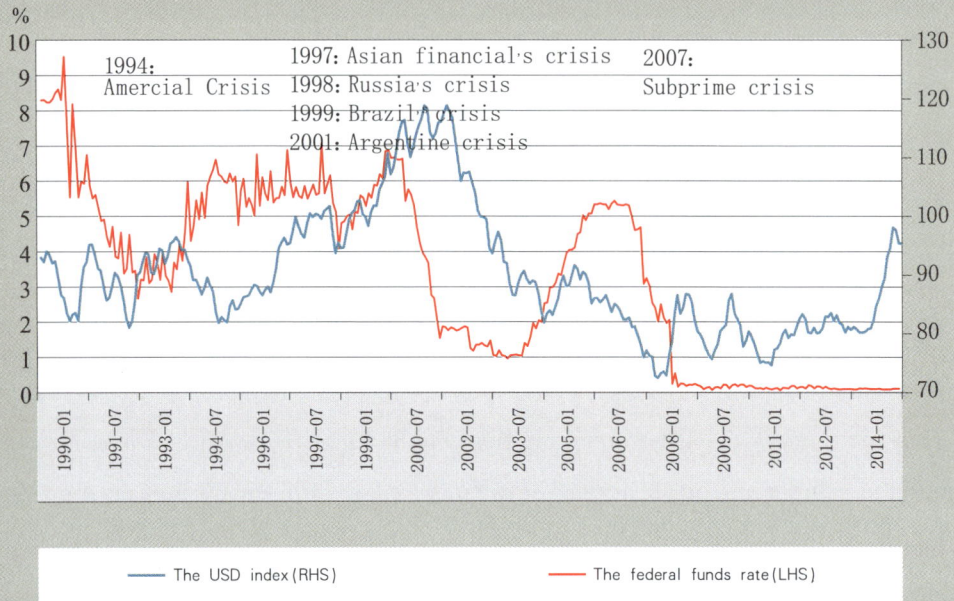

1994: Amercial Crisis
1997: Asian financial's crisis
1998: Russia's crisis
1999: Brazil's crisis
2001: Argentine crisis
2007: Subprime crisis

The USD index (RHS)　　The federal funds rate (LHS)

Sources: CEIC.

During the next stage, the foreign-exchange administration will continue to implement the arrangements of the Central Party and the State Council, to adhere to balance reform and innovation, and to actively adapt to the new normal in economic development. The administration will simplify administration, balance between foreign-exchange management and liberalization, improve services and deepen reform, creatively conduct interim and ex-post monitoring, and remain dedicated to foreign-exchange administration. First, the authorities will continue to simplify administration, to deepen the reforms in important foreign-exchange areas, and to foster capital-account convertibility to support the development of the real economy. Second, they will improve monitoring, analysis, and forecasting of cross-border capital flows, strengthen the foundation for the data system, and combat illegal activities in the field of foreign exchange to reinforce their duty to guard against risks. Third, they will continue to strengthen management of foreign-exchange reserves to ensure the safety, liquidity, and appreciation of the assets.

附　录　统计资料
Appendix　Statistics

一、国际收支[1]

I. Balance of Payments

亿 美 元
USD 100 million

%

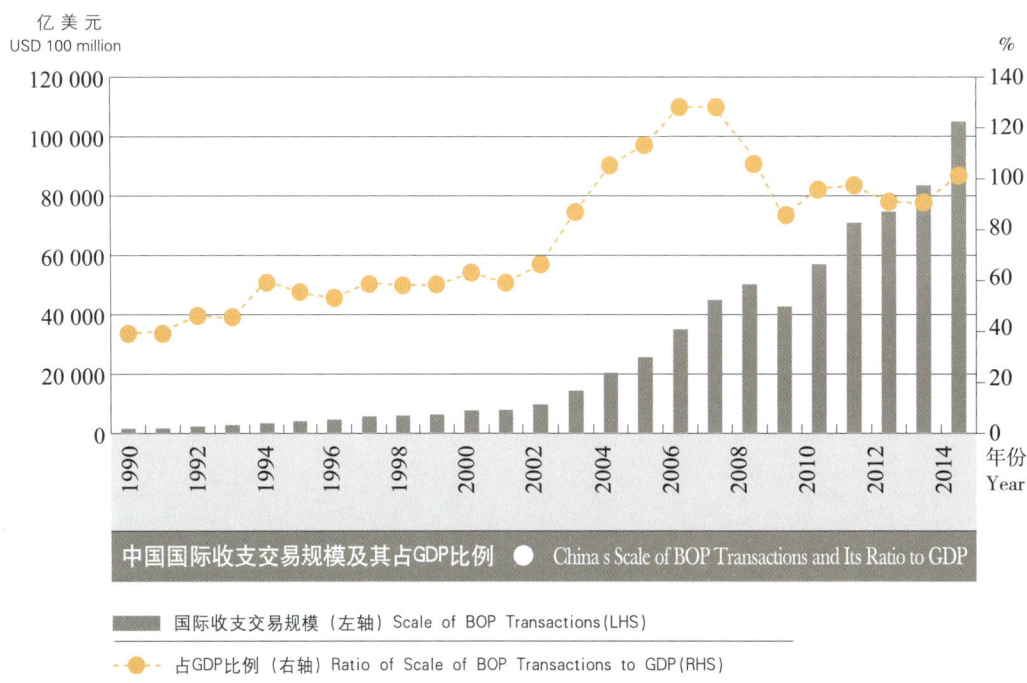

中国国际收支交易规模及其占GDP比例 ● China's Scale of BOP Transactions and Its Ratio to GDP

■ 国际收支交易规模（左轴）Scale of BOP Transactions（LHS）

─●─ 占GDP比例（右轴）Ratio of Scale of BOP Transactions to GDP（RHS）

---

① 资料来源：国家外汇管理局；IMF《国际收支统计》、《国际金融统计》；环亚经济数据库。
Sources: State Administration of Foreign Exchange; IMF, Balance of Payments Statistics, International Financial Statistics; CEIC Database.

亿 美 元
USD 100 million

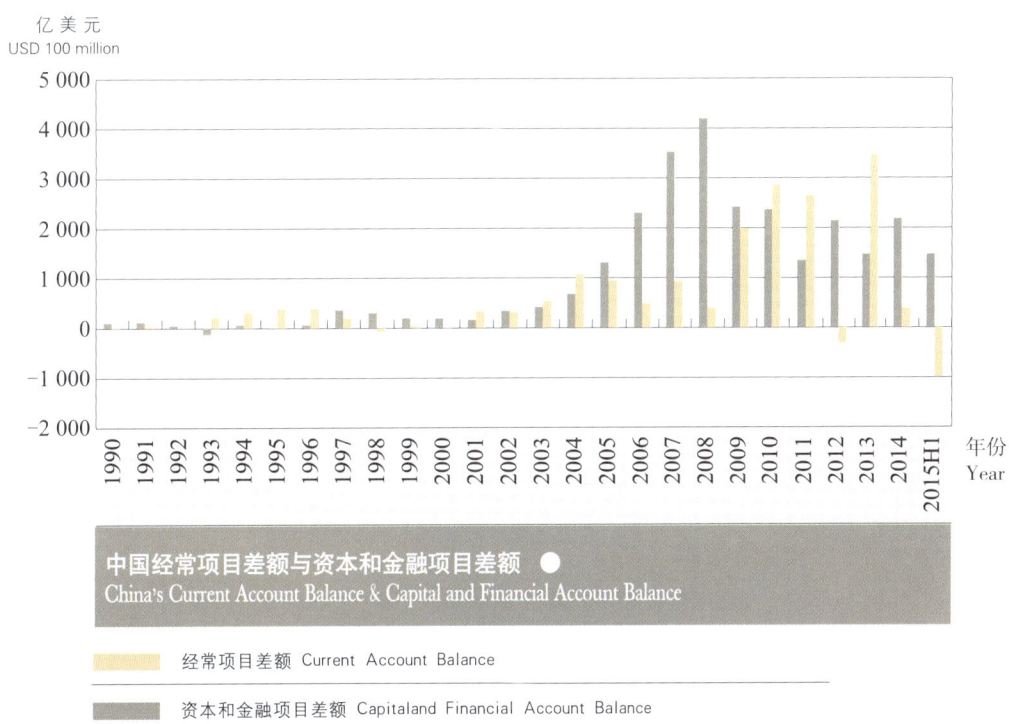

中国经常项目差额与资本和金融项目差额 ●
China's Current Account Balance & Capital and Financial Account Balance

经常项目差额 Current Account Balance

资本和金融项目差额 Capitaland Financial Account Balance

中国国际收支概览表（1）

China's Balance of Payments Abridged

项目　　　年份 Item/Year	1982	1983	1984	1985	1986	1987
1.经常账户	57	42	20	−114	−70	3
贷方	243	240	273	276	276	354
借方	−186	−198	−253	−390	−347	−351
A.货物和服务	48	26	1	−125	−74	3
贷方	226	220	248	258	262	341
借方	−178	−194	−247	−383	−336	−338
a.货物	42	18	−2	−131	−90	−13
贷方	199	192	217	227	223	300
借方	−158	−174	−219	−358	−313	−313
b.服务	6	8	2	6	16	16
贷方	27	28	31	31	39	41
借方	−20	−20	−29	−25	−23	−25
B.初次收入	4	12	15	8	0	−2
贷方	10	15	19	14	9	10
借方	−6	−3	−4	−5	−9	−12
C.二次收入	5	5	4	2	4	2
贷方	7	6	6	4	5	4
借方	−2	−1	−2	−2	−1	−2
2.资本和金融账户	−60	−41	−32	139	83	11
2.1 资本账户	0	0	0	0	0	0
贷方	0	0	0	0	0	0
借方	0	0	0	0	0	0
2.2 金融账户	−60	−41	−32	139	83	11

单位：亿美元
Unit: USD 100 million

项目　年份 Item/Year	1982	1983	1984	1985	1986	1987
资产	−71	−54	−58	50	13	−58
负债	11	13	25	89	70	69
2.2.1 非储备性质的金融账户	−17	−14	−38	85	65	27
资产	−29	−27	−63	−4	−4	−42
负债	11	13	25	89	70	69
直接投资	4	8	13	13	18	17
资产	0	−1	−1	−6	−5	−6
负债	4	9	14	20	22	23
证券投资	0	−6	−16	30	16	11
资产	0	−6	−17	23	0	−1
负债	0	0	1	8	16	12
金融衍生工具	0	0	0	0	0	0
资产	0	0	0	0	0	0
负债	0	0	0	0	0	0
其他投资	−21	−16	−34	41	32	0
资产	−28	−19	−44	−20	1	−34
负债	6	4	10	62	31	34
2.2.2 储备资产	−42	−27	5	54	17	−17
其中:外汇储备	−43	−19	7	56	12	−15
3.净误差与遗漏	3	−2	12	−25	−12	−14

中国国际收支概览表（2）

China's Balance of Payments Abridged(2)

项目 年份 Item/Year	1994	1995	1996	1997	1998	1999
1.经常账户	77	16	72	370	315	211
贷方	1 121	1 389	1 645	1 986	1 990	2 124
借方	−1 045	−1 373	−1 573	−1 617	−1 675	−1 913
A.货物和服务	74	120	176	428	438	306
贷方	1 046	1 319	1 548	1 874	1 888	1 987
借方	−973	−1 199	−1 373	−1 446	−1 449	−1 681
a.货物	35	128	122	366	456	329
贷方	844	1 074	1 268	1 532	1 637	1 693
借方	−810	−947	−1 147	−1 167	−1 181	−1 364
b.服务	39	−8	54	63	−18	−23
贷方	202	244	280	342	251	294
借方	−163	−252	−226	−280	−268	−317
B.初次收入	−10	−118	−124	−110	−166	−145
贷方	57	52	73	57	56	83
借方	−68	−170	−198	−167	−222	−228
C.二次收入	13	14	21	51	43	49
贷方	18	18	24	55	47	54
借方	−4	−4	−2	−3	−4	−4
2.资本和金融账户	21	162	83	−147	−127	−33
2.1 资本账户	0	0	0	0	0	0
贷方	0	0	0	0	0	0
借方	0	0	0	0	0	0
2.2 金融账户	21	162	83	−147	−127	−33

单位：亿美元
Unit: USD 100 million

项目 年份 Item/Year	1994	1995	1996	1997	1998	1999
资产	-367	-247	-357	-788	-479	-452
负债	389	409	440	641	352	419
2.2.1 非储备性质的 金融账户	326	387	400	210	-63	52
资产	-62	-22	-40	-431	-415	-367
负债	389	409	440	641	352	419
直接投资	318	338	381	417	411	370
资产	-20	-20	-21	-26	-26	-18
负债	338	358	402	442	438	388
证券投资	35	8	17	69	-37	-112
资产	-4	1	-6	-9	-38	-105
负债	39	7	24	78	1	-7
金融衍生工具	0	0	0	0	0	0
资产	0	0	0	0	0	0
负债	0	0	0	0	0	0
其他投资	-27	40	2	-276	-437	-205
资产	-38	-3	-13	-396	-350	-244
负债	12	43	15	120	-86	39
2.2.2 储备资产	-305	-225	-317	-357	-64	-85
其中:外汇储备	-304	-220	-315	-349	-51	-97
3.净误差与遗漏	-98	-178	-155	-223	-187	-178

中国国际收支概览表 (3)

China's Balance of Payments Abridged (3)

项目 年份 Item/Year	2000	2001	2002	2003	2004	2005
1.经常账户	204	174	354	431	689	1 324
贷方	2 725	2 906	3 551	4 825	6 522	8 403
借方	−2 521	−2 732	−3 197	−4 395	−5 833	−7 080
A.货物和服务	288	281	374	358	512	1 246
贷方	2 531	2 721	3 330	4 480	6 074	7 733
借方	−2 243	−2 440	−2 956	−4 121	−5 562	−6 487
a.货物	299	282	377	398	594	1 301
贷方	2 181	2 329	2 868	3 966	5 429	6 949
借方	−1 881	−2 047	−2 491	−3 568	−4 835	−5 647
b.服务	−11	−1	−3	−40	−82	−55
贷方	350	392	462	513	645	785
借方	−362	−393	−465	−553	−727	−840
B.初次收入	−147	−192	−149	−102	−51	−161
贷方	126	94	83	161	206	393
借方	−272	−286	−233	−263	−257	−554
C.二次收入	63	85	130	174	229	239
贷方	69	91	138	185	243	277
借方	−5	−6	−8	−10	−14	−39
2.资本和金融账户	−86	−125	−432	−513	−819	−1 553
2.1 资本账户	0	−1	0	0	−1	41
贷方	0	0	0	0	0	42
借方	0	−1	0	0	−1	−1
2.2 金融账户	−86	−125	−432	−512	−818	−1 594

单位：亿美元
Unit: USD 100 million

项目　年份 Item/Year	2000	2001	2002	2003	2004	2005
资产	−666	−541	−932	−1 212	−1 916	−3 352
负债	580	416	500	699	1 098	1 758
2.2.1 非储备性质的金融账户	20	348	323	549	1 082	912
资产	−561	−67	−177	−150	−16	−845
负债	580	416	500	699	1 098	1 758
直接投资	375	374	468	494	601	904
资产	−9	−69	−25	0	−20	−137
负债	384	442	493	495	621	1 041
证券投资	−40	−194	−103	114	197	−47
资产	−113	−207	−121	30	65	−262
负债	73	12	18	84	132	214
金融衍生工具	0	0	0	0	0	0
资产	0	0	0	0	0	0
负债	0	0	0	0	0	0
其他投资	−315	169	−41	−60	283	56
资产	−439	208	−31	−180	−61	−447
负债	123	−39	−10	120	345	502
2.2.2 储备资产	−105	−473	−755	−1 061	−1 901	−2 506
其中:外汇储备	−109	−466	−742	−1 060	−1 904	−2 526
3.净误差与遗漏	−119	−49	78	82	130	229

中国国际收支概览表（4）

China's Balance of Payments Abridged (4)

项目　　年份 Item/Year	2006	2007	2008	2009	2010	2011
1.经常账户	2 318	3 532	4 206	2 433	2 378	1 361
贷方	10 779	13 832	16 597	14 006	17 959	22 087
借方	−8 460	−10 300	−12 391	−11 574	−15 581	−20 726
A.货物和服务	2 089	3 080	3 488	2 201	2 230	1 819
贷方	9 917	12 571	14 953	12 497	16 039	20 089
借方	−7 828	−9 490	−11 465	−10 296	−13 809	−18 269
a.货物	2 157	3 117	3 599	2 435	2 464	2 287
贷方	8 977	11 316	13 500	11 272	14 864	18 078
借方	−6 820	−8 199	−9 901	−8 836	−12 400	−15 791
b.服务	−68	−37	−111	−234	−234	−468
贷方	941	1 254	1 453	1 226	1 175	2 010
借方	−1 008	−1 291	−1 564	−1 460	−1 409	−2 478
B.初次收入	−51	80	286	−85	−259	−703
贷方	546	835	1 118	1 083	1 424	1 443
借方	−597	−754	−832	−1 168	−1 683	−2 146
C.二次收入	281	371	432	317	407	245
贷方	316	426	526	426	495	556
借方	−35	−55	−94	−110	−88	−311
2.资本和金融账户	−2 355	−3 665	−4 394	−2 019	−1 849	−1 223
2.1 资本账户	40	31	31	39	46	54
贷方	41	33	33	42	48	56
借方	−1	−2	−3	−3	−2	−2
2.2 金融账户	−2 395	−3 696	−4 425	−2 058	−1 895	−1 278

单位：亿美元
Unit: USD 100 million

项目 年份 Item/Year	2006	2007	2008	2009	2010	2011
资产	−4 519	−6 371	−6 087	−4 283	−6 536	−6 136
负债	2 124	2 676	1 662	2 225	4 641	4 858
2.2.1 非储备性质的金融账户	453	911	371	1 945	2 822	2 600
资产	−1 671	−1 764	−1 291	−280	−1 819	−2 258
负债	2 124	2 676	1 662	2 225	4 641	4 858
直接投资	1 001	1 391	1 148	872	1 857	2 317
资产	−239	−172	−567	−439	−580	−484
负债	1 241	1 562	1 715	1 311	2 437	2 801
证券投资	−684	164	349	271	240	196
资产	−1 113	−45	252	−25	−76	62
负债	429	210	97	296	317	134
金融衍生工具	0	0	0	0	0	0
资产	0	0	0	0	0	0
负债	0	0	0	0	0	0
其他投资	136	−644	−1 126	803	724	87
资产	−319	−1 548	−976	184	−1 163	−1 836
负债	455	904	−150	619	1 887	1 923
2.2.2 储备资产	−2 848	−4 607	−4 795	−4 003	−4 717	−3 878
其中:外汇储备	−2 853	−4 609	−4 783	−3 821	−4 696	−3 848
3.净误差与遗漏	36	133	188	−414	−529	−138

中国国际收支概览表 (5)

China's Balance of Payments Abridged (5)

项目　　年份 Item/Year	2012	2013	2014	2015H1
1.经常账户	2 154	1 482	2 197	1 486
贷方	23 933	25 927	27 299	12 728
借方	-21 779	-24 445	-25 102	-11 242
A.货物和服务	2 318	2 354	2 840	1 621
贷方	21 751	23 556	24 758	11 234
借方	-19 432	-21 202	-21 917	-9 613
a.货物	3 116	3 590	4 350	2 566
贷方	19 735	21 486	22 438	10 112
借方	-16 619	-17 896	-18 087	-7 546
b.服务	-797	-1 236	-1 510	-945
贷方	2 016	2 070	2 320	1 122
借方	-2 813	-3 306	-3 830	-2 067
B.初次收入	-199	-784	-341	-104
贷方	1 670	1 840	2 130	1 310
借方	-1 869	-2 624	-2 471	-1 414
C.二次收入	34	-87	-302	-32
贷方	512	532	411	184
借方	-477	-619	-714	-215
2.资本和金融账户	-1 283	-853	-795	-585
2.1 资本账户	43	31	0	3
贷方	45	45	19	4
借方	-3	-14	-20	-1
2.2 金融账户	-1 326	-883	-795	-587

单位：亿美元
Unit: USD 100 million

项目 年份 Item/Year	2012	2013	2014	2015H1
资产	−3 996	−6 517	−5 120	−1 084
负债	2 670	5 633	4 325	497
2.2.1 非储备性质的金融账户	−360	3 430	383	−1 259
资产	−3 030	−2 203	−3 942	−1 756
负债	2 670	5 633	4 325	497
直接投资	1 763	2 180	2 087	920
资产	−650	−730	−804	−529
负债	2 412	2 909	2 891	1 449
证券投资	478	529	824	−241
资产	−64	−54	−108	−572
负债	542	582	932	331
金融衍生工具	0	0	0	−7
资产	0	0	0	−23
负债	0	0	0	16
其他投资	−2 601	722	−2 528	−1 931
资产	−2 317	−1 420	−3 030	−632
负债	−284	2 142	502	−1 299
2.2.2 储备资产	−966	−4 314	−1 178	671
其中：外汇储备	−987	−4 327	−1 188	666
3.净误差与遗漏	−871	−629	−1 401	−901

2015年上半年中国国际收支平衡表

China's Balance of Payments in the First Half of 2015

项目	行次	2015年上半年
1. 经常账户	1	1 486
贷方	2	12 728
借方	3	-11 242
1.A 货物和服务	4	1 621
贷方	5	11 234
借方	6	-9 613
1.A.a 货物	7	2 566
贷方	8	10 112
借方	9	-7 546
1.A.b 服务	10	-945
贷方	11	1 122
借方	12	-2 067
1.A.b.1 加工服务	13	97
贷方	14	98
借方	15	-1
1.A.b.2 维护和维修服务	16	11
贷方	17	17
借方	18	-6
1.A.b.3 运输	19	-220
贷方	20	198
借方	21	-418
1.A.b.4 旅行	22	-892
贷方	23	277
借方	24	-1 169
1.A.b.5 建设	25	31
贷方	26	82
借方	27	-51
1.A.b.6 保险和养老金服务	28	-14
贷方	29	20

项目	行次	2015年上半年
借方	30	−34
1.A.b.7 金融服务	31	−4
贷方	32	11
借方	33	−15
1.A.b.8 知识产权使用费	34	−99
贷方	35	6
借方	36	−105
1.A.b.9 电信、计算机和信息服务	37	59
贷方	38	114
借方	39	−55
1.A.b.10 其他商业服务	40	100
贷方	41	290
借方	42	−190
1.A.b.11 个人、文化和娱乐服务	43	−4
贷方	44	4
借方	45	−8
1.A.b.12 别处未提及的政府服务	46	−9
贷方	47	5
借方	48	−14
1.B 初次收入	49	−104
贷方	50	1 310
借方	51	−1 414
1.B.1 雇员报酬	52	151
贷方	53	179
借方	54	−28
1.B.2 投资收益	55	−258
贷方	56	1 127
借方	57	−1 385
1.B.3 其他初次收入	58	4

2015年上半年中国国际收支平衡表

China's Balance of Payments in the First Half of 2015

项目	行次	2015年上半年
贷方	59	4
借方	60	−1
1.C 二次收入	61	−32
贷方	62	184
借方	63	−215
2. 资本和金融账户	64	−585
2.1 资本账户	65	3
贷方	66	4
借方	67	−1
2.2 金融账户	68	−587
资产	69	−1 084
负债	70	497
2.2.1 非储备性质的金融账户	71	−1 259
资产	72	−1 756
负债	73	497
2.2.1.1 直接投资	74	920
2.2.1.1.1 直接投资资产	75	−529
2.2.1.1.1.1 股权	76	−495
2.2.1.1.1.2 关联企业债务	77	−34
2.2.1.1.2 直接投资负债	78	1 449
2.2.1.1.2.1 股权	79	1 233
2.2.1.1.2.2 关联企业债务	80	215
2.2.1.2 证券投资	81	−241
2.2.1.2.1 资产	82	−572
2.2.1.2.1.1 股权	83	−326
2.2.1.2.1.2 债券	84	−247
2.2.1.2.2 负债	85	331
2.2.1.2.2.1 股权	86	212

单位：亿美元
Unit: USD 100 million

项目	行次	2015年上半年
2.2.1.2.2.2 债券	87	120
2.2.1.3 金融衍生工具	88	−7
2.2.1.3.1 资产	89	−23
2.2.1.3.2 负债	90	16
2.2.1.4 其他投资	91	−1 931
2.2.1.4.1 资产	92	−632
2.2.1.4.1.1 其他股权	93	0
2.2.1.4.1.2 货币和存款	94	−152
2.2.1.4.1.3 贷款	95	−541
2.2.1.4.1.4 保险和养老金	96	−56
2.2.1.4.1.5 贸易信贷	97	130
2.2.1.4.1.6 其他应收款	98	−13
2.2.1.4.2 负债	99	−1 299
2.2.1.4.2.1 其他股权	100	0
2.2.1.4.2.2 货币和存款	101	−175
2.2.1.4.2.3 贷款	102	−759
2.2.1.4.2.4 保险和养老金	103	14
2.2.1.4.2.5 贸易信贷	104	−357
2.2.1.4.2.6 其他应付款	105	−23
2.2.1.4.2.7 特别提款权	106	0
2.2.2 储备资产	107	671
2.2.2.1 货币黄金	108	0
2.2.2.2 特别提款权	109	−4
2.2.2.3 在国际货币基金组织的储备头寸	110	10
2.2.2.4 外汇储备	111	666
2.2.2.5 其他储备资产	112	0
3.净误差与遗漏	113	−901

中国国际投资头寸表[①]

China's International Investment Position

项目	2008年末	2009年末	2010年末	2011年末	2012年末	2013年末	2014年末	2015年上半年末
净头寸	14 938	14 905	16 880	16 884	18 665	19 960	17 764	14 640
A.资产	29 567	34 369	41 189	47 345	52 132	59 861	64 087	64 337
1.直接投资	1 857	2 458	3 172	4 248	5 319	6 605	7 443	10 129
1.1 股权	–	–	–	–	–	–	–	8 309
1.2 关联企业债务	–	–	–	–	–	–	–	1 820
2.证券投资	2 525	2 428	2 571	2 044	2 406	2 585	2 625	2 760
2.1 股权	214	546	630	864	1 298	1 530	1 613	1 777
2.2 债券	2 311	1 882	1 941	1 180	1 108	1 055	1 012	983
3.金融衍生工具	–	–	–	–	–	–	–	39
4.其他投资	5 523	4 952	6 304	8 495	10 527	11 867	15 026	13 695
4.1 其他股权	–	–	–	–	–	–	–	1
4.2 货币和存款	1 529	1 310	2 051	2 942	3 906	3 751	5 541	3 125
4.3 贷款	1 071	974	1 174	2 232	2 778	3 089	3 747	4 658
4.4 保险和养老金	–	–	–	–	–	–	–	200
4.5 贸易信贷	1 102	1 444	2 060	2 769	3 387	3 990	4 677	4 547
4.6 其他应收款	1 821	1 224	1 018	552	457	1 038	1 061	1 165
5.储备资产	19 662	24 532	29 142	32 558	33 879	38 804	38 993	37 713
5.1 货币黄金	169	371	481	530	567	408	401	624
5.2 特别提款权	12	125	123	119	114	112	105	105
5.3 在国际货币基金组织的储备头寸	20	44	64	98	82	71	57	46
5.4 外汇储备	19 460	23 992	28 473	31 811	33 116	38 213	38 430	36 938

① 从 2015 年开始，国际收支平衡表及国际投资头寸表按照国际货币基金组织《国际收支和国际投资头寸手册》(第六版)标准进行编制和列示。往期数据未进行追溯调整。

项目	2008年末	2009年末	2010年末	2011年末	2012年末	2013年末	2014年末	2015年上半年末
5.5 其他储备资产	–	–	–	–	–	–	–	0
B.负债	14 629	19 464	24 308	30 461	33 467	39 901	46 323	49 697
1.直接投资	9 155	13 148	15 696	19 069	20 680	23 312	26 779	28 274
1.1 股权	–	–	–	–	–	–	–	26 027
1.2 关联企业债务	–	–	–	–	–	–	–	2 247
2.证券投资	1 677	1 900	2 239	2 485	3 361	3 865	5 143	8 997
2.1 股权	1 505	1 748	2 061	2 114	2 619	2 977	3 693	6 727
2.2 债券	172	152	178	371	742	889	1 449	2 270
3.金融衍生工具	–	–	–	–	–	–	–	108
4.其他投资	3 796	4 416	6 373	8 907	9 426	12 724	14 402	12 318
4.1 其他股权	–	–	–	–	–	–	–	0
4.2 货币和存款	918	937	1 650	2 477	2 446	3 466	5 030	4 611
4.3 贷款	1 030	1 636	2 389	3 724	3 680	5 642	5 720	4 341
4.4 保险和养老金	–	–	–	–	–	–	–	85
4.5 贸易信贷	1 296	1 617	2 112	2 492	2 915	3 365	3 344	2 987
4.6 其他应付款	552	121	106	106	277	144	207	195
4.7 特别提款权	–	106	116	107	107	108	101	98

外汇储备

Foreign Exchange Reserves

单位：亿美元
Unit: USD 100 million

年份 year	外汇储备余额 Foreign Exchange Reserves	外汇储备增加额 Increase of Foreign Exchange Reserves
1990	111	55
1991	217	106
1992	194	−23
1993	212	18
1994	516	304
1995	736	220
1996	1 050	315
1997	1 399	348
1998	1 450	51
1999	1 547	97
2000	1 656	109
2001	2 122	466
2002	2 864	742
2003	4 033	1 168
2004	6 099	2 067
2005	8 189	2 090
2006	10 663	2 475
2007	15 282	4 619
2008	19 460	4 178
2009	23 992	4 531
2010	28 473	4 481
2011	31 811	3 338
2012	33 116	1 304
2013	38 213	5 097
2014	38 430	217
2015H1	36 938	−1 492

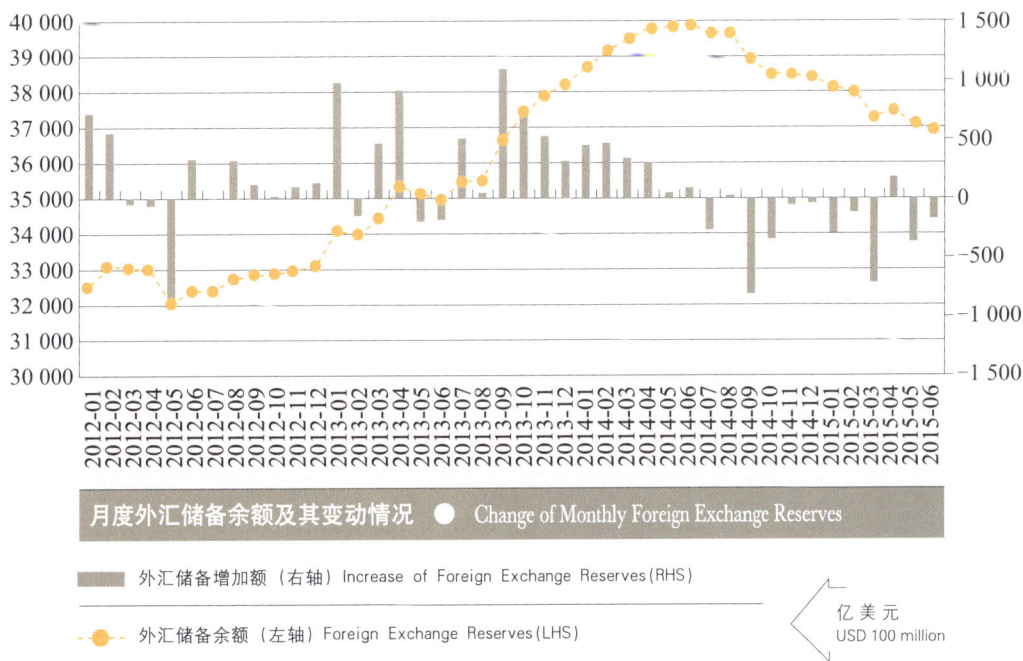

月度外汇储备余额及其变动情况　●　Change of Monthly Foreign Exchange Reserves

外汇储备增加额（右轴）Increase of Foreign Exchange Reserves（RHS）

外汇储备余额（左轴）Foreign Exchange Reserves（LHS）

亿美元
USD 100 million

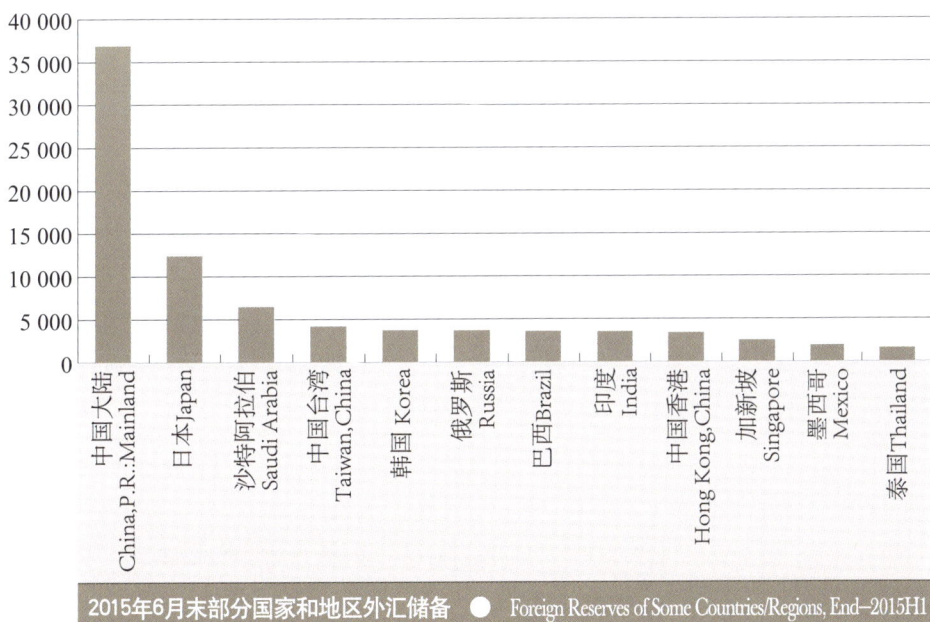

2015年6月末部分国家和地区外汇储备　●　Foreign Reserves of Some Countries/Regions, End—2015H1

亿美元
USD 100 million

二、对外贸易①

Ⅱ. Foreign Trade

2014年世界货物贸易出口前十名

Top 10 Countries/Regions of Goods Export in 2014

国家/地区 Countries/Regions	出口额（10亿美元） Export（USD billions）	增长 Increase（%）	占世界出口总额比重 Ratio to total export of the world（%）	2013年排名 Ranking in 2013
世界World	18 935	0.8	100	
1.中国P.R.C	2 343	6.1	12.4	1
2.美国U.S.A	1 623	2.8	8.6	2
3.德国Germany	1 511	4.0	8.0	3
4.日本Japan	684	−4.3	3.6	4
5.荷兰Netherlands	672	1.2	3.6	5
6.法国France	583	0.5	3.1	6
7.韩国Korea	573	2.3	3.0	7
8.意大利Italy	529	2.1	2.8	11
9.中国香港HongKong,China	524	−2.2	2.8	9
10.英国UK	507	−6.3	2.7	8

① 数据来源：海关总署；世界贸易组织。
Sources: General Administration of Customs; World Trade Organization.

2014年世界货物贸易进口前十名

Top 10 Countries/Regions of Goods Import in 2014

国家/地区 Countries/Regions	进口额（10亿美元） Import（USD billions）	增长 Increase（%）	占世界进口总额比重 Ratio to total Import of the world（%）	2013年排名 Ranking in 2013
世界World	19 024	0.8	100	
1.美国U.S.A	2 409	3.3	12.7	1
2.中国P.R.C	1 960	0.5	10.3	2
3.德国Germany	1 217	2.5	6.4	3
4.日本Japan	822	−1.3	4.3	4
5.英国UK	683	4.4	3.6	6
6.法国France	679	−0.3	3.6	5
7.中国香港HongKong,China	601	−3.4	3.2	7
8.荷兰Netherlands	587	−0.5	3.1	8
9.韩国Korea	526	1.9	2.8	9
10.加拿大Canada	475	0.2	2.5	11

中国进出口总值

China's Total Value of Import & Export

单位：亿美元
Unit: USD 100 million

年度 Year	进出口 Import & Export	出口 Export	进口 Import	差额 Balance
1981	440	220	220	0
1982	416	223	193	30
1983	436	222	214	8
1984	535	261	274	−13
1985	696	274	423	−149
1986	738	309	429	−120
1987	827	394	432	−38
1988	1 028	475	553	−78
1989	1 117	525	591	−66
1990	1 154	621	534	87
1991	1 357	719	638	81
1992	1 655	849	806	44
1993	1 957	917	1 040	−122
1994	2 366	1 210	1 156	54
1995	2 809	1 488	1 321	167
1996	2 899	1 511	1 388	122
1997	3 252	1 828	1 424	404
1998	3 239	1 837	1 402	435
1999	3 606	1 949	1 657	292
2000	4 743	2 492	2 251	241
2001	5 097	2 661	2 436	226
2002	6 208	3 256	2 952	304
2003	8 510	4 382	4 128	255
2004	11 546	5 933	5 612	321
2005	14 219	7 620	6 600	1 020
2006	17 604	9 689	7 915	1 775
2007	21 766	12 205	9 561	2 643
2008	25 633	14 307	11 326	2 981
2009	22 072	12 017	10 059	1 957
2010	29 728	15 779	13 948	1 831
2011	36 421	18 986	17 435	1 551
2012	38 668	20 489	18 178	2 311
2013	41 603	22 100	19 503	2 598
2014	43 030	23 427	19 603	3 825
2015H1	18 805	10 719	8 086	2 633

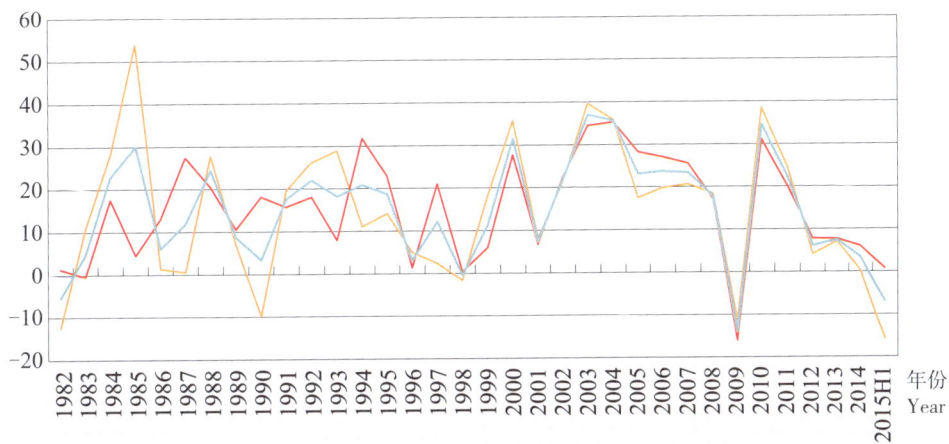

进出口增长率 ● Growth Rate of Import & Export

—— 进出口Export & Import　　—— 出口Export　　—— 进口Import

增长率 (%)
Growth Rate (%)

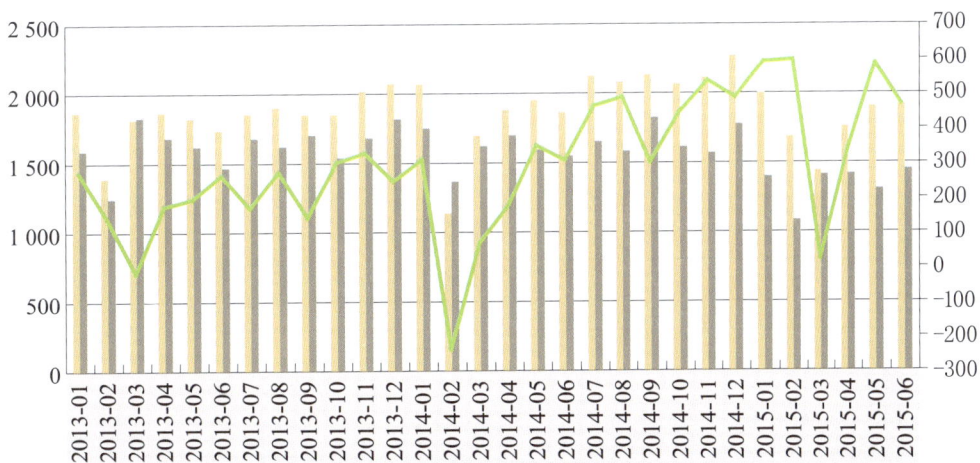

月度进口、出口和进出口差额 ● Monthly Import　Export　Import & Export Balance

▭ 出口（左轴）Export(LHS)　　▭ 进口（左轴）Import(LHS)

—— 进出口差额（右轴）Trade Balance(RHS)

亿美元
USD 100 million

按贸易方式分类进出口

Import & Export by Trading Forms

贸易方式Trading Forms	2005	2006	2007	2008	2009	2010	2011	2012	2013	2014	2015H1
进口Import	**660 118**	**791 614**	**955 818**	**1 133 086**	**1 005 555**	**1 394 829**	**1 743 458**	**1 817 826**	**1 950 289**	**1 960 290**	**808 623**
一般贸易Ordinary Trade	279 719	333 181	428 648	572 677	533 872	767 978	1 007 464	1 021 819	1 109 718	1 109 513	456 995
国家间、国际组织间无偿援助和捐赠的物资 Foreign Aid and Donation by Overseas	49	65	35	49	43	22	16	27	21	38	7
其他捐赠物资 Other Donations	19	22	10	58	136	185	266	338	11	10	16
来料加工装配贸易 Processing and Assembling Trade	67 029	73 834	89 165	90 162	75 993	99 295	93 635	84 459	87 543	97 537	42 754
进料加工贸易 Processing with Imported Materials	206 997	247 662	279 228	288 243	246 345	318 134	376 161	396 710	409 447	426 843	167 585
寄售代销贸易 Goods on Consignment	6	3	2	2	2	2	2	1	0	0	0
边境小额贸易 Border trade	5 721	6 214	7 589	8 975	7 196	9 634	14 448	15 289	14 065	9 856	3 580
加工贸易进口设备 Equipment Imported for Processing & Assembling	2 862	2 817	3 277	2 859	953	1 212	885	912	969	687	287
租赁贸易 Goods on Lease	3 681	8 067	8 280	6 932	3 448	5 628	5 459	6 760	8 656	10 212	4 792
外商投资企业作为投资进口的设备物品 Equipment or Materials Imported as Investment by Foreign-invested Enterprises	27 674	27 823	25 906	27 677	15 176	16 312	17 508	13 429	9 835	9 059	3 371
出料加工贸易 Outward Processing Trade	33	33	39	160	78	126	73	236	252	307	144
易货贸易 Barter Trade	3	6	4	1	8	1	2	0	1	3	2
免税外汇商品 Duty Free Commodities on Payment of Foreign Exchange	8	6	6	6	5	10	13	26	28	20	8
保税监管场所进出境货物 Customs Warehousing Trade	20 065	32 018	41 720	57 277	54 392	61 099	79 658	83 969	84 844	99 870	42 413
海关特殊监管区域物流货物 Entrepot Trade by Bonded Area	44 255	55 508	66 910	73 739	64 259	109 241	140 831	185 132	218 448	186 689	81 864
海关特殊监管区域进口设备 Equipment Imported into Export Processing Zone	1 411	3 623	4 108	3 118	2 113	3 994	4 741	6 094	3 993	5 133	2 932
其他 Others	586	732	890	1 150	1 535	1 957	2 296	2 624	2 458	2 950	1 070

单位：百万美元
Unit: USD million

贸易方式Trading Forms	2005	2006	2007	2008	2009	2010	2011	2012	2013	2014	2015H1
出口Export	761 999	969 073	1 218 015	1 428 546	1 201 663	1 577 932	1 898 600	2 048 935	2 210 042	2 342 747	1 071 871
一般贸易 Ordinary Trade	315 091	416 318	538 576	662 584	529 833	720 733	917 124	988 007	1 087 553	1 203 682	583 099
国家间、国际组织间无偿援助和捐赠的物资 Foreign Aid and Donation by overseas	225	211	201	231	291	294	471	551	456	478	228
其他捐赠物资 Other Donations	0	0	0	2	8	3	11	2	8	6	0
补偿贸易 Compensation Trade	0	1	0	0	0	0	0	0	0	0	0
来料加工装配贸易 Processing and Assembling Trade	83 970	94 483	116 043	110 520	93 423	112 317	107 653	98 866	92 479	90 692	38 534
进料加工贸易 Processing with Imported Materials	332 511	415 892	501 613	564 663	493 558	628 017	727 763	763 913	768 337	793 668	334 348
寄售代销贸易 Goods on Consignment	1	2	4	4	6	1	2	4	1	0	0
边境小额贸易 Border trade	7 409	9 943	13 739	21 904	13 667	16 408	20 203	24 216	30 929	37 207	13 802
对外承包工程出口货物 Contracting Projects	1 705	3 071	5 188	10 963	13 357	12 617	14 923	14 782	16 011	16 326	8 470
租赁贸易 Goods on Lease	90	214	84	189	117	145	166	562	305	327	94
出料加工贸易 Outward Processing Trade	27	24	44	118	46	185	198	196	199	235	101
易货贸易 Barter Trade	17	19	48	16	1	1	1	1	2	3	1
保税监管场所进出境货物 Customs Warehousing Trade	7 956	13 069	18 624	28 404	26 793	35 366	43 294	42 477	46 510	53 288	23 798
海关特殊监管区域物流货物 Entrepot Trade by Bonded Area	11 615	14 463	20 977	23 937	21 476	36 502	49 655	94 819	141 990	110 395	47 706
其他 Others	1 380	1 361	2 916	5 011	9 088	15 343	17 135	20 540	25 262	36 438	21 686

按企业类型分类进出口

Import & Export by Type of Enterprises

单位：亿美元
Unit: USD 100 million

企业类型Type of Enterprises	2005	2006	2007	2008	2009	2010	2011	2012	2013	2014	2015H1
进口Import	**6 601**	**7 916**	**9 558**	**11 331**	**10 056**	**13 948**	**17 435**	**18 178**	**19 503**	**19 603**	**8 086**
国有企业State-owned Enterprises	1 972	2 252	2 697	3 538	2 885	3 876	4 934	4 954	4 990	4 911	2 040
外商投资企业 Foreign-funded Enterprises	3 875	4 726	5 594	6 200	5 452	7 380	8 648	8 712	8 748	9 093	4 035
中外合作 Sino-foreign Contractual Joint Ventures	96	99	88	88	66	74	86	82	83	87	31
中外合资 Sino-foreign Equity Joint Ventures	1 184	1 356	1 549	1 818	1 586	2 095	2 561	2 748	2 842	2 858	1 212
外商独资 Foreign Investment Enterprises	2 595	3 270	3 957	4 294	3 799	5 212	6 002	5 883	5 823	6 149	2 792
集体企业/私营企业 Collective Enterprises/Private owned Enterprises	205	200	232	289	265	349	407	353	4 368	4 475	1 891
其他Other Enterprises	549	738	1 035	1 304	1 454	2 343	3 445	4 158	1 397	1 124	121
出口Export	**7 620**	**9 691**	**12 180**	**14 285**	**12 017**	**15 779**	**18 986**	**20 489**	**22 100**	**23 427**	**10 719**
国有企业State-owned Enterprises	1 688	1 913	2 248	2 572	1 910	2 344	2 672	2 563	2 490	2 565	1 175
外商投资企业 Foreign-funded Enterprises	4 442	5 638	6 955	7 906	6 722	8 623	9 953	10 227	10 443	10 747	4 804
中外合作 Sino-foreign Contractual Joint Ventures	157	177	181	183	146	165	177	162	157	136	57
中外合资 Sino-foreign Equity Joint Ventures	1 360	1 638	1 988	2 269	1 824	2 376	2 731	2 873	3 009	3 055	1 378
外商独资 Foreign Investment Enterprises	2 925	3 824	4 786	5 454	4 752	6 082	7 046	7 193	7 277	7 556	3 369
集体企业/私营企业 Collective Enterprises/Private owned Enterprises	365	411	469	547	405	499	554	509	8 633	9 547	4 480
其他Other Enterprises	1 125	1 728	2 508	3 260	2 979	4 314	5 807	7 190	534	958	260
差额Balance	**1 019**	**1 775**	**2 622**	**2 955**	**1 961**	**1 831**	**1 551**	**2 311**	**2 598**	**3 825**	**2 633**
国有企业State-owned Enterprises	-284	-339	-449	-966	-975	-1 532	-2 262	-2 391	-2 500	-2 346	-865
外商投资企业 Foreign-funded Enterprises	567	912	1 361	1 706	1 270	1 243	1 305	1 515	1 695	1 654	769
中外合作 Sino-foreign Contractual Joint Ventures	61	78	93	95	80	91	91	80	74	49	26
中外合资 Sino-foreign Equity Joint Ventures	176	281	439	451	238	281	170	125	167	197	166
外商独资 Foreign Investment Enterprises	330	553	829	1 160	953	870	1 044	1 310	1 454	1 407	577
集体企业/私营企业 Collective Enterprises/Private owned Enterprises	160	211	237	258	140	150	147	156	4 265	5 072	2 589
其他Other Enterprises	576	990	1 473	1 956	1 525	1 971	2 362	3 032	-863	-166	139

2015年上半年按贸易方式分类的进口构成
Components of Import by Trading Forms in the First Half of 2015

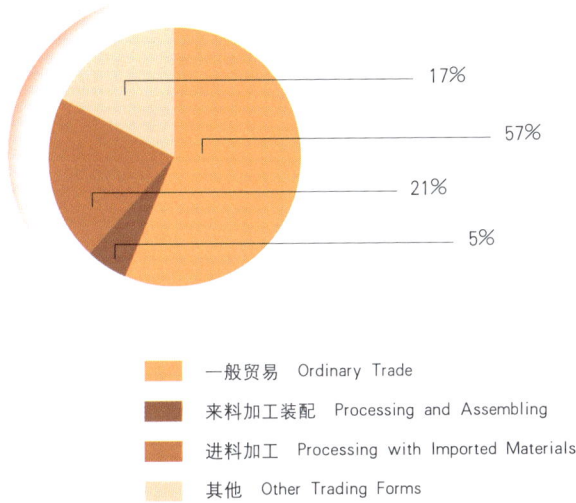

17%
57%
21%
5%

一般贸易 Ordinary Trade
来料加工装配 Processing and Assembling
进料加工 Processing with Imported Materials
其他 Other Trading Forms

2015年上半年按贸易方式分类的出口构成
Components of Export by Trading Forms in the First Half of 2015

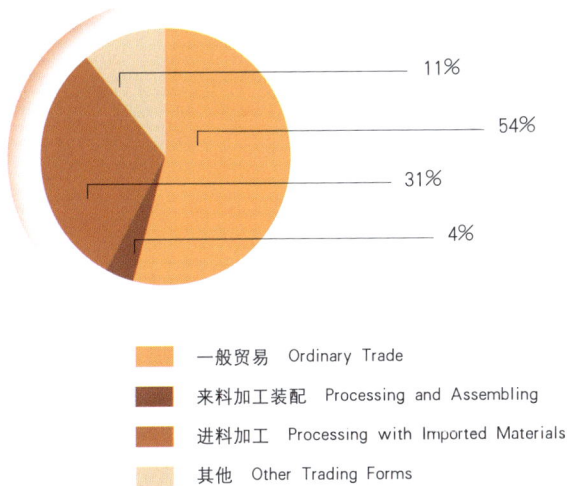

11%
54%
31%
4%

一般贸易 Ordinary Trade
来料加工装配 Processing and Assembling
进料加工 Processing with Imported Materials
其他 Other Trading Forms

2015年上半年按企业类型分类的进口构成
Components of Import by Type of Enterprises in the First Half of 2015

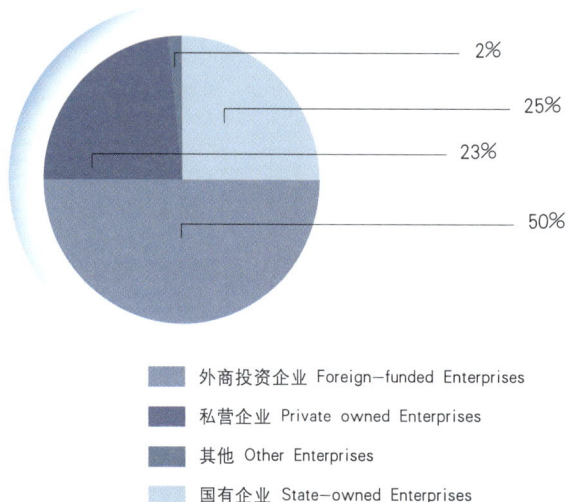

2%

25%

23%

50%

外商投资企业 Foreign-funded Enterprises

私营企业 Private owned Enterprises

其他 Other Enterprises

国有企业 State-owned Enterprises

2015年上半年按企业类型分类的出口构成
Components of Export by Type of Enterprises in the First Half of 2015

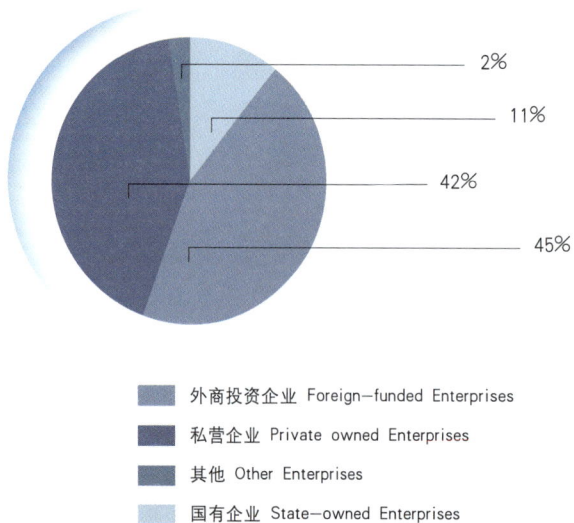

2%

11%

42%

45%

外商投资企业 Foreign-funded Enterprises

私营企业 Private owned Enterprises

其他 Other Enterprises

国有企业 State-owned Enterprises

2015年上半年进出口按贸易方式分类

Import & Export by Trading Forms in the First Half of 2015

单位：亿美元
Unit: USD 100 million

贸易方式　Trading Forms	进口 Import 金额Value	同比（%）Increase	出口 Export 金额Value	同比（%）Increase	进出口差额 Import & Export Balance
总值 **Total Value**	8 086	−15.6	10 719	0.9	2 633
一般贸易 Ordinary Trade	4 570	−18.7	5 831	6.3	1 261
加工贸易 Processing Trade	2 104	10.7	3 728	−7.5	1 624
来料加工装配 Processing and Assembling	428	−4.2	385	−7.9	−43
进料加工 Processing with imported materials	1 676	−12.3	3 343	−7.5	1 667
其他贸易 Dther trading forms	1 412	−12.4	1 159	5.4	−253

2015年上半年进出口按企业类型分类

Import & Export by Type of Enterprises in the First Half of 2015

单位：亿美元
Unit: USD 100 million

企业类型 Type of Enterprises	进口 Import 金额Value	同比（%）Increase	出口 Export 金额Value	同比（%）Increase	进出口差额 Import & Export Balance
总值 Total Value	8 086	−15.6	10 719	0.9	2 633
国有企业 State-owned Enterprises	2 040	−19.2	1 175	−3	−865
外资企业 Foreign-funded Enterprises	4 035	−6.7	4 804	−3.4	769
私营和其他企业 Private Owned and other Enterprises	2 011	−26.6	4 740	6.8	2 729

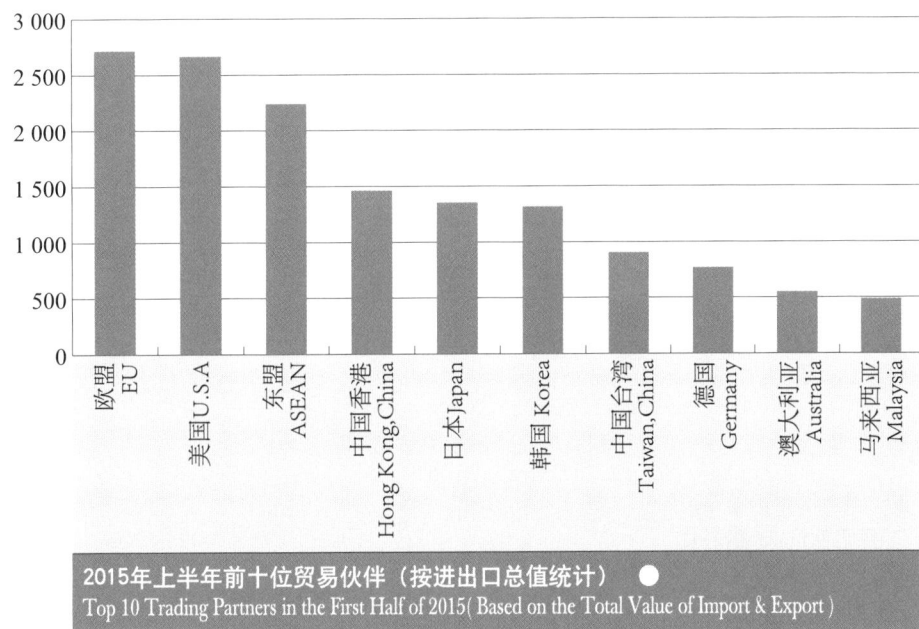

2015年上半年前十位贸易伙伴（按进出口总值统计） ●
Top 10 Trading Partners in the First Half of 2015(Based on the Total Value of Import & Export)

亿 美 元
USD 100 million

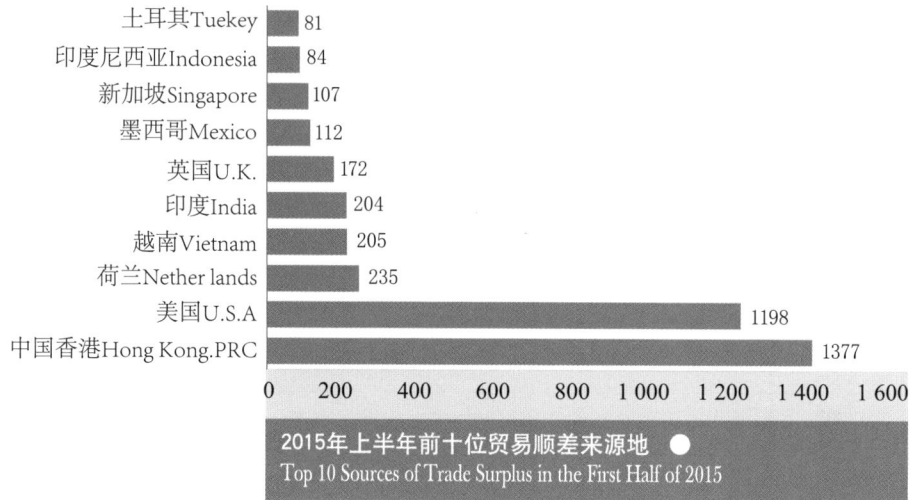

2015年上半年前十位贸易顺差来源地 ●
Top 10 Sources of Trade Surplus in the First Half of 2015

亿 美 元
USD 100 million

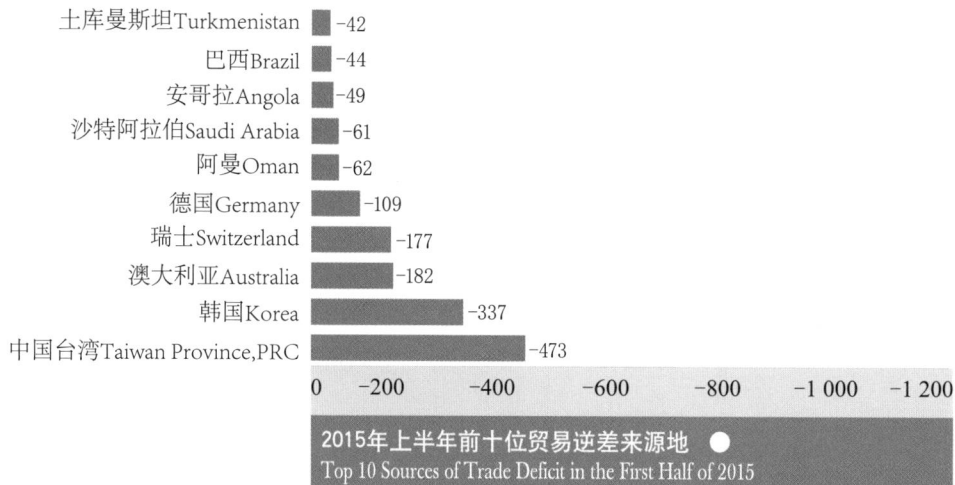

2015年上半年前十位贸易逆差来源地 ●
Top 10 Sources of Trade Deficit in the First Half of 2015

亿 美 元
USD 100 million

三、外汇市场和人民币汇率①

III．Foreign Exchange Market and Exchange Rate of Renminbi

人民币对美元交易中间价月平均汇价

人民币元/100美元
RMB per 100 USD

Monthly Average Transaction Mid Rates of Renminbi against US dollar，1980—2014

年份Year 月份Month	1980	1981	1982	1983	1984	1985	1986	1987	1988	1989	1990
1月/Jan.	149.37	154.87	176.77	192.01	204.12	280.88	320.15	372.21	372.21	372.21	472.21
2月/Feb.	150.05	161.06	181.74	196.03	205.72	282.51	320.70	372.21	372.21	372.21	472.21
3月/Mar.	155.12	162.80	183.79	197.80	206.08	284.51	321.20	372.21	372.21	372.21	472.21
4月/Apr.	155.70	166.20	185.19	198.72	208.91	284.11	320.61	372.21	372.21	372.21	472.21
5月/May	149.06	172.27	180.97	198.52	218.21	284.75	319.44	372.21	372.21	372.21	472.21
6月/Jun.	146.50	176.05	189.70	198.95	221.22	286.25	320.35	372.21	372.21	372.21	472.21
7月/Jul.	145.25	175.98	192.36	198.88	229.39	287.38	363.82	372.21	372.21	372.21	472.21
8月/Aug.	147.26	179.52	193.87	198.00	236.43	290.23	370.36	372.21	372.21	372.21	472.21
9月/Sept.	146.81	175.01	195.04	198.14	253.26	296.26	370.66	372.21	372.21	372.21	472.21
10月/Oct.	148.03	175.05	198.22	196.17	264.00	306.73	371.64	372.21	372.21	372.21	472.21
11月/Nov.	151.73	173.46	199.41	198.90	266.16	320.15	372.21	372.21	372.21	372.21	495.54
12月/Dec.	154.19	173.78	193.99	198.69	278.91	320.15	372.21	372.21	372.21	423.82	522.21
年平均 Annual Average	**149.84**	**170.50**	**189.25**	**197.57**	**232.70**	**293.66**	**345.28**	**372.21**	**372.21**	**376.51**	**478.32**

①资料来源：国家外汇管理局。
Source：State Administration of Foreign Exchange.

人民币对美元交易中间价月平均汇价

人民币元/100美元
RMB per 100 USD

Monthly Average Transaction Mid Rates of Renminbi against US dollar，1980—2014

年份Year 月份Month	1991	1992	1993	1994	1995	1996	1997	1998	1999	2000	2001
1月/Jan.	522.21	544.81	576.40	870.00	844.13	831.86	829.63	827.91	827.90	827.93	827.71
2月/Feb.	522.21	546.35	576.99	870.28	843.54	831.32	829.29	827.91	827.80	827.79	827.70
3月/Mar.	522.21	547.34	573.13	870.23	842.76	832.89	829.57	827.92	827.91	827.86	827.76
4月/Apr.	526.59	549.65	570.63	869.55	842.25	833.15	829.57	827.92	827.92	827.93	827.71
5月/May	531.39	550.36	572.17	866.49	831.28	832.88	829.29	827.90	827.85	827.77	827.72
6月/Jun.	535.35	547.51	573.74	865.72	830.08	832.26	829.21	827.97	827.80	827.72	827.71
7月/Jul.	535.55	544.32	576.12	864.03	830.07	831.60	829.11	827.98	827.77	827.93	827.69
8月/Aug.	537.35	542.87	577.64	858.98	830.75	830.81	828.94	827.99	827.73	827.96	827.70
9月/Sept.	537.35	549.48	578.70	854.03	831.88	830.44	828.72	827.89	827.74	827.86	827.68
10月/Oct.	537.90	553.69	578.68	852.93	831.55	830.00	828.38	827.78	827.74	827.85	827.68
11月/Nov.	538.58	561.31	579.47	851.69	831.35	829.93	828.11	827.78	827.82	827.74	827.69
12月/Dec.	541.31	579.82	580.68	848.45	831.56	829.90	827.96	827.79	827.93	827.72	827.68
年平均 Annual Average	532.33	551.46	576.20	861.87	835.10	831.42	828.98	827.91	827.83	827.84	827.70

人民币对美元交易中间价月平均汇价

人民币元/100美元
RMB per 100 USD

Monthly Average Transaction Mid Rates of Renminbi against US dollar，1980—2014

年份Year 月份Month	2002	2003	2004	2005	2006	2007	2008	2009	2010	2011	2012	2013	2014
1 月/Jan.	827.67	827.68	827.69	827.65	806.68	778.98	724.78	683.82	682.73	660.27	631.68	627.87	610.43
2 月/Feb.	827.66	827.73	827.71	827.65	804.93	775.46	716.01	683.57	682.70	658.31	630.00	628.42	611.28
3 月/Mar.	827.70	827.72	827.71	827.65	803.50	773.90	707.52	683.41	682.64	656.62	630.81	627.43	613.58
4 月/Apr.	827.72	827.71	827.69	827.65	801.56	772.47	700.07	683.12	682.62	652.92	629.66	624.71	615.53
5 月/May	827.69	827.69	827.71	827.65	801.52	767.04	697.24	682.45	682.74	649.88	630.62	619.70	616.36
6 月/Jun.	827.70	827.71	827.67	827.65	800.67	763.30	689.71	683.32	681.65	647.78	631.78	617.18	615.57
7 月/Jul.	827.68	827.73	827.67	822.90	799.10	758.05	683.76	683.20	677.75	646.14	632.35	617.25	615.69
8 月/Aug.	827.67	827.70	827.68	810.19	797.33	757.53	685.15	683.22	679.01	640.9	634.04	617.08	616.06
9 月/Sept.	827.70	827.71	827.67	809.22	793.68	752.58	683.07	682.89	674.62	638.33	633.95	615.88	615.28
10 月/Oct.	827.69	827.67	827.65	808.89	790.32	750.12	683.16	682.75	667.32	635.66	631.44	613.93	614.41
11月/Nov.	827.71	827.69	827.65	808.40	786.52	742.33	682.86	682.74	665.58	634.08	629.53	613.72	614.32
12月/Dec.	827.72	827.70	827.65	807.59	782.38	736.76	684.24	682.79	665.15	632.81	629.00	611.60	612.38
年平均 Annual Average	**827.70**	**827.70**	**827.68**	**819.42**	**797.18**	**760.40**	**694.51**	**683.10**	**676.95**	**646.14**	**631.25**	**619.32**	614.28

2015年1-6月人民币市场汇率汇总表

林吉特、卢布单位：外币/100人民币
其他7种币种单位：人民币元/100外币
MYR, RUB Unit: foreign currency per 100 RMB
Other 7 Currency unit: RMB per 100 foreign currency

Transaction Mid Rates of Renminbi in the First Half of 2015

月份Month	币种Currency	期初价 Beginning of Period	期末价 End of Period	最高价 Highest	最低价 Lowest	期平均 Period Average	累计平均 Accumulative Average
1月Jan	美元USD	612.48	613.70	613.84	611.88	612.72	612.72
	港币HKD	78.97	79.17	79.18	78.92	79.03	79.03
	日元JPY	5.12	5.21	5.28	5.12	5.20	5.20
	欧元EUR	734.61	696.78	734.61	687.44	713.57	713.57
	英镑GBP	939.89	927.53	939.89	922.83	930.07	930.07
	澳元AUD	497.17	478.76	505.12	478.76	496.23	496.23
	加元CAD	520.13	486.60	520.95	486.60	506.77	506.77
	林吉特MYR	57.10	58.67	58.72	57.10	58.06	58.06
	卢布RUB	952.92	1 105.19	1 105.19	952.92	1 037.71	1 037.71
2月Feb	美元USD	613.85	614.75	614.75	612.61	613.39	613.05
	港币HKD	79.18	79.27	79.27	79.01	79.10	79.07
	日元JPY	5.25	5.18	5.25	5.12	5.20	5.20
	欧元EUR	696.26	692.56	705.31	692.56	698.77	706.17
	英镑GBP	928.51	951.90	957.51	925.74	941.13	935.60
	澳元AUD	478.98	482.19	485.25	472.17	479.22	487.73
	加元CAD	483.18	491.68	493.56	483.18	490.02	498.39
	林吉特MYR	58.60	56.88	58.60	56.61	57.32	57.69
	卢布RUB	1 113.97	986.35	1 113.97	986.35	1 049.67	1 043.69
3月Mar	美元USD	615.13	614.22	616.17	613.75	615.07	613.72
	港币HKD	79.33	79.21	79.38	79.14	79.28	79.14
	日元JPY	5.16	5.13	5.17	5.09	5.13	5.18
	欧元EUR	689.07	666.48	690.14	648.52	668.71	693.68
	英镑GBP	951.15	911.08	951.15	909.28	924.78	931.99
	澳元AUD	480.79	471.10	484.13	470.14	477.09	484.18
	加元CAD	491.40	484.52	495.16	481.14	487.99	494.93
	林吉特MYR	57.56	59.35	59.35	57.56	58.57	57.98
	卢布RUB	992.46	930.89	1 007.18	925.24	970.30	1 019.22
4月Apr	美元USD	614.34	611.37	614.34	611.37	613.02	613.59
	港币HKD	79.23	78.88	79.23	78.88	79.09	79.13
	日元JPY	5.14	5.15	5.17	5.11	5.14	5.16
	欧元EUR	661.47	680.82	680.82	651.63	662.61	684.35
	英镑GBP	912.76	945.50	945.50	901.10	917.78	927.40
	澳元AUD	469.37	490.58	490.59	465.63	474.64	481.75
	加元CAD	484.23	508.75	508.75	484.23	496.16	495.40
	林吉特MYR	59.24	57.00	59.24	57.00	58.40	58.15
	卢布RUB	940.77	821.92	940.77	804.15	855.88	972.04

2015年1-6月人民币市场汇率汇总表

林吉特、卢布单位：外币/100人民币
其他7种币种单位：人民币元/100外币
MYR, RUB Unit: foreign currency per 100 RMB
Other 7 Currency unit: RMB per 100 foreign currency

Transaction Mid Rates of Renminbi in the First Half of 2015

月份Month	币种 Currency	期初价 Beginning of Period	期末价 End of Period	最高价 Highest	最低价 Lowest	期平均 Period Average	累计平均 Accumulative Average
5月May	美元USD	611.65	611.96	612.02	610.79	611.43	613.15
	港币HKD	78.91	78.93	78.94	78.80	78.87	79.08
	日元JPY	5.11	4.96	5.14	4.96	5.08	5.15
	欧元EUR	685.72	671.89	700.22	667.35	683.94	684.27
	英镑GBP	928.48	939.32	965.53	927.61	948.05	931.61
	澳元AUD	479.43	469.28	497.07	469.28	483.97	482.20
	加元CAD	502.75	492.76	510.81	476.34	501.49	496.64
	林吉特MYR	57.23	58.59	58.64	57.23	57.89	58.10
	卢布RUB	826.19	850.83	850.83	796.96	816.74	940.34
6月Jun	美元USD	612.07	611.36	612.25	611.04	611.61	612.88
	港币HKD	78.95	78.86	78.95	78.82	78.89	79.04
	日元JPY	4.94	5.01	5.01	4.91	4.96	5.11
	欧元EUR	671.30	686.99	696.98	670.25	687.11	684.77
	英镑GBP	936.85	964.22	973.45	932.59	953.19	935.42
	澳元AUD	468.84	469.93	477.42	467.60	472.67	480.52
	加元CAD	490.83	492.32	499.95	488.67	494.64	496.29
	林吉特MYR	58.98	61.02	61.02	58.98	60.19	58.47
	卢布RUB	846.16	903.15	905.76	846.16	879.43	929.59

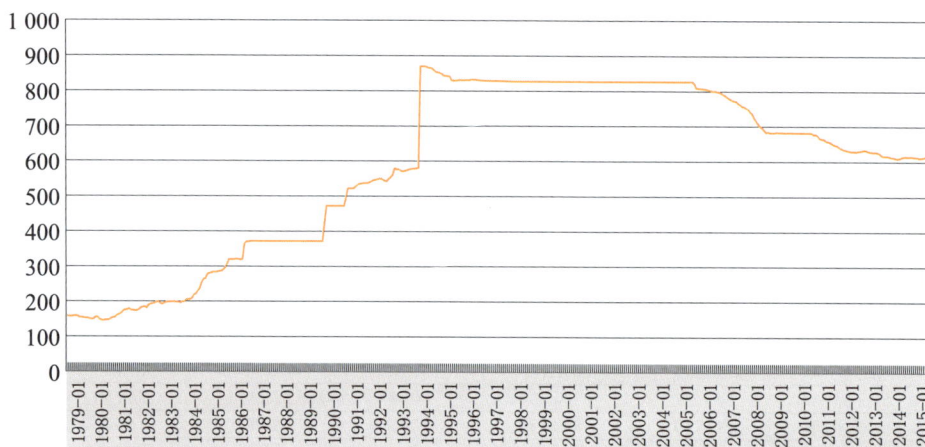

1979–2015年上半年人民币对美元交易中间价月平均汇价 ●
Monthly Average Transaction Mid Rates of Renminbi Against US dollar,1979–2015H1

人民币元/100美元
RMB per 100 USD

四、利用外资①

Ⅳ. Foreign Investment Utilization

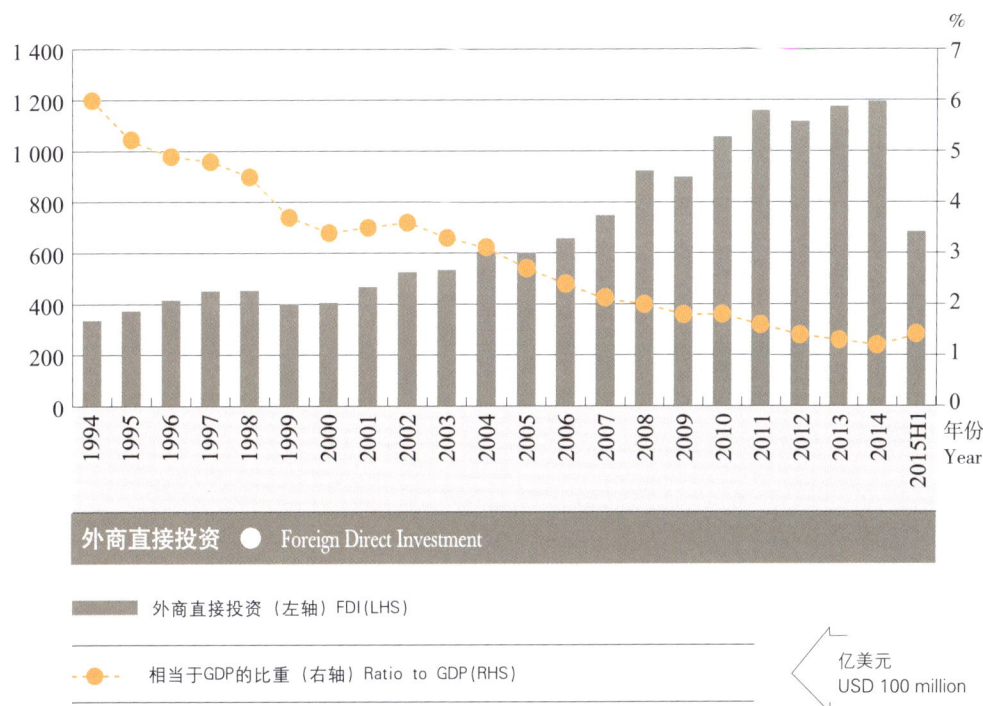

外商直接投资 ● Foreign Direct Investment

外商直接投资（左轴）FDI（LHS）

相当于GDP的比重（右轴）Ratio to GDP（RHS）

亿美元
USD 100 million

①资料来源：商务部。
Source: Ministry of Commerce.

2015年上半年利用外资

Foreign Direct Investment in the first half of 2015

单位：亿美元
Unit: USD 100 million

利用外资方式 Mode of Foreign Investment Utilization	本年批准外资项目数 Approved Foreign Investment Programs		本年实际使用外资 Actual Utilization of Foreign Investment	
	本年累计 Accumulative in This Year	同比增长(%) Increase	本年累计 Accumulative in This Year	同比增长(%) Increase
总计 Total	11 914	8.6	684.1	7.8
一、外商直接投资 Direct Foreign Investment	11 914	8.6	684.1	8
中外合资企业 Sino-Foreign Equity Joint Venture	2 623	17.3	134.5	11.6
中外合作企业 Sino-Foreign Contractual Joint Venture	52	0	9.6	30.5
外资企业 Foreign Investment Enterprise	9 209	6.3	525.2	6.2
外商投资股份制 Stock-Holding by Foreign Investment	30	25	14.8	37.6
合作开发 Cooperation Exploitation	0	0	0	0
其他 Others	0	0	0	0
二、外商其他投资 Other Foreign Investment	0	0	0	−100
对外发行股票 Issue Stocks to the Outside	0	0	0	0
国际租赁 International Tenancy	0	0	0	0
补偿贸易 Compensative Trade	0	0	0	0
加工装配 Processing & Assembling	0	0	0	−100

注：统计数据为非金融领域。
Note: The data is subject to non-financial sectors.

五、外债[①]

V. External Debt

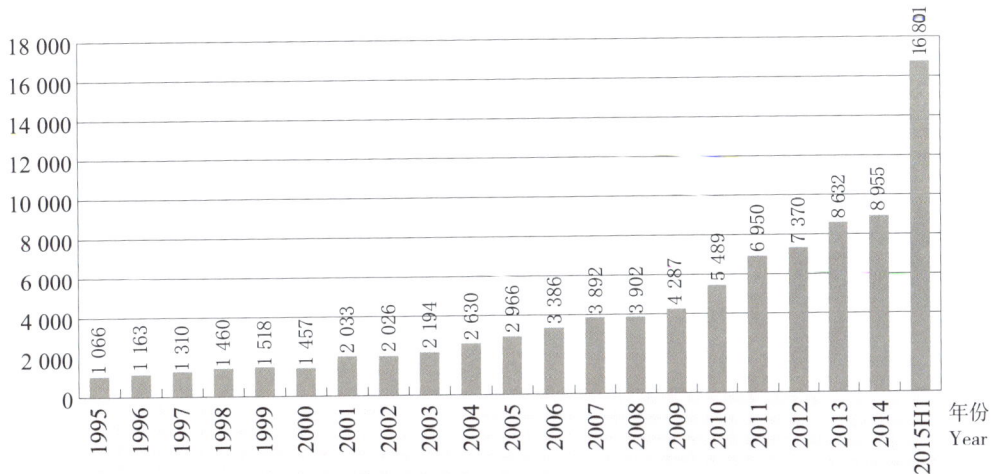

外债余额 ● External Debt

亿美元
USD 100 million

(Data values by year: 1995: 1 066; 1996: 1 163; 1997: 1 310; 1998: 1 460; 1999: 1 518; 2000: 1 457; 2001: 2 033; 2002: 2 026; 2003: 2 194; 2004: 2 630; 2005: 2 966; 2006: 3 386; 2007: 3 892; 2008: 3 902; 2009: 4 287; 2010: 5 489; 2011: 6 950; 2012: 7 370; 2013: 8 632; 2014: 8 955; 2015H1: 16 801)

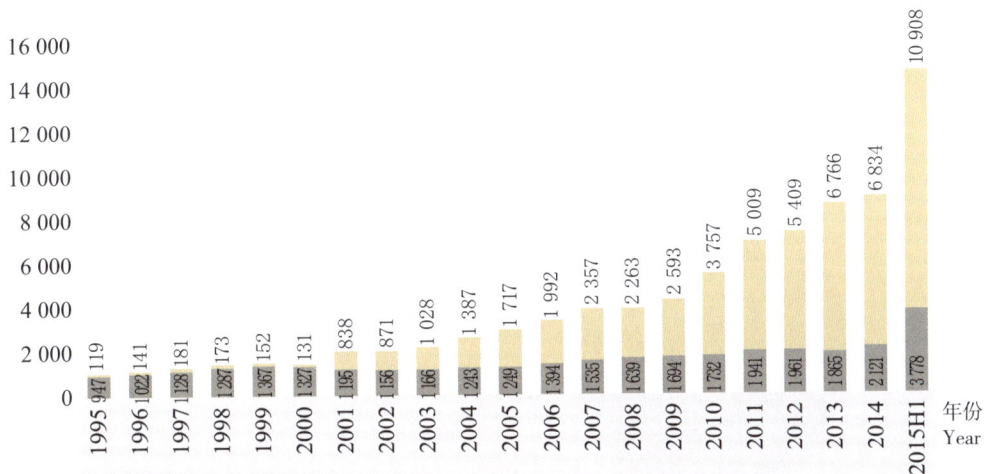

外债余额期限结构（剩余期限） ●
Components of External Debt by Period Structure (Residual Maturity)

■ 中长期外债余额 Long-and Medium-term External Debt

■ 短期外债余额 Short-term External Debt

亿美元
USD 100 million

(Long/Medium-term and Short-term by year — 1995: 947 / 119; 1996: 1 022 / 141; 1997: 1 128 / 181; 1998: 1 287 / 173; 1999: 1 367 / 152; 2000: 1 327 / 131; 2001: 1 195 / 838; 2002: 1 156 / 871; 2003: 1 166 / 1 028; 2004: 1 243 / 1 387; 2005: 1 249 / 1 717; 2006: 1 394 / 1 992; 2007: 1 535 / 2 357; 2008: 1 639 / 2 263; 2009: 1 694 / 2 593; 2010: 1 732 / 3 757; 2011: 1 941 / 5 009; 2012: 1 961 / 5 409; 2013: 1 865 / 6 766; 2014: 2 121 / 6 834; 2015H1: 3 778 / 10 908)

① 数据来源：国家外汇管理局。
Sources: State Administration of Foreign Exchange.

2015年上半年末外债余额期限结构（剩余期限）
Components of External Debt by Period Structure (Residual Maturity)，End—2015H1

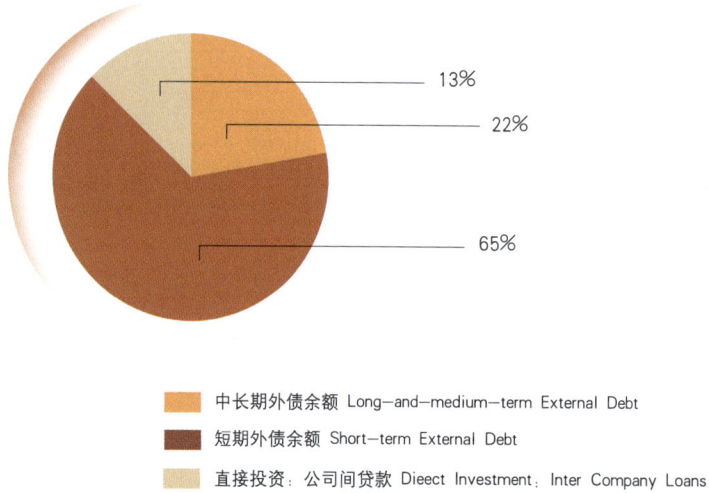

13%

22%

65%

■ 中长期外债余额 Long—and—medium—term External Debt
■ 短期外债余额 Short—term External Debt
■ 直接投资：公司间贷款 Dieect Investment：Inter Company Loans

2015年上半年末登记外债余额主体结构
Components of Registered External Debt by Type of Debtor，End—2015H1

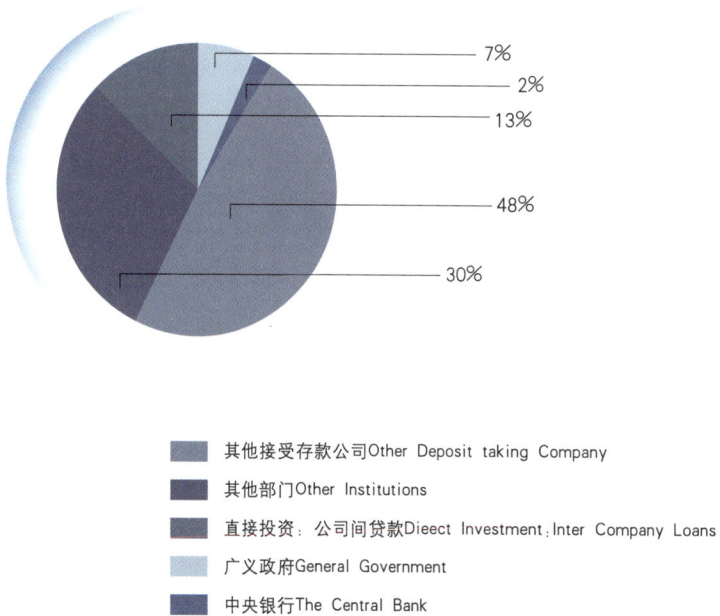

7%

2%

13%

48%

30%

■ 其他接受存款公司Other Deposit taking Company
■ 其他部门Other Institutions
■ 直接投资：公司间贷款Dieect Investment：Inter Company Loans
■ 广义政府General Government
■ 中央银行The Central Bank

六、国际旅游[①]

Ⅵ. International Tourism

入境过夜旅游者人数和旅游外汇收入

Number of Inbound Stay—over Tourists and Foreign Exchange Income from Tourism

年份 Year	入境过夜旅游（万人次） Inbound Stay-over Tourists(10 000 persons)	旅游外汇收入（亿美元） Foreign Exchange Income from Tourism(USD 100 million)	年份 Year	入境过夜旅游（万人次） Inbound Stay-over Tourists(10 000 persons)	旅游外汇收入（亿美元） Foreign Exchange Income from Tourism(USD 100 million)
1978	71.6	2.63	1997	2 377.0	120.74
1979	152.9	4.49	1998	2 507.3	126.02
1980	350.0	6.17	1999	2 704.7	140.99
1981	367.7	7.85	2000	3 122.9	162.24
1982	392.4	8.43	2001	3 316.7	177.92
1983	379.1	9.41	2002	3 680.3	203.85
1984	514.1	11.31	2003	3 297.1	174.06
1985	713.3	12.50	2004	4 176.1	257.39
1986	900.1	15.31	2005	4 680.9	292.96
1987	1 076.0	18.62	2006	4 991.0	339.49
1988	1 236.1	22.47	2007	5 472.0	419.19
1989	936.1	18.60	2008	5 304.9	408.43
1990	1 048.4	22.18	2009	5 087.5	396.75
1991	1 246.4	28.45	2010	5 566.5	458.14
1992	1 651.2	39.47	2011	5 758.1	484.64
1993	1 898.2	46.83	2012	5 772.5	500.28
1994	2 107.0	73.23	2013	5 568.6	516.64
1995	2 003.4	87.33	2014	5 562.2	569.13
1996	2 276.5	102.00	2015H1	2768	275.34

①资料来源：国家旅游局。
Soicrce: China National Tourism Administration.

七、世界经济增长状况①

Ⅶ. Growth of World Economics

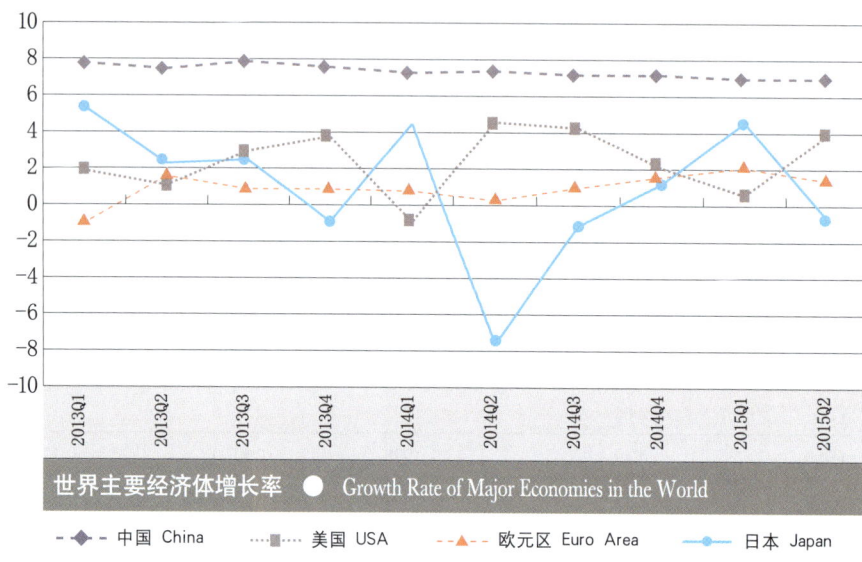

世界主要经济体增长率 ● Growth Rate of Major Economies in the World

- - ◆ - - 中国 China   ……■…… 美国 USA   - - ▲ - - 欧元区 Euro Area   —●— 日本 Japan

经济增长率 (%)
Growth Rate of Economy (%)

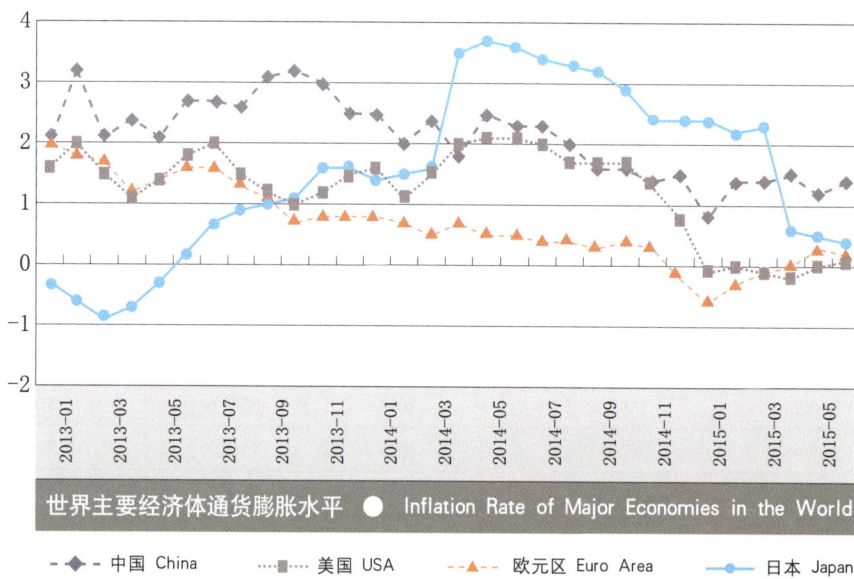

世界主要经济体通货膨胀水平 ● Inflation Rate of Major Economies in the World

- - ◆ - - 中国 China   ……■…… 美国 USA   - - ▲ - - 欧元区 Euro Area   —●— 日本 Japan

居民消费价格指数
CPI（%）

①资料来源：彭博资讯；CEIC Asia Database。
Sources：Bloomberg, CEIC Asia Database.

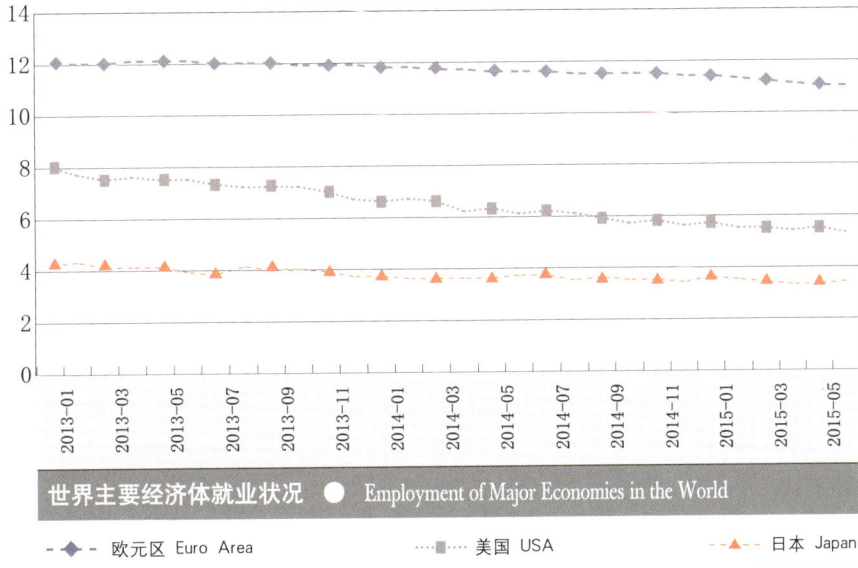

世界主要经济体就业状况 ● Employment of Major Economies in the World

- ◆- 欧元区 Euro Area   ···■··· 美国 USA   -▲- 日本 Japan

失业率 (%)
Unemployment Rate (%)

八、国际金融市场状况①

Ⅷ. International Financial Market

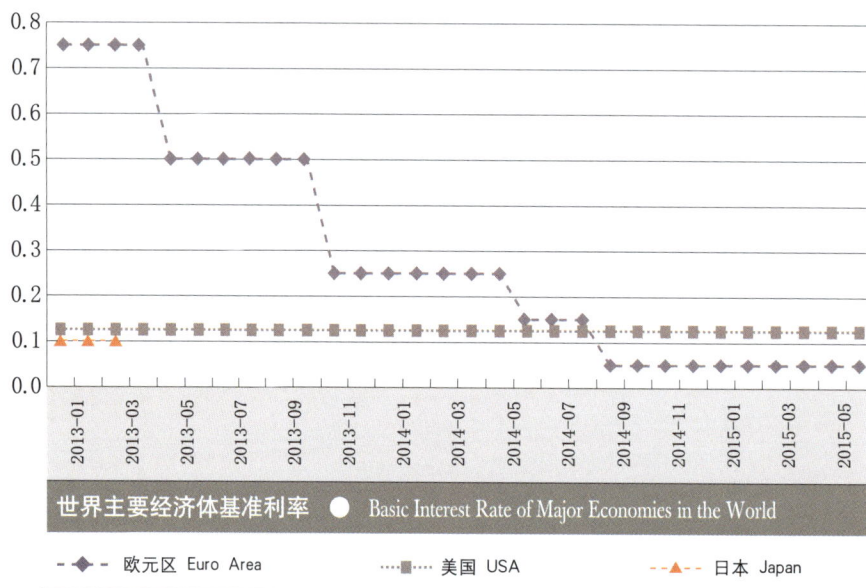

世界主要经济体基准利率 ● Basic Interest Rate of Major Economies in the World

- ◆ - 欧元区 Euro Area   ⋯■⋯ 美国 USA   - ▲ - 日本 Japan

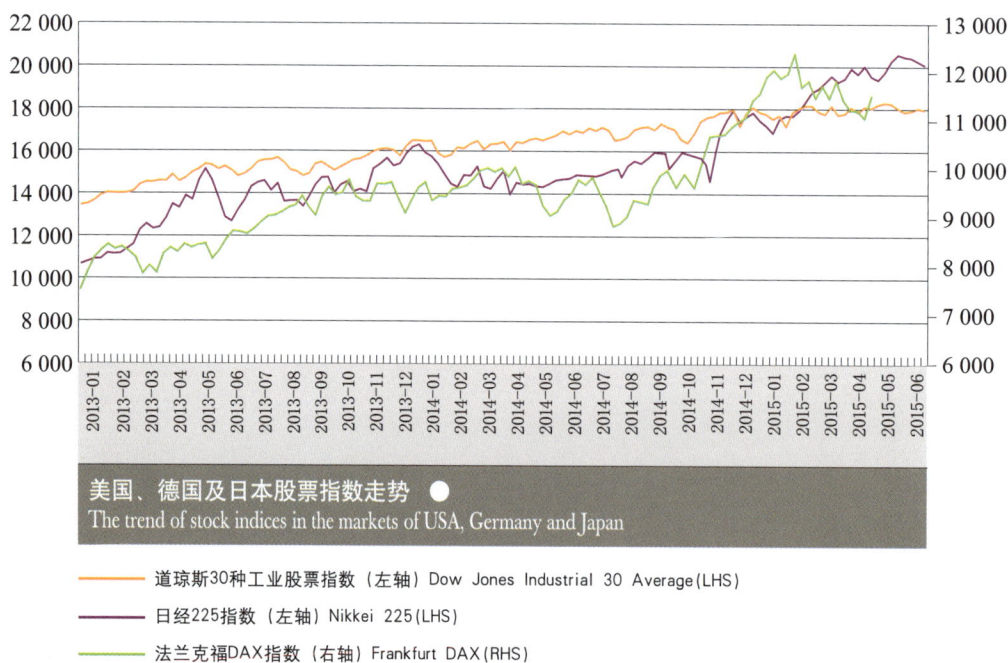

美国、德国及日本股票指数走势 ●
The trend of stock indices in the markets of USA, Germany and Japan

── 道琼斯30种工业股票指数（左轴）Dow Jones Industrial 30 Average(LHS)

── 日经225指数（左轴）Nikkei 225(LHS)

── 法兰克福DAX指数（右轴）Frankfurt DAX(RHS)

①资料来源：彭博资讯。
Sources：Bloomberg.

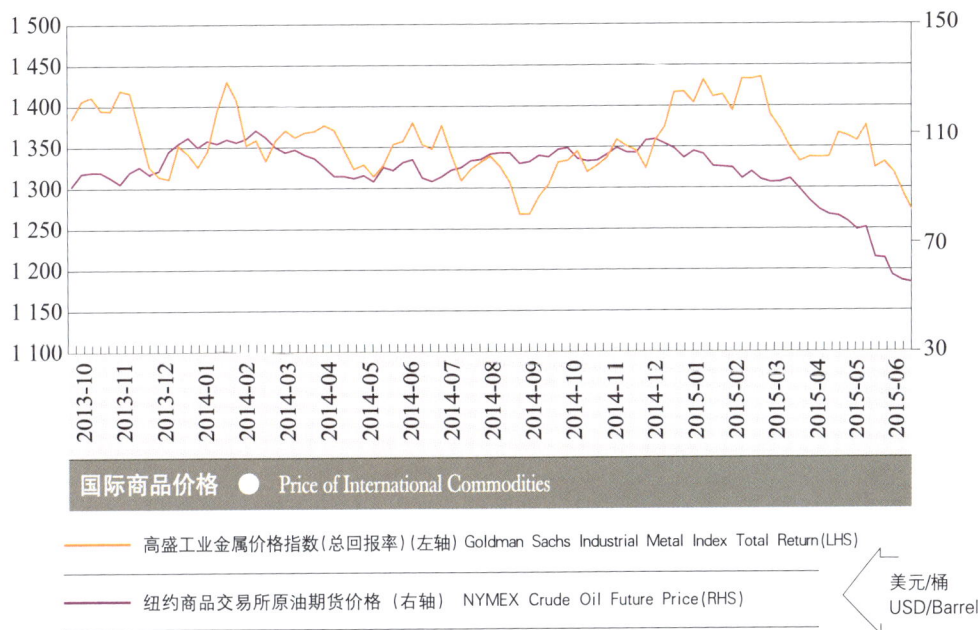

国际商品价格 ● Price of International Commodities

—— 高盛工业金属价格指数（总回报率）（左轴）Goldman Sachs Industrial Metal Index Total Return(LHS)

—— 纽约商品交易所原油期货价格（右轴） NYMEX Crude Oil Future Price(RHS)

美元/桶
USD/Barrel

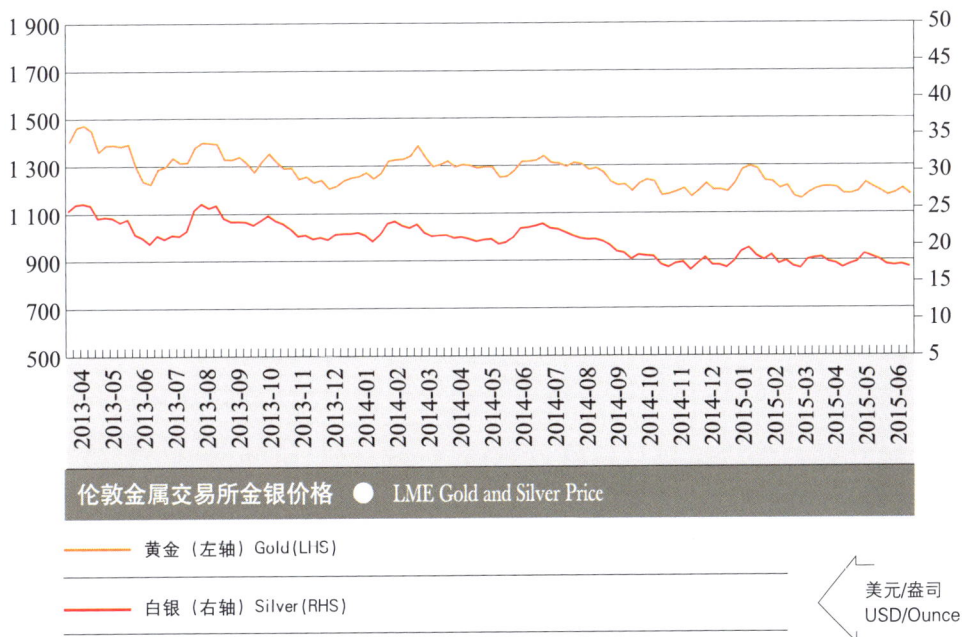

伦敦金属交易所金银价格 ● LME Gold and Silver Price

—— 黄金（左轴）Gold(LHS)

—— 白银（右轴）Silver(RHS)

美元/盎司
USD/Ounce